Contents

SECOND EDITION

LEADING
FOR RESULTS

Transforming Teaching, Learning,
and Relationships in Schools

DENNIS SPARKS

A JOINT PUBLICATION

CORWIN PRESS
A SAGE Publications Company
Thousand Oaks, CA 91320

For information:

Corwin Press
A Sage Publications Company
2455 Teller Road
Thousand Oaks, California 91320
www.corwinpress.com

Sage Publications Ltd.
1 Oliver's Yard
55 City Road
London EC1Y 1SP
United Kingdom

Sage Publications India Pvt. Ltd.
B-42, Panchsheel Enclave
Post Box 4109
New Delhi 110 017 India

Printed in the United States of America on acid-free paper

Library of Congress Cataloging-in-Publication Data

Sparks, Dennis.
Leading for results : transforming teaching, learning, and relationships in schools / Dennis Sparks.
        p. cm.
Includes bibliographical references and index.
ISBN 1-4129-4969-6 or 978-1-4129-4969-9 (cloth) &
ISBN 1-4129-4970-x or 978-1-4129-4970-5 (pbk.)
    1. School management and organization. 2. Educational leadership. I. Title.

LB2805.S735 2005
371.2—dc22

                                        2004019866

This book is printed on acid-free paper.

07   08   09   10   10   9   8   7   6   5   4   3   2

Acquisitions Editor:	Rachel Livsey
Editorial Assistant:	Phyllis Cappello
Production Editor:	Sanford Robinson
Typesetter:	C&M Digitals (P) Ltd.
Indexer:	Kirsten Kite
Cover Designer:	Anthony Paular
Graphic Artist:	Lisa Riley

Acknowledgments

I am immensely grateful to Dave Ellis and Bill Rentz, president and vice president, respectively, of the Brande Foundation, for stimulating many of the ideas in this book. Through the foundation, Dave gave me the deeply appreciated gift of life coaching and demonstrated in his own writing and speaking the power of clarity of thought and of simply expressed ideas. Bill Rentz served ably as my life coach and partner in the development of a "results skills" curriculum out of which a section of this book grew. Dave's and Bill's deep belief in the capacity of individuals and groups to create the life of their dreams has informed and inspired my work.

I want to thank the National Staff Development Council (NSDC) trustees, past and present, who encouraged me and other Council staff members to extend our thinking into new areas and to disseminate our ideas widely. I have been truly honored to work with these individuals and to benefit from their leadership regarding NSDC's ambitious goals for professional learning in schools.

I owe a huge debt of gratitude to the core professional staff of the National Staff Development Council—Stephanie Hirsh, Joan Richardson, Joellen Killion, and Leslie Miller—whose incredible competence and ability to work both independently and as part of various teams make it possible for me to have the intellectual space necessary to prepare a book such as this one. In particular, I want to thank Joan Richardson, NSDC's director of publications, and Tracy Crow, the Council's Web editor, whose careful and thoughtful editing of the first and second editions of this book, respectively, and coordination of this project with Corwin Press have made significant contributions to the quality of this book.

In addition, I would like to extend my appreciation to Rachel Livsey of Corwin Press and Sanford Robinson of Sage Publications for their valuable contribution to this effort. Though the author's name appears on book covers, the individuals who work invisibly behind the scenes have a large effect on the quality of the book you hold in your hands.

Whatever value this book holds for its readers is due in large part to the tens of thousands of educators with whom I have interacted over the years. Their perspectives and experiences have shaped my views and kept me grounded in the day-to-day lives of teachers and school leaders whose work gives purpose to my writing.

About the Author

Dennis Sparks has been executive director of the 11,000-member National Staff Development Council (NSDC) since 1984. Before this position, he was an independent educational consultant and director of the Northwest Staff Development Center, a state- and federally funded teacher center in Livonia, Michigan.

Dr. Sparks has also been a teacher, counselor, and codirector of an alternative high school. He completed his PhD in counseling at the University of Michigan in 1976. He speaks frequently throughout North America on topics such as powerful staff development and school leadership.

He is the author of *Designing Powerful Professional Development for Teachers and Principals* (NSDC, 2002); *Conversations That Matter* (NSDC, 2001), a collection of his JSD interviews since 1991; coauthor with Stephanie Hirsh of *Learning to Lead, Leading to Learn* (NSDC, 2000); coauthor with Joan Richardson of *What Is Staff Development Anyway?* (NSDC, 1998); and coauthor with Stephanie Hirsh of *A New Vision for Staff Development* (ASCD/NSDC, 1997).

Dr. Sparks's column appears each month in the newsletter *The Learning Principal*, a publication of the NSDC. In addition, his articles have appeared in a variety of publications, including *Educational Leadership, Phi Delta Kappan, The American School Board Journal, The Principal,* and *The School Administrator.*

Many of Dr. Sparks's articles and interviews with educational leaders are accessible on the NSDC Web site at www.nsdc.org/library/authors/sparks.cfm.

Introduction

Change Ourselves to Change Organizations

[E]very day of your life is filled with opportunities to be creative, to act with purpose and potency. You don't need an elevated position or a title of great importance to assume a leadership role.

—Larraine Matusak

One who sees the invisible can do the impossible.

—Frank Gaines

L eaders matter. What leaders think, say, and do—and who they are when they come to work each day—profoundly affects organizational performance, the satisfaction they and those with whom they interact derive from their work, and their ability to sustain engagement with their work over the period of time necessary to oversee significant improvements. Leaders' thoughts and actions shape the culture of their organizations and set the direction and pace for the professional learning and teamwork that are essential in improving organizational performance.

Significant change in organizations begins, therefore, with significant change in what leaders think, say, and do. *Leading for Results: Transforming Teaching, Learning, and Relationships in Schools* offers my view on the nature of these changes and how they can be initiated, deepened over time, and used to produce changes in teaching and relationships that benefit all students. Underneath this view, of course, is my belief that the knowledge, skills, understandings, and attitudes described in this book can be developed and nurtured through both formal and informal means.

The type of leadership discussed here might be labeled transformational or authentic. Transformational leadership has as its goal fundamental changes in individuals, organizations, and society. Authentic leadership flows from self-awareness regarding intentions, values, and feelings and wields its influence through actions congruent with that self-awareness. Both transformational and authentic leadership are founded on the belief that individuals can have a profound influence on one another and their organization through particular kinds of interactions and creative processes. Such leadership may be provided by both an organization's official leaders and others within the organization who apply the beliefs and skills presented in these pages.

The type of leadership I advocate activates latent potential within organizations and energizes those who live and work within them. It promotes extraordinary performance in otherwise "ordinary" people. These ideas are developed throughout the book.

AN INNER DEPARTURE

In *The Cultural Creatives: How 50 Million People Are Changing the World*, Paul Ray and Sherry Ruth Anderson (2000) described the inner departures or turning points that shape our lives:

> Whether your inner departure is sparked by something you saw on TV or in the morning paper, or by a personal shock and loss; whether it started in childhood or in the middle of your life or at retirement—at some point, the previously accepted explanation of how things came to be the way they are doesn't satisfy you anymore. (p. 48)

Over a number of years, I came to realize that my work to improve the quality of teacher and administrator professional learning for the benefit of students was not producing the results I desired. During those years, I talked with thousands of educators in countless settings about the importance of high-quality professional learning and the nature of the professional development that led to that learning. I presented research findings, quoted experts, provided practical tips on how to do those things, answered questions, and asked participants to discuss what they were learning and to set goals.

I gradually came to see that this approach was not working, but I did not know another way to create the results I desired. So I lived for several years in an uncomfortable in-between state, convinced that what I was doing wasn't working and feeling frustrated and rudderless because I did not know of another way.

Over time, with the assistance of many people, I began to develop the ideas I present in this book. I offer these ideas to you not as the truth but as an invitation to explore them with an open mind and a sense of possibility that they may lead you to the things you most value and want in your school and life. I hope that you will give each of these ideas careful examination and a thoughtful appraisal as you experiment with them in whatever settings seem most appropriate.

Make the Invisible Visible

I believe deeply in the importance of actualizing human ability and of the critical role that organizational leaders play in both the development and full use of that potential. Before it is actualized, though, that potential is invisible. It lies latent, unnoticed, waiting to be manifested.

Likewise, the human energy required to actualize potential often lies invisible and dormant until it is aroused through the means described in this book. These means include connections with others in ways that enrich and energize us, clarity of thought regarding our values and beliefs, commitment to a compelling purpose, the magnet-like force of a richly detailed vision of that which we desire to create, and the motivation produced by an expanded set of possibilities. Human potential and energy become visible as they manifest through our words and actions and the world changes.

Three of the most significant barriers to the realization of human potential—lack of clarity, resignation, and dependency—are also often invisible to the casual observer. By recognizing and naming them, we begin the process of shifting from lack of clarity to clarity, from resignation to possibility, and from dependency to interdependency and a sense of personal power.

FOCUS ON LEADERS

This book focuses on the leader's role in actualizing human potential and unleashing individual and organizational energy. Leaders do so by connecting people to larger purposes and to one another and by cultivating in their organizations transformational professional learning and breakthrough thinking. I focus on leaders—a category that in schools includes teacher leaders as well as principals and district administrators—because I believe that both formal and informal leaders have the capacity to make a tremendous difference in their organizations through their beliefs, values, intentions, and interactions.

A leader's work in actualizing human potential and unlocking energy is both personal and intensely interpersonal. It begins within each of us and radiates outward as we clarify our purposes and ideas, represent our views to others, improve the quality of our relationships, and shape the culture of our organizations. It is about individuals making a profound difference in the world around them, whether that world is their friends and families, their organizations, their communities, their nation, or the planet.

Because leaders' thoughts, emotions, and behaviors affect the moods and performance of countless others, this book views these qualities as critical but often neglected attributes of leadership. "Every one of our thoughts, emotions, and behaviors has an energy consequence, for better or for worse," Jim Loehr and Tony Schwarz (2003) pointed out in *The Power of Full Engagement.* "The ultimate measure of our lives is not how much time we spend on the planet, but rather how much energy we invest in the time we have" (p. 4).

Jane Dutton (2003) added another dimension to this topic in *Energize Your Workplace:*

[L]eaders can make a profound difference in activating and renewing energy by building and sustaining high-quality connections. . . . High-quality connections contribute substantially to individuals' well-being and work performance. They also contribute significantly to an organization's capacity for collaboration, coordination, learning, and adaptation, as well as its ability to keep people committed and loyal. ("Executive Summary")

In *Shaking Up the Schoolhouse* (2001), Phil Schlechty argued that it is imperative that school leaders be transformational rather than transactional: "Transformational leadership requires the leader to embrace and cause others to embrace new and revolutionary assumptions [rather than] only to improve operational effectiveness based on well-established and commonly accepted assumptions" (p. 164).

The 11th edition of *Merriam Webster's Collegiate Dictionary* (2003) defines *transform* as a "change in composition or structure" and says it "implies a major change in form, nature, or function" (p. 1328). It defines *breakthrough* as "a sudden advance especially in knowledge or technique." David Perkins (2000) stated that breakthrough thinking is a "cognitive snap" and "creativity that makes a decisive break with the past" (p. 6). It is my goal to assist the reader in generating breakthrough thinking that transforms relationships among everyone in schools and dramatically improves the quality of student and educator learning.

Breakthroughs and transformations occur in many ways. Sometimes urgency in the face of life-and-death problems creates breakthroughs, as has been the case in wartime when bold new procedures were tried in the field to save lives. Sometimes it is a powerful moment of individual epiphany and reevaluation such as that experienced by an attorney who said he was led to a career in the ministry after he sat in a beautiful natural setting listening to a performance of the World Youth Symphony Orchestra. At other times, it is a subtle or not-so-subtle shift in perspective that comes from the words of another, such as those reported by Marlo Thomas (2002) in *The Right Words at the Right Time*. For instance, she cited film director Mike Nichols's experience of breakthrough:

> Two or three times in my life, I have read or heard something that seemed in a moment to change me so palpably that I actually heard or felt a click, a sound, tumblers falling into place. . . . [I]t is simply the experience of becoming somebody slightly different, somebody new, the next you. (p. 238)

More than ever, educational leaders live in a results-oriented world with unprecedented external expectations for high levels of student achievement on standardized tests. My aim in *Leading for Results* is not only to help you meet those expectations but also to assist you in creating the additional results you value in your school, school system, and life. Because I believe significant change in organizations begins with transformational change in their leaders—as Gandhi put it, "We must become the change we seek in the world"— this book assists you in developing ways of thinking, speaking, and acting that are particularly powerful in achieving your goals.

Although leadership that promotes continuous improvements in student and adult learning includes many attributes and qualities, the most important of these, I believe, can be reduced to a set of beliefs and abilities that I term *results skills:*

- Clarity of thought regarding intentions and assumptions
- Deep understanding of important subjects
- The capacity to create
- Empowering beliefs
- The concise and consistent expression of those intentions and beliefs in the spirit of dialogue
- Committed listening
- Continuous innovation in the methods used to achieve our goals

I explore each of these results skills in the chapters that follow. I recognize that the readers of this book are already likely to possess highly developed skills. You may have one or more college degrees and hold a responsible position within the education community and may serve on important committees. Because I start with the assumption that you are already successful, this book provides a series of invitations to experiment with one or more of the ideas or skills presented here to determine if they will aid you in achieving that which is most important to you.

My Assumptions

The views I express in *Leading for Results* are grounded in the following assumptions:

> **Leaders matter. Therefore, significant changes in organizations begin with significant changes in what leaders think (depth of understanding and beliefs), say (both the content and form of our speech), and do (a continuous flow of powerful actions within a culture of interpersonal accountability).**

The habits that produce significant advances in schooling—particularly improvements in teaching and learning—begin with significant change in leaders. That means leaders first consider how their own assumptions, understanding of significant issues, and behaviors may be preserving current practices. They then initiate a disciplined process of developing habits of mind and practice that will assist them in achieving their purposes.

> **Lack of clarity, resignation, and dependency on the part of principals and teachers are major barriers to quality teaching in all classrooms and the successful learning of all students.**

When spoken by teachers and principals, the phrases "I don't know what to do," "There's nothing I can do," and "Tell me what to do" are among the most damaging and disempowering unintended consequences of school reform efforts. The ideas and skills I present in this book are a means by which school leaders can move themselves and those with whom they interact to more empowered and enabling points of view.

> **High-quality professional interactions within a high-performance culture are a prerequisite to quality teaching in all classrooms.**

Most of the important forms of professional learning occur in the daily and routine interactions among teachers in which they work together to improve lessons, deepen one another's understanding of content, analyze student work, examine various data sources on student performance, and solve the myriad of problems they face each day. From this perspective, sustained teacher-to-teacher communication about teaching and learning is the most powerful source of professional learning and instructional improvement. Consequently, one of the most important responsibilities of school leaders is the development of a high-performance culture that has at its heart mutual respect and trust, collaboration, continuous improvement, and a climate in which generative human connections can thrive.

> **Because instructional and cultural change are intensely interpersonal, it is essential that leaders consistently apply communication and problem-solving skills that promote productive relationships founded on qualities such as clarity of values and purpose, authenticity, candor, trust, and integrity.**

Deep and far-reaching improvements originate in relationships formed within strong, purpose-focused, accountable, and action-oriented communities. Improving instruction and building culture are relationship intensive and often conflict ridden. Unless leaders successfully address the complex and often emotionally laden interpersonal demands of school leadership, schools won't achieve long-term improvements in teaching and student achievement. Such improvements require principals and teachers to take the lead in establishing a high-performance culture.

> **Organizations are successful and most likely to sustain that success over time when leaders at all levels serve as teachers of others. Such leaders establish teaching and learning for everyone as an organizational norm.**

Some leaders believe that the best way to "run" an organization is to issue directives, monitor compliance, and provide rewards and sanctions as appropriate. Communication flows from the top down and fear is a primary motivator. Another approach, one that I believe is more successful in producing results and strengthening relationships, is for leaders to see themselves as their organizations' "head teachers." They teach not by telling or directing those with whom they work, but by engaging them in dialogue about important issues based on leaders' clearly formulated and expressed points of view.

In *The Cycle of Leadership: How Great Leaders Teach Their Companies to Win*, Noel Tichy (2002) describes organizations with this style of leadership as "teaching organizations," the dialogue-based interactions as "interactive teaching," and leaders' clarity of thought as a "teachable point of view." Leaders lead by teaching, not by commanding, Tichy argues. "A Teaching Organization is one in which everyone is a teacher, everyone is a learner, and as a result, everyone gets smarter every day," Tichy writes.

> **The intellectual and creative capacity of educators—particularly principals and teachers—to make significant improvements in teaching and learning is an underdeveloped and untapped resource.**

The most successful schools are innovation machines, in which students and adults continually invent better ways of achieving their purposes and which amplify the best practices of teachers across the faculty. Teachers in such schools tap research and best practice, but they do so as peers and partners with researchers and policy makers who recognize and value their contributions and talents. Unless such appreciative and respectful relationships are in place, we cannot create schools in which all students and teachers learn and perform at high levels.

> **Sustained action-oriented professional learning by all principals and teachers is essential in creating schools with quality teaching in every classroom.**

High-quality professional development is intellectually rigorous, attends to both content knowledge and teaching methods, enhances the quality of professional judgment, and embeds teachers in a supportive community of professional practice. High-quality professional development enables teachers to bridge the "knowing-doing" gap that is prevalent in virtually all schools so that new practices are initiated and sustained in classrooms.

> **Planning and implementation decisions about professional learning matter—whether those decisions are made at the federal, district, state, or school level. This means that district administrators, principals, and teachers must consistently advocate for the most powerful forms of professional learning.**

Visa founder Dee Hock provided a standard against which policy may be measured: "Have a simple, clear purpose," he said, "which gives rise to complex, intelligent behavior rather than complex rules and regulations that give rise to simplistic thinking and stupid behavior." Effective planning and policy decisions, therefore, provide a clear, compelling purpose grounded in improved practice and student learning; develops in teachers and administrators complex, intelligent behavior; and provides resources to maintain this effort over many years.

Planning and policy decisions made by school improvement committees, district staff development committees, and policy-making bodies can guide teachers and principals toward the most powerful forms of professional learning or lead them toward low-level learning and the dependency and resignation discussed earlier. (I recommend that readers preview the section titled "How to Use This Book," before engaging in the following activities.)

EXAMINE YOUR ASSUMPTIONS

Write your assumptions regarding the significance of what leaders think, say, and do, stating them as succinctly and powerfully as possible. Make simple, declarative statements of your beliefs. For instance, you may believe that leaders really don't matter because teachers are the ones who ultimately affect student learning. Share your assumptions with colleagues in the spirit of dialogue.

_____

_____

_____

_____

_____

_____

DEEPEN YOUR UNDERSTANDING

Clarify in writing your views on the impact of leaders in achieving organizational goals and the qualities of leaders that produce that effect. Discuss your views with others.

_____

_____

_____

_____

_____

_____

ENGAGE IN NEXT ACTION THINKING

Specify actions you will take to apply what you have learned in this chapter about leadership and by what date you will take those actions.

_____

_____

_____

_____

_____

_____

_____

REFERENCES

Dutton, J. (2003). *Energize your workplace.* San Francisco: Jossey-Bass.

Loehr, J., & Schwarz, T. (2003). *The power of full engagement.* New York: Free Press.

Merriam Webster. (2003). *Merriam-Webster's collegiate dictionary* (11th ed.). Springfield, MA: Author.

Perkins, D. (2000). *The eureka effect: The art and logic of breakthrough thinking.* New York: W.W. Norton.

Ray, P., & Anderson, S. R. (2000). *The cultural creatives: How 50 million people are changing the world.* New York: Three Rivers Press.

Schlechty, P. (2001). *Shaking up the schoolhouse.* San Francisco: Jossey-Bass.

Thomas, M. (2002). *The right words at the right time.* New York: Atria.

Tichy, N. (2002). *The cycle of leadership: How great leaders teach their companies to win.* New York: HarperCollins Publishers.

How to Use This Book

All acts of understanding require accessing prior knowledge and apply-
ing it to guide the noticing, framing, and connecting of new ideas and
events to what is already encoded in memory. This is an active process,
not a passive encoding of information.

—James Spillane, Brian Reiser, & Todd Reimer

Only when students can articulate in writing the basic principles they
are learning . . . can we be sure that they are internalizing those prin-
ciples in an intellectually coherent way.

—Richard Paul

> **My assumptions: The major purposes of professional learning
> are to deepen understanding, transform beliefs and assump-
> tions, and create a stream of continuous actions that changes
> habits and affects practice. Such learning most often occurs
> through sustained attention, study, and action.**

I intend *Leading for Results: Transforming Teaching, Learning, and
Relationships in Schools* to be a tool to inform your professional
learning and guide your actions. From my perspective, the major
purposes of professional learning are to deepen understanding,
transform beliefs and assumptions, and create a stream of continuous
actions that changes habits and affects practice. To those ends, I bring
you what I regard as leading-edge ideas and practices about improving the quality of leadership, teaching, and student learning and ask

you to seriously consider their implications for your work through sustained attention, study, and action of the kind promoted in this book.

Although there is no single correct way to use this book, I believe its value will best be realized when used by a study group whose members are committed to improving professional learning, teaching, and leadership in their school or school system. Chapters may be studied in any order or used in combination as starting points for dialogue, professional learning, and action related to the topic at hand.

In subsequent chapters, I seldom include citations to the work of others because I intend this book to be an expression of my views based on my reading and experience in the field. I want you to interact with the ideas to develop your own views rather than simply surrender your point of view to "experts." Quotations are highlighted to stimulate your thinking and promote dialogue. Readers interested in a fuller exploration of most of the ideas presented here will be able to find countless columns, articles, and books that address them, including my earlier book, *Designing Powerful Professional Development for Teachers and Principals,* available at www.nsdc.org/library/leaders/sparksbook.cfm.

Some of my favorite nonfiction books use stories or anecdotes to illustrate important points. (See Chapter 9 to consider the value of stories in promoting improvement.) I have shied away from such examples here, however, because the appropriate use of the ideas and skills presented here are context bound. That makes it difficult to provide a succinct example to illustrate external variables and internal thought processes that affect a particular course of action. In addition, some of my most compelling illustrations come from real-life situations and would be virtually impossible to recount without compromising the anonymity of those involved. So, to the best of your ability, please reflect on your own personal and professional lives as a source of stories that illustrate and make personally meaningful the ideas I present.

WHAT'S NEW IN THIS EDITION

Since the publication of the first edition of *Leading for Results: Transforming Teaching, Learning, and Relationships in Schools*, I have had the opportunity to teach its contents to education leaders at every level. The more I worked with leaders, the more I became convinced that the power to change schools lies in their hands, and that through clarity, dialogue, and meaningful interactions, learning teams can create solutions to almost any challenge.

While the fundamental premises of the book haven't changed, I have been fortunate to encounter exciting ideas and useful practices that I believe can be useful in improving relationships and transforming learning in schools. I developed 18 new chapters for this edition, which led to some reordering and an additional section.

As with the first edition, I offer the "Introduction" and this section as starting points for the book. From there, individual readers or study groups may determine what chapters will best help them achieve their goals.

ORGANIZATION OF THE BOOK

Leading for Results is divided into four parts:

"Transformation Through Clarity and Creation" addresses the power of clarity of thought, breakthrough thinking, and human creativity. These chapters describe ways to develop clarity regarding intentions, values, assumptions, and actions.

"Transformation Through Interpersonal Influence" provides insight into specific results-oriented ways of speaking, listening, and interacting. These chapters present ways to use these skills to achieve a school's most important purposes.

"Transformation Through a Culture That Promotes Professional Learning, Teamwork, and Continuous Improvement" covers the environment in which teaching and learning takes place. These chapters address attitudes, emotions, and barriers to learning in order to improve teaching and learning.

"Transformation Through Professional Learning and Doing" provides an overview of the attributes of the most effective forms of professional development for improving staff and student learning. These chapters consider how to develop new professional habits of thought and behavior and bridge the knowing-doing gap.

Each chapter promotes deeper understanding, transformational learning, and "next action thinking" as described below.

Deeper Understanding: Some forms of professional learning are shallow. Because of the design of the experience, participants' learning skims across the surface of complex topics. Although superficial learning has its place in creating awareness of issues, it is far too often the sum and substance of professional development for teachers and administrators.

A common example is teachers who attend an introductory workshop on cooperative learning and leave knowing only that the process involves students working together in small groups. Likewise, principals may superficially learn the procedures of "walk-throughs" as an instructional leadership activity but not truly understand the subtleties of what they might observe or how to discuss their observations with teachers.

Therefore, each chapter asks you to more fully engage your brain by elaborating your learning in various ways to deepen your understanding and to create meaning and a context for the learning. Deep understanding typically requires sustained thought and engagement with a subject. Such engagement asks learners of all ages to paraphrase what they are learning, draw inferences from it, and connect new learning to prior knowledge and experience. It also asks them to synthesize and evaluate what they are learning; to write, speak, and prepare mind maps and other graphic organizers; to engage in dialogue; and to develop action plans for applying their learning.

Transformational Learning: Because beliefs and assumptions (what we hold to be true about a subject) exert a powerful force on our behavior and professional practice, it is critically important that leaders examine their own beliefs to determine if they are furthering their purposes or impeding them. Transformational learning at the level of beliefs and assumptions can occur through many means, but two of the most common are dialogue and engagement in activities that evoke strong emotions or create cognitive dissonance, or both. In dialogue, participants surface and explore their assumptions in a non-threatening setting and gradually open themselves to seeing the world from the perspective of others. Strong emotion and cognitive dissonance may be evoked when leaders make site visits, shadow or interview students, or are confronted by disaggregated data that break through walls of denial.

For the purposes of this book, I encourage you to use dialogue whenever possible to deepen your understanding of the topic and to promote transformational learning. To stimulate this form of interaction, I include my own assumptions in each chapter whenever appropriate. In the spirit of dialogue, I invite you to identify and express your own assumptions on those topics and to encourage others with whom you interact to do the same. To stimulate and clarify your thinking and to provide balance, I provide in the "Examine Your Assumptions" section of each chapter beliefs that I have heard expressed by educators that are contrary to my own.

"Dialogue . . . imposes a rigorous discipline on the participants," Daniel Yankelovich (1999) wrote in *The Magic of Dialogue: Transforming Conflict Into Cooperation.* He added:

> [W]hen dialogue is done skillfully, the results can be extraordinary: long-standing stereotypes dissolved, mistrust overcome, mutual understanding achieved, visions shaped and grounded in shared purpose, people previously at odds with one another aligned on objectives and strategies, new common ground discovered, new perspectives and insights gained, new levels of creativity stimulated, and bonds of community strengthened. (p. 16)

The discipline that Yankelovich (1999) recommended (and that I suggest you use in discussing this and other chapters) includes equality among participants, an absence of coercive influences, empathic listening, and the ability to bring assumptions into the open while suspending judgment. Those seeking to maximize the benefits they receive from this book may wish to read *The Magic of Dialogue,* by Yankelovich, or *Dialogue: Rediscovering the Transforming Power of Conversation* by Linda Ellinor and Glenna Gerard (1998).

Next Action Thinking: A stream of continuous actions is required to change habits to improve leadership and instructional practices. Deep understanding and clarity regarding assumptions are of limited value unless they are followed by commitments to such actions and a sense of interpersonal accountability for completing them. In *Getting Things Done: The Art of Stress-Free Productivity* (2001), David Allen wrote, "Over the years, I have noticed an extraordinary shift in energy and productivity whenever individuals and groups installed 'What's the next action?' as a fundamental and consistently asked question" (p. 236). The result, he says, would be that "no meeting or discussion will end, and no interaction cease, without a clear determination of whether or not some action is needed—and if it is, what it will be, or at least who has responsibility for it" (p. 236). Allen argued that "shifting your focus to something that your mind perceives as a doable, completable task will create a real increase in positive energy, direction, and motivation" (p. 242).

My goal is that you use this book to deepen your understanding of its topics, shift your beliefs to empower yourself and others, and set in motion a stream of powerful goal-focused actions within a system of interpersonal accountability that includes regular reflection on the impact of those actions. To aid you in implementing the ideas and skills in this book, I offer its content in bite-size chapters that can be digested over a period of weeks or months.

Simply reading these entries, however, is unlikely to improve your understanding or use of these ideas. I encourage you to slow down to ponder the meaning and implications of what you are reading so you can intellectually interact with the ideas. Write about and teach others what you are learning. Creatively combine these ideas for your unique purposes. Of ultimate importance are the quality of discussion and intensity of motivation provided by a study group, your depth of engagement with the ideas, and the actions you take as a consequence of that understanding.

EXAMINE YOUR ASSUMPTIONS

Write your assumptions regarding the significance of what leaders think, say, and do, stating them as succinctly and powerfully as possible. Make simple, declarative statements of your beliefs. For instance, you may believe that the major reason and only purpose for professional development is to meet district, state, and federal requirements. Share your assumptions with colleagues in the spirit of dialogue.

_____

_____

_____

_____

_____

_____

DEEPEN YOUR UNDERSTANDING

Describe in writing and discuss with others the methods you use when you want to understand a subject more deeply. Consider which of them might be most effective in promoting your learning from this book.

_____

_____

_____

_____

_____

_____

ENGAGE IN NEXT ACTION THINKING

Specify actions you will take to apply those learning methods as you study this book.

_____

_____

_____

_____

_____

_____

REFERENCES

Allen, D. (2001). *Getting things done: The art of stress-free productivity.* New York: Viking.

Ellinor, L., & Gerard, G. (1998). *Dialogue: Rediscovering the transforming power of conversation.* New York: John Wiley & Sons.

Yankelovich, D. (1999). *The magic of dialogue: Transforming conflict into cooperation.* New York: Simon & Schuster.

PART I

Transformation Through Clarity and Creation

Long-distance winners often have disarmingly simple mission statements. When the question was put to Jonas Salk, he replied: "To reduce human suffering."

—John R. O'Neil

People with clear minds are like magnets.

—Wilma Mankiller

The chapters in Part I: Transformation Through Clarity and Creation are based on a few simple premises:

- We affect the world through clarity regarding our most fundamental values and purposes.
- Intentions aligned with our individual and collective values and purposes are particularly powerful in producing the results we most desire.
- Having multiple, well-considered pathways to achieving large, important goals significantly increases the likelihood of producing those results.
- Educators' capacity to invent solutions to educational problems is a powerful, untapped resource for improvement.

Because school leaders' most important responsibilities are helping schools set inspiring goals and engaging staff members in creating the means to achieve them, leaders' intentions and the way they are expressed have a profound effect on the organizations they lead. Consequently, one of the most important skills possessed by leaders is clarity of thought and speech about what they believe and want to create. And because the clarity and the sense of empowerment leaders provide are contagious, individuals and organizations are transformed when these qualities are brought with persistence to various settings.

Here is a famous example of the power of the succinct expression of intention aligned with a fundamental purpose: In 1940, Winston Churchill spoke to the British House of Commons. In his first speech as Prime Minister, he said: "I would say to the House, as I said to those who have joined this government: 'I have nothing to offer but blood, toil, tears, and sweat.' . . . You ask, what is our policy? I can say: It is to wage war, by sea, land, and air, with all our might and with all the strength that God can give us. . . . You ask, what is our aim? I can answer in one word: It is victory, victory at all costs, victory in spite of all terror, victory, however long and hard the road may be; for without victory, there is no survival."

While we all do not possess the oratorical skills of Winston Churchill nor do we lead in lofty matters of state, Churchill's passionate commitment to his purpose and the clarity of his aim are qualities each of us can adapt to our own settings. And when leaders assist teachers in connecting with deeper purposes and tapping into their own creative powers, the passion and commitment that are generated will fuel sustained professional learning and continuous improvement in teaching and learning.

CHAPTER 1

Use Fundamental Choices to Create Your Life

Either you are creating your life, or circumstances are.

—Thomas Leonard

One fundamental choice is the primary influence on all other choices; every day you can choose consciously to move consistently, persistently, and boldly in the direction of your dreams.

—David McNally & Karl Speak

My assumptions: Leaders' fundamental choices—their basic orientation toward life and their work—affect their everyday actions in profound and often invisible ways. Consciously choosing one's fundamental choice based on heartfelt values and intentions is a powerful leadership tool.

A while back, I had lunch with a group of principals, during which one of them described a recent presentation he had attended on job-embedded professional learning, in which a participant had aggressively countered every suggestion offered by the presenter with a reason why it couldn't be done. I responded, "Until someone has made a fundamental choice to do something, there's always a reason not to do it," a thought I undoubtedly had acquired from a wise person somewhere along the way. What that

> When people make a fundamental choice to be true to what is highest in them, or when they make a choice to fulfill a purpose in their life, they can easily accomplish many changes that seemed impossible or improbable in the past.
>
> —Robert Fritz

means to me in this situation is that until a principal or other leader has chosen at a basic level to have all teachers experience high-quality professional learning as part of their daily work, there will always be reasons why it can't be done. The same could be said about many other worthy goals.

In *The Path of Least Resistance*, Robert Fritz (1989) defined *fundamental choice* as "a choice in which you commit yourself to a basic life orientation or a basic state of being" (p. 188). Fundamental choices are like magnets that align and organize our goals and daily actions. Usually, a single fundamental choice governs our entire life, but sometimes individuals select one for their personal lives and another for their professional lives.

> How different our lives are when we really know what is deeply important to us, and, keeping that picture in mind, we manage ourselves each day to be and do what really matters.
>
> —Stephen Covey

For instance, I made a fundamental choice for my life in general to "have an A+ day, every day." That means that as I consider each day's activities and the moment-to-moment decisions about what I will think, say, or do, I consider whether they lead me to that goal or away from it. While in many instances I don't succeed in realizing that aspiration, it nonetheless guides me to a more fulfilling life than I would experience without it.

While Fritz's (1989) notion of a fundamental choice as a basic life orientation implies only one such guiding aspiration, some educators find it helpful, at least initially, to create a fundamental choice for both their personal and professional lives. I define my professional fundamental choice to do all that I can in my sphere of influence to create a system of schools in which each of us would send our own child to any classroom in any school.

Over the years, I have collected quotations that represent examples of fundamental choices made by well-known and not so well-known individuals:

> *To affect the quality of the day—that is highest of arts.*
>
> —Thoreau

I wish to be up and doing, I wish to face each day with resolution and purpose. I wish to use every waking hour to give encouragement, to bless those whose burdens are heavy, to build faith and strength of testimony. It is the presence of wonderful people which stimulates the adrenaline. It is the look of love in their eyes which gives me energy.

—Gordon Hinckley, age 92 years

A pebble cast into a pond causes ripples that spread in all directions. Each one of our thoughts, words, and deeds is like that. We won't sit down and feel hopeless. There's too much work to do.

—Dorothy Day

To feel joy requires a decision on our part—it is a chosen approach to life, a chosen attitude, a chosen awareness.

—Jaroldeen Asplund Edwards

We won't be the instrument of other people's intentions.

—Peter Yarrow

One must have the adventurous daring to accept oneself as a bundle of possibilities and undertake the most interesting game in the world— making the most of one's best.

—Harry Emerson Fosdick

If there is a soul, it is a mistake to believe that it is given to us fully created. It is created here, throughout a whole life.

—Albert Camus

Take care of yourself; take care of others; take care of this place.

—Dee Hock

Stephen Covey (2004) provided several strategies that may help you identify your fundamental choice:

- assume you've had a heart attack, now live accordingly;
- assume that the half-life of your profession is two years, now prepare accordingly;
- assume everything you say about another, they can overhear, now speak accordingly;
- assume you have a one-on-one visit with your Creator every quarter, now live accordingly. (p. 58)

EXAMINE YOUR ASSUMPTIONS

Write your assumptions regarding fundamental choices. For instance, you may believe that school leaders are too busy to ponder their fundamental choices, and even if they did find the time, too many uncontrollable forces exist to knock them off course. Share your assumptions with colleagues in the spirit of dialogue.

_____

_____

_____

_____

_____

_____

_____

DEEPEN YOUR UNDERSTANDING

Reflect on the fundamental choices that have governed your life to this point, whether you have been aware of them or not. Consider the fundamental choices of others whom you respect, including those who have served as role models, even though you may never have met them.

_____

_____

_____

_____

_____

_____

_____

ENGAGE IN NEXT ACTION THINKING

Formulate in writing a fundamental choice for your life or fundamental choices you wish to guide your personal and professional lives. To further clarify your fundamental choice, share it with others and, if it would be useful, revise it.

_____

_____

_____

_____

_____

_____

_____

REFERENCES

Covey, S. (2004). *The 8th habit: From effectiveness to greatness.* New York: Free Press.

Fritz, R. (1989). *The path of least resistance.* New York: Fawcett Columbine.

CHAPTER 2

Clarify Your Intentions

You will bring into your life whatever it is that you have the most clarity about. The trouble is, most people have a great deal of clarity about what it is they don't want.

—Susan Scott

Man's vitality is as great as his intentionality: they are interdependent.

—Paul Tillich

My assumptions: Clearly formulated and expressed intentions and pride about what we want are powerful tools in creating the results we desire. Almost always, our desires are trusted guides for the future of our organizations.

Knowing what we want and being proud of it increases the likelihood we will achieve the results we seek. Intentions described in rich detail offer direction for their achievement and make it more likely we will recognize valuable opportunities.

Telling the truth about what we want in our lives is essential to being effective leaders and human beings in relationship to one another. Naming and describing our desires and generating multiple pathways to realizing them (about which more will be said in Chapter 7) empowers us. Our empowerment, in turn, empowers those with whom we interact.

A method I use to identify and clarify my intentions is to write them on three-by-five-inch index cards, one per card. A computer might be used for the same purpose. I begin with the sentence stem, "I want . . . ," and write whatever comes to mind. At the end of a 15-minute session, I may have 20 to 25 intentions, some of which

I will simply throw away upon second thought. I might use such a session for the broad purpose of gathering intentions related to all subjects that come to mind or in a more focused way related to a particular problem or issue. I use the back of index cards to add descriptive detail regarding the intention and possible action steps.

> No wind favors him who has no destined port.
>
> —Montaigne

I encourage you to capture in writing your intention, specific details or images of attaining that goal, and the steps you will take to reach it. Writing can crystallize and freeze our thinking so we can examine and strengthen it. I recommend writing a brief essay or constructing a mind map about what achieving the goal would look and feel like and the effects it will have on people who encounter it.

Our complaints (and those of others) are another means of better understanding our intentions and commitments. One way of addressing the dispiriting effects of complaints, particularly about professional issues, is to recognize that behind most complaints lies a commitment to something of value to the individual. Thwarting that commitment activates the complaint. Allowing individuals and groups to identify and express these intentions and commitments and to consider ways of realizing them is a powerful tool for achieving results.

> Dare to be remarkable.
>
> —Jane Gentry

Robert Kegan and Lisa Lahey (2001) describe this phenomenon in *How the Way We Talk Can Change the Way We Work*. "[F]or every commitment we genuinely hold to bring about some important change, there is another commitment we hold that has the effect of preventing the change," they write (p. 63). For instance, a principal who is committed to ensuring quality teaching for all students may find that she also has a not entirely conscious countervailing commitment to avoiding conflict with staff members.

Kegan and Lahey also contend that "Big Assumptions" firmly hold these countervailing commitments in place. They say individuals treat these assumptions as accurate representations of reality and believe dire consequences will follow if they are violated.

> You maximize the likelihood of developing creative and innovative solutions by setting aside presumed human, physical, information, and financial constraints that limit your vision.
>
> —Gerald Nadler & Shozo Hibino

Big Assumptions derive their influence because they typically pass under the radar of our conscious awareness and because they presume dire consequences. For instance, in the example above, the principal may believe conflict will quickly escalate out of control and result in anger, hurt feelings, or even irreparably damaged relationships.

Kegan and Lahey recommend that individuals and groups:

- Explore their countervailing commitments (I'm committed to quality teaching for all students in this school, but I'm also committed to minimizing conflict and getting along with everyone);
- Examine the "Big Assumptions" that anchor the competing commitment (If I truthfully say my views, it will provoke conflict and the consequences will be horrible); and
- Design simple, low-risk experiments to determine the validity of their assumptions (At a grade-level meeting, explaining her views on ways to strengthen teaching).

EXAMINE YOUR ASSUMPTIONS

Write your assumptions regarding the value of clarifying what you want, stating them as succinctly and powerfully as possible. For instance, you may believe "My job as a leader is to serve other people so that they get what they want. My desires are secondary to their purposes." Share your assumptions with colleagues in the spirit of dialogue.

_____

_____

_____

_____

_____

_____

_____

DEEPEN YOUR UNDERSTANDING

Teach one or more people about the value of clarifying our professional and personal intentions.

If possible, provide one or more examples of how clarity of intent helped you achieve your goals.

> Many of us hold ourselves back from imagining a desired outcome unless someone can show us how to get there. Unfortunately, that's backwards in terms of how our minds work to generate and recognize solutions and methods.
>
> —David Allen

ENGAGE IN NEXT ACTION THINKING

List at least 10 things you want at work. List everything that comes to mind. Make a second list of things you want in your personal life. Add details to improve the clarity of your intentions. Review your list each day, adding, deleting, or revising items as appropriate. Set a goal to have at least 50 items on each list within a month.

_____

_____

_____

_____

_____

_____

_____

REFERENCE

Kegan, R., & Lahey, L. (2001). *How the way we talk can change the way we work.* San Francisco: Jossey-Bass.

CHAPTER 3

Establish
Stretch Goals

Make no little plans; they have no magic to stir men's blood and probably in themselves will not be realized. Make big plans; aim high in hope and work remembering that a noble, logical diagram once recorded will never die.

—Daniel Hudson Burnham

If you limit your choices to what seems possible or reasonable, you disconnect yourself from what you truly want, and what is left is a compromise.

—Robert Fritz

> **My assumption: Ambitious goals are more likely to produce the deep changes in beliefs and practices that are essential in improving the learning of all students and in sustaining those changes over time.**

One theory of goal setting recommends setting modest, incremental goals because people are more likely to achieve them and to experience the motivation provided by that success. This motivation, in turn, leads to continued improvement.

Another theory says "stretch goals"—goals so large they seem impossible to achieve—and the deep changes they require for their attainment are more valuable in producing significant, lasting improvements in schools. The benefits of both processes can be obtained, however, when their strengths are blended. Stretch goals can stimulate deep change, while incremental "milestone" goals can provide mid-course markers of improvement (which could be viewed as incremental goals) and offer opportunities to celebrate success and experience the motivation provided by achieving them.

> [Big Hairy Audacious Goals] . . . may be daunting and perhaps risky, but the adventure, excitement, and challenge of it grabs people in the gut, gets their juices flowing, and creates immense forward momentum.
>
> —James Collins & Jerry Porras

Stretch goals are important because most individuals and organizations underestimate their ability to improve. For instance, teachers or administrators may believe students from particular families or ethnic and racial groups are less capable of certain types of learning. That's why leaders in this field like Dave Ellis ask educators to set goals for "paradise" and then to reset them for "paradise times four" and David Allen encourages us to envision "wild success."

> Part of an organization's vision can be an ideal toward which we always strive without ever reaching it. Part of a vision must be attainable, lest the group lose hope.
>
> —Max DePree

Stretch goals by their very nature require important, deep changes in the organization. Achieving stretch goals (some individuals use the term "BHAG" to prompt themselves to establish *Big, Hairy, Audacious Goals*) requires unrelenting focus, clarity of thought, consistent communication, alignment of resources, innovation, discipline, and teamwork. For example, the goal that all students will read at grade level or higher when they leave this school is likely to require significant alterations in curriculum, assessment, teaching methods, leadership practices, after-school programs, and engagement with parents.

> Leaders who get the best results combine an ability to set inspiring goals and a willingness to admit that they don't know exactly how to accomplish those goals.
>
> —Kate Sweetman

EXAMINE YOUR ASSUMPTIONS

> [C]onstriction of the possible could be the single largest obstacle in the way of renewal.
>
> —John O'Neil

> In striving to attain big things, the little things become easy, but in striving to attain only little things, even they become hard.
>
> —C. T. Gilbreath

Write your assumptions regarding the value of stretch goals in stimulating significant improvement, stating them as succinctly and powerfully as possible. For instance, you may believe "Stretch goals by their very nature set up teachers for dispiriting frustration and failure, feelings that are a major barrier to continuous improvement." Share your assumptions with colleagues in the spirit of dialogue.

_____

_____

_____

_____

_____

_____

_____

DEEPEN YOUR UNDERSTANDING

> When we have successfully experienced a deep change, it inspires us to encourage others to undergo a similar experience. We are all potential change agents. As we discipline our talents, we deepen our perceptions about what is possible.
>
> —Robert Quinn

Stretch your intentions by detailing the qualities and characteristics of the school you would create if you knew you could not fail in its implementation. As you conceptualize this school, plan it without knowing whether you would be a student, teacher, or principal and that you would play this role forever. Consider how your description might inform your current school improvement efforts.

_____

_____

_____

_____

_____

_____

_____

ENGAGE IN NEXT ACTION THINKING

Establish one or more stretch goals for your work or for your school, specifying actions you will take and by what date you will take those actions.

_____

_____

_____

_____

_____

_____

_____

CHAPTER 4

Identify Multiple Ways to Achieve Your Goals

The problem with trying to figure out how to achieve a goal before becoming committed to it is that the most effective means to a goal usually are invented in the process of achieving the goal itself.

—Dave Ellis

Most situations in life don't have a single right answer.... In my experience, the most effective actions arise when we live the question, 'What do we want to create?' ... The key to all this is really pretty simple—believing that every person has the capacity to create.

—Peter Senge

> **My assumptions: Most goals can be achieved in many ways. This awareness frees us from "one-right-way" thinking and a dependence on "experts" to "advise" us. It also engages our creative capacities and promotes responsibility for selecting the most powerful strategies.**

For some people, realizing that most goals can be reached in many ways is a breakthrough thought. Thinking that there is a single right answer to complex educational problems and that "science" or an "expert" knows it—even though researchers and other experts often disagree—diminishes educators' belief in their capacity to innovate and their sense of responsibility for producing results. Dependency and resignation can easily become by-products of such thinking.

While educators' dependence on expert advice is often debilitating, reasoned opinion and the research and professional literature upon which it is based have their place in decision making. They can inform our assumptions, provide the substance for brainstorming during planning, and help us assess improvement strategies to determine their power and likelihood for achieving the desired result.

Getting a good idea begins with getting your hands on many ideas, Jonas Salk is credited with observing. Sometimes these ideas originate in our prior knowledge or experience. At other times, we may glean ideas from the professional literature, from consultants or other experts, or have conversations with those who have gone down this road before us. Our goal during this phase is not to find the "right" solution, but to expand the options for consideration. Some authorities on the creative process call this phase "saturation" as we fill our minds with information methodically sought from numerous sources.

> Stimulate your creativity by allowing for several alternative solutions and keeping them viable for as long as possible.
>
> —Gerald Nadler & Shozo Hibino

A common problem at this stage is for individual or groups to settle too quickly on the first strategy that comes to mind rather than seriously weighing the pros and cons of various approaches. Groups enter the "zone of wishful thinking" when they select a course of action without first determining its effectiveness. Another common problem in strategy selection is "group think," which occurs when individuals accede to the views of the group even though they doubt the wisdom of the decision.

Individuals and school groups can use a number of processes to improve the quality of the strategies they select. One way is to expand group thinking by brainstorming ways to achieve the goal. This process can sometimes be aided by first reviewing research and other professional literature. Brainstorming is most effective, of course, when far-out, creative ideas are encouraged and participants feel emotionally safe to contribute to the process. Some facilitators prefer asking participants to create their own lists of ideas before the group begins brainstorming. Brainstorming honors the expertise that exists within the person or group, recognizes that most problems have more than one possible solution, and prevents us from prematurely selecting the first solution that comes to mind.

Sometimes a quick review of a brainstormed list reveals items for immediate action. At other times, it is critical to stand back from the list to determine the most powerful strategies, particularly when money and time for strategy implementation are in short supply. One way to do this is to apply the "80/20 principle," which holds that

80% of the benefits will be found among 20% of the items on the list. A thoughtful discussion about which 20% of the items would produce 80% of the benefits may provide guidance about where to begin. In some situations, it may be helpful to further refine the strategies by using each item on the "20%" list as a source for further brainstorming. The "80/20 principle" could again be applied to each list to identify the items likely to produce the maximum benefit. I write more about this strategy in Chapter 6.

Another means of vetting the original brainstormed list is to create a filter, such as a rubric or decision matrix, through which items must pass before being implemented. Research and perspectives gained from professional literature may provide a basis for the filter. Other considerations may be included as well, such as expense and professional judgment regarding the strategy's impact. A simple process for doing this is asking individuals to indicate with a vote of one to five fingers their views on how successful the strategy or combination of strategies will be in achieving the intended result.

> The most interesting thing I've noticed is that there's a consistent order to the quality of ideas. You'd think the sixtieth idea would be the most lame, but for my purposes, which are to trigger leaps of imagination, it's often opposite. . . . The closer they get to the sixtieth idea, the more imaginative they become—because they have been forced to stretch their thinking.
>
> —Twyla Tharp

A way to double-check the power of the selected strategies is to articulate a "theory of change" that explains to someone outside the group its assumptions about how the proposed actions will accomplish its purposes. The process of making explicit these assumptions often reveals significant gaps in the plan that, if left unattended, would lead to failure. I have more to say on this topic in Chapter 9.

> [A] key characteristic distinguishing high-performing teams from lesser-performing ones is the ability to generate more options. This requires time for expansive thinking and idea generation from narrowing options through analysis and evaluation.
>
> —M. Kathryn Clubb

Discussions at this level of specificity often reveal the depth of the group's commitment to doing whatever is necessary to achieve the goal. Participants will sometimes report at this point that they thought the goal-setting and strategy development process was just another exercise to fulfill a bureaucratic requirement that no one had taken very seriously.

Individuals or groups typically find it useful to establish bench-marks to help measure progress and to help them know early on whether strategies are beginning to have their desired effect. These benchmarks also are a reminder to regularly celebrate progress.

Candor is important during this process, particularly when the efficacy of various approaches is being weighed and strategies selected. Group members often have views about a strategy that are unexpressed because of the power of group opinion, the desire to minimize conflict with colleagues, or a lack of psychological safety and trust in the group. Waiting for the optimal conditions before speaking our truth may mean less effective ideas will be accepted, squandering precious resources and the goodwill of those affected by the decision. Chapter 9 addresses this subject.

EXAMINE YOUR ASSUMPTIONS

Write your assumptions regarding "one-right-way thinking" and the value of generating many methods to achieve a goal or solve a problem, stating them as succinctly and powerfully as possible. For instance, you may believe "For most school improvement goals there is a right way to achieve success and it can be found in educational research." Share your assumptions with colleagues in the spirit of dialogue.

_____

_____

_____

_____

_____

_____

DEEPEN YOUR UNDERSTANDING

Describe your experiences with brainstorming and with other methods of generating ideas. Discuss methods you have used for selecting the most promising approaches from initial lists of ideas. For example, you may recall the generation of ideas that occurred as you selected strategies to use in your school or district improvement efforts, or you may consider a personal experience such as identifying places to visit or activities for a family vacation.

_____

_____

_____

_____

_____

_____

_____

Engage in Next Action Thinking

Specify actions you will take to identify multiple pathways to achieve a goal, the methods you will use to select the most powerful approaches, and by what dates you will take those actions.

_____

_____

_____

_____

_____

_____

_____

CHAPTER 5

Find the Trim Tab

The balance of circumstances can be shifted in a major way by a minor action. Only a few decisions really matter. Those that do, matter a great deal. Choice can always be exercised.

—Richard Koch

We must not, in trying to think about how we can make a big difference, ignore the small daily differences we can make which, over time, add up to big differences that we often cannot foresee.

—Marian Wright Edelman

> **My assumptions: When leaders focus on a small number of carefully considered "trim tabs," they are more likely to use their energy efficiently in achieving important goals.**

Fifteen years ago, I was profoundly influenced by Peter Senge's (1990) discussion of leverage and "trim tabs" in *The Fifth Discipline.* These concepts gave me tools with which I could think in fresh ways about increasing the effectiveness of my work and consider the most efficient means for increasing my influence.

"Small changes can produce big results—but the areas of highest leverage are often the least obvious," Senge wrote (1990, p. 63). He used the term *leverage* to describe the "small well-focused actions" that "can sometimes produce significant, enduring improvements, if they're in the right place. . . . Tackling a difficult problem is often a matter of see- ing where the high leverage lies, a change which—with a minimum of effort—would lead to lasting significant improvement" (p. 64).

To further explain this idea, Senge (1990) cited Buckminster Fuller's concept of a trim tab—"a small rudder on the rudder of a

> We make the most lasting and vivid impression when people witness us being true to our beliefs, staying in alignment with who and what we really are.
> —David McNally & Karl Speak

ship" whose function it is "to make it easier to turn the rudder, which, then, makes it easier to turn the ship" (p. 64). When I approach my work now, I consider the rudder—a place of leverage—and the trim tab that makes it easier for me to affect the rudder.

Stephen Covey (2004) said a trim tab is a way "of taking initiative to expand your influence in every opportunity around you" (p. 118). He offered as an example the power of switching our view from "they are the problem" to "I am the problem." "Remember that every time you think the problem is out there, *that* very thought is the problem," Covey wrote (p. 131).

Let's assume a school leader has as an overarching goal the continuous improvement of teaching and learning. The leader views instructional leadership as the rudder that will steer his or her efforts. I offer the following as examples of possible trim tabs on that rudder:

- Examining the quality of student work during classroom visits, rather than focusing on teacher actions; using student work as the primary subject of conversation in postobservation conferences
- Linking teachers to one another in small teams that create a limited number of common instructional goals and in which team members assist one another in achieving those goals
- Using faculty meetings for substantive discussions of teaching and learning rather than "administrivia."

Each trim tab that I've identified may also have its own small, well-focused actions, as Senge (1990) would describe it. For instance, a school leader who selected "using faculty meetings for substantive discussions of teaching and learning rather than 'administrivia'" might invite grade-level or department teams on a rotating basis to present an instructional challenge they are addressing and the methods they have used or are using to overcome it.

EXAMINE YOUR ASSUMPTIONS

Write your assumptions regarding the significance of trim tabs. For instance, you may believe that because schools are very complex and highly reactive organizations it is impossible for busy school leaders to isolate trim tabs and to maintain a focus on affecting them. Share your assumptions with colleagues in the spirit of dialogue.

_____

_____

_____

_____

_____

_____

DEEPEN YOUR UNDERSTANDING

Write about a highly leveraged action you took in the past that produced significant results. As a means of better understanding how you selected that trim tab, describe the analysis that led to that action.

_____

_____

_____

_____

_____

_____

ENGAGE IN NEXT ACTION THINKING

Identify an important goal in your work and a rudder that is important in affecting it. Then determine a trim tab that will make a significant contribution in that area. To produce greater clarity and accountability, discuss it with a colleague and determine a date when the action or actions will be initiated.

REFERENCES

Covey, S. (2004). *The 8th habit: From effectiveness to greatness.* New York: Free Press.
Senge, P. (1990). *The fifth discipline: The art and practice of the learning organization.* New York: Doubleday Currency.

CHAPTER 6

Apply the 80/20 Principle

We must learn to distinguish between what is "merely important" and what is "wildly important."

—Stephen Covey (2004, p. 281)

Much of our present struggles with our organizations have to do with remembering what is essential and placing it back in the center of our lives.

—David Whyte

> **My assumptions: The majority of the results we achieve in our work and personal lives comes from a small portion of our actions and resources. Results-oriented leaders focus on the few things that are most influential in achieving their most important goals.**

Some things we do as leaders make an important contribution to the achievement of our goals. Other things we do make little difference. The ability to discriminate between these two categories of things and to focus our efforts on the former category is essential in producing results and in achieving those results more efficiently. That, in turn, leads to a more balanced and less stressful style of work and life. A term given to this way of thinking is the *80/20 principle*, also known as the Pareto principle.

"The 80/20 principle asserts that a minority of causes, inputs, or effort usually lead to a majority of the results, outputs, or rewards,"

> Suppose you have an 80 percent chance of achieving any particular goal with excellence. Add a second goal to that first goal, and research shows your chances of achieving both goals drop to 64 percent. Keep adding goals and the probability of achieving them plunges steeply.
>
> —Stephen Covey

Richard Koch claimed in *The 80/20 Principle: The Secret to Success by Achieving More with Less* (1998, p. 4). He added, "Every person I have known who has taken the 80/20 principle seriously has emerged with useful, and in some case life-changing, insights." He added, "Unless you use the 80/20 principle to redirect your strategy, you can be pretty sure that the strategy is badly flawed" (pp. 24–25).

Koch's (1998) views can be summarized this way:

- "Most efforts do not realize their intended results" (p. 116).
- "A few things are always much more important than most things" (p. 125).
- "80 percent of achievement is attained in 20 percent of the time taken. . . . 80 percent of happiness is experienced in 20 percent of life. . . . Remember that these are hypotheses to be tested against your experience. It doesn't matter what the exact percentages are and in any case it is almost impossible to measure them precisely. The key question is whether there is a major imbalance between the time spent on the one hand and achievement or happiness on the other" (pp. 146–147).
- "The objective of 80/20 thinking is to generate action which will make sharp improvements in your life and that of others" (p. 136).
- "For the 80 percent of activities that give you only 20 percent of results, the ideal is to eliminate them. You may need to do this before allocating more time to the high-value activities. . . . There is normally great scope to do things differently within your existing circumstances. . . . [B]e unconventional and eccentric in how you use your time. Do not follow the herd. . . . Since there is little value in the activities you want to displace, people may not actually notice if you stop doing them" (p. 158).
- "There is no shortage of time. If fact, we are positively awash in with it. And for the most talented individuals, it is often tiny amounts of time that make all the difference. . . . The 80/20 principle says that we should act less. Action drives out thought. . . . It is not the shortage of time that should worry us, but the tendency for the majority of time to be spent in

low-quality ways. Speeding up or being more 'efficient' with our use of time will not help us; indeed, such ways of thinking are more the problem than the solution" (p. 149).

Here's a simple illustration that if implemented could make a large difference in the professional life of many busy school leaders: Koch argues that "80 percent of the value of a book can be found in 20 percent or fewer of its pages and absorbed in 20 percent of the time most people would take to read it through" (p. 25). In my case, I have changed the estimate to 90/10: Ten percent of the material can produce 90% of the benefit. With a few exceptions for particular subjects and purposes (e.g., reading poetry or wanting to go deeply in a subject that is very important to my work), I have found that by taking a few minutes to identify the paragraphs or pages that convey the vast majority of an article or book's meaning, I can in a relatively brief amount of time gain an understanding of an author's key ideas. That means I can read about 10 books in the same amount of time I previously read one, with only a modest loss of understanding. These are rough estimates, of course, but they provide a sense of the power of applying this principle to common but important professional tasks.

Examine Your Assumptions

Write your assumptions regarding the 80/20 principle. For instance, you may believe that all actions initiated by leaders are important or they wouldn't be undertaken and that, for the most part, the only way to determine if an action will produce results is by doing it. Share your assumptions with colleagues in the spirit of dialogue.

_____

_____

_____

_____

_____

_____

DEEPEN YOUR UNDERSTANDING

List activities in which you engage that you believe produce a disproportionate share of the results you most value (the 20% that produce 80% of your results) and those that could be diminished or eliminated (the 80% that produce only 20% of your results).

_____

_____

_____

_____

_____

_____

_____

ENGAGE IN NEXT ACTION THINKING

Describe to someone the 80% actions you will reduce or eliminate and the 20% activities you will increase. Make a commitment and set a deadline to initiate your plan.

_____

_____

_____

_____

_____

_____

_____

REFERENCES

Covey, S. (2004). _The 8th habit: From effectiveness to greatness._ New York: Free Press.

Koch, R. (1998). _The 80/20 principle: The secret to success by achieving more with less._ New York: Currency.

CHAPTER 7

Practice "Satisficing"

The best is the enemy of the good.

—Unknown

The man who insists upon seeing with perfect clearness before he decides, never decides.

—Henri Frederic Amiel

> **My assumptions: Approaching more educational decisions from a "good enough" perspective based on clearly defined, high standards will improve the quality of decision making, planning, and practice.**

Most leaders are familiar with the phrase "the good is the enemy of the best." But in many day-to-day situations that leaders face, the phrase "the best is the enemy of the good" might be more appropriate. In *The Paradox of Choice*, Barry Schwartz (2004) provided a rationale for this view and explained why the abundance of choice that many individuals face today is a source of discontent as well as a benefit of freedom and autonomy. That is certainly true in the overwhelming number of options school leaders face as they try to determine the best means to improve teaching and learning in their schools.

Schwartz (2004) suggested that addressing the distress of choice overload requires "practice, discipline, and perhaps a new way of thinking. . . . To manage the problem of excessive choice, we must decide which choices in our lives really matter and focus our time energy there, letting many other opportunities pass us by" (pp. 221–222). The ability

> Everybody gets so much information all day long that they lose their common sense.
>
> —Gertrude Stein

and discipline to focus on what really matters are discussed in Chapters 5, 6, and 8.

Schwartz stated that making wise choices starts with a clear understanding of our goals and that our first choice is between aspiring to the absolute best or to something that is good enough. He applied the term *maximizer* to those who seek the absolute best and *satisficer* to those who develop standards and criteria for their choice and stop searching when those standards are met. Maximizers are willing to spend a great deal of time and effort in finding the perfect selection and in being just right in everything they do.

> Have a bias toward action—let's see something happen now. You can break that big plan into small steps and take the first step right away.
>
> —Indira Gandhi

Schwartz acknowledged that to many maximizers, the act of satisficing may seem like settling for mediocrity. "A satisficer may be just as discriminating as a maximizer," he notes. "The difference between the two types is that the satisficer is content with the merely excellent as opposed to the absolute best" (p. 78). He added, "Satisficers may have very high standards. It's just that they allow themselves to be satisfied once experiences meet those standards" (p. 89).

Though acknowledging the value of maximizing in some situations, Schwartz argued that maximizers pay a cost for their exhaustive searches—sometimes a heavy one—in time and other resources, stress, and overall diminishment of well-being. "I believe that the goal of maximizing is a source of great dissatisfaction, that it can make people miserable—especially in a world that insists on providing an overwhelming number of choices, both trivial and not so trivial," he argued (p. 79). "To become a satisficer, however, requires that you think carefully about your goals and aspirations, and that you develop well-defined standards for what is 'good enough' whenever you face a decision" (pp. 225–226).

Problems can arise when school leaders approach every school improvement and professional learning decision from a maximizer orientation. For instance, leaders who insist that every *i* be dotted and every *t* crossed before any work can begin on a multiyear plan may diminish the sense of urgency and energy established by the planning process. Or maximizer leaders may search at great length for the very best tool or method or piece of research and be reluctant to act until they are confident they possess it. That often leads them to a seemingly endless list of articles, books, and workshops. As a result, they defer taking meaningful action until all areas have been fully explored and understood. In the meantime, momentum is lost, current practice continues, and student learning languishes. To the extent that my perception is accurate, it's not hard to understand why many leaders report that they feel overwhelmed, stressed, and discouraged.

EXAMINE YOUR ASSUMPTIONS

Write your assumptions regarding the value and place of satisficing in your leadership work. For instance, you may believe that settling for anything less than the very best in any situation is a recipe for mediocrity and organizational decline. Share your assumptions with colleagues in the spirit of dialogue.

_____

_____

_____

_____

_____

_____

_____

DEEPEN YOUR UNDERSTANDING

Describe several situations in which you used a "good enough" or satisficing approach to decision making and the positive and negative consequences of that approach.

_____

_____

_____

_____

_____

_____

_____

ENGAGE IN NEXT ACTION THINKING

Identify an important decision that you think might be best made from a "good enough" perspective. Discuss it with others and, if appropriate, make the decision from that orientation.

_____

_____

_____

_____

_____

_____

REFERENCE

Schwartz, B. (2004). *The paradox of choice: Why more is less.* New York: HarperCollins.

CHAPTER 8

Determine Root Causes

[O]ur significant challenges cannot be solved with simplistic little quick-fix programs-of-the-month or psyche-up slogans and formulas. We must earn a comprehension of the nature and root of the problems we face in organizations.

—Stephen Covey

Problems cannot be solved at the same level of awareness that created them.

—Albert Einstein

> **My assumptions: Dissolving the often-invisible roots of a persistent problem is usually the most effective use of the limited resources available to school leaders. Without such an approach, the problem is likely to continue and manifest in various forms.**

When faced with a significant problem, school leaders or faculty groups sometimes move too quickly to implement a solution without first clearly defining the problem and understanding its roots. As a result, they address symptoms rather than underlying causal factors, which often means the problem will recur in similar or different forms. Root cause analysis (RCA) "offers a pause between problem identification and solution that allows for reflection and focusing on the issues of causation," Paul Preuss (2003) wrote. "Proper solutions must be aimed at causation, not at symptoms" (p. 43).

> Fix the problem, not the blame.
>
> —Japanese proverb

Preuss (2003) defined *root cause* as "the deepest underlying cause, or causes, of positive or negative symptoms within any process that, if dissolved, would result in elimination, or substantial reduction, of the symptom" (p. 3). He advocated focusing on "dissolving the root rather than 'fixing' the symptom with a patch" (p. 5). "In complex social systems, such as schools," Preuss

> We recognize that the world changes only when individuals shift to living with a new set of values, beliefs, attitudes, and assumptions.
>
> —George Land & Beth Jarman

(2003) wrote, "it may be difficult, if not impossible, to identify a single, specific, root cause. Often, there are clusters of causal factors that each contribute to the problem. Sometimes, dissolution of any one of the causal factors is sufficient to substantially reduce or totally eliminate the problem" (p. 7). Acknowledging the various restraints of insufficient data and time, he added that nonetheless "teams can usually arrive at a proximate area of cause or causes that if dissolved, or reduced, will remedy or reduce the symptom" (p. 13).

John Dew (2003) offered a definition of root cause that extends the analysis into the organization's mental models:

> A root cause is a basic causal factor, which if corrected or removed, will prevent recurrence of a situation. . . . What some practitioners are reluctant to admit is that root causes reside in the values and beliefs of an organization. Until the analysis moves to this level, an organization has not begun to grapple with root causes. . . . [D]ig until you reach the point of admitting something really embarrassing about the organization. (p. 59)

A common approach to root cause analysis is the "five whys" approach. To dig deeply into underlying causes, the question "Why?" is posed in relation to the problem statement. That answer is again queried with "Why?" This process continues at least five times to dig deeper into the problem's roots.

I offer for your consideration a modification of this process that I sometimes use with individuals or groups. Step 1 engages participants in defining the problem (e.g., "Teachers are not excited about professional development, and a good number of them actively resist it"). Step 2 asks, "Why?" Group members are asked to generate as many answers as come to mind, viewing each as a hypothesis. For instance, participants might offer the following ideas: (1) teachers do not see the relevance or impact of staff development on the core day-to-day tasks of teaching, (2) teachers are not meaningfully involved in selecting the goals and methods of professional development, (3) a small number of negative teachers infect others with their attitudes, and (4) traditional methods such as large-group lectures are used rather than more engaging small-group, hands-on problem-based learning. The group can again ask "Why?" for each of the four possible causes or select just one or two particularly promising causes for further exploration. The process continues in this way until one or two underlying causes emerge on which the group focuses its problem-solving efforts. As Preuss (2003) pointed out, "Sometimes, dissolution of any one of the causal factors is sufficient to substantially reduce or totally eliminate the problem" (p. 7).

Examine Your Assumptions

Write your assumptions regarding the value of root cause analysis. For instance, you may believe that the causes of most important problems are self-evident, as are their solutions, and that the school leader's primary job is to get followers to implement the solution as rapidly as possible. Share your assumptions with colleagues in the spirit of dialogue.

_____

_____

_____

_____

_____

_____

Deepen Your Understanding

Describe a time when you used root cause analysis (or a variation of it) and the effects of the process on understanding and resolving the problem.

_____

_____

_____

_____

_____

_____

ENGAGE IN NEXT ACTION THINKING

Identify one or more problems in your school or school system that would benefit from root cause analysis. Determine which individuals or groups will conduct the analysis and a due date for completion of their work.

_____

_____

_____

_____

_____

_____

REFERENCES

Dew, J. (2003, September). The seven deadly sins of quality management. *Quality Progress*, 59.

Preuss, P. (2003). *School leader's guide to root cause analysis: Using data to dissolve problems.* Larchmont, NY: Eye on Education.

CHAPTER 9

Develop a Theory of Action and Use Storytelling to Communicate It

Every school improvement program reflects beliefs and assumptions about how students learn, how schools should be run, and how change takes place. . . . Taken together, these beliefs and assumptions constitute a program's or organization's 'theories of action'—implicit and explicit understandings of how a school or program can accomplish its goals. . . . [W]hile many schools have goals, mission statements, and strategic plans, few have clearly articulated or well-examined theories of action.

—Thomas Hatch

We are defined by our stories, which continually form us and make us vital and give us hope.

—Max DePree

> **My assumptions: Improvement efforts are shaped by theories of action, whether or not we are aware of them. Leaders who develop and communicate clear, coherent, and compelling theories of action through stories and other means are more likely to produce the results they desire.**

Think of a theory of action as a set of underlying assumptions about how the organization will move from its current state to its desired future. A theory of action lays out for examination each of the links in a chain of causal events and the underlying assumptions that support them. We decide to do "x" because we believe "y." For instance, we may reduce class size in the primary grades because we believe students will benefit academically and socially in such settings.

These assumptions affect improvement efforts whether they are hidden from us because we have never consciously considered them or are explicit because we have thoughtfully reflected upon their efficacy and articulated them to others. Even if unarticulated, our current theories of action can sometimes be inferred from actions we take to achieve our goals. For example, an elementary school's primary strategy to improve student reading may be the creation of a parent newsletter devoted to tips on improving literacy at home. An inference about the school's theory of action might be that reading will improve for all or most students because (1) parent engagement is the most effective means to improve reading performance, (2) the strategies contained within the newsletter are sufficiently powerful that if used in the home they will improve reading, (3) all or most parents will read the newsletter, (4) parents who have read the newsletter will understand what it asks them to do, and (5) parents will apply what they have learned with sufficient consistency that reading will improve. This is, of course, a simplified example. But many schools use one or more relatively weak interventions to pursue substantial goals and have theories of action that would not survive professional scrutiny if they were surfaced and discussed.

> The telling of stories leads to shared meaning and emotional experience that changes something profoundly.
>
> —John Kao

> The universal love of stories is not a coincidence; our brains function by constructing narratives. Adults and children alike live, learn, and relate to others through stories. Unlike other forms of writing, stories engage our emotions and imagination in the process of learning.
>
> —Editors of *American Educator*

Once school leaders and teachers have a theory of action that is sufficiently robust to produce the desired result, that theory must be repeatedly shared in many places over a long period to motivate and guide improvement efforts. Communication may include letters to staff members and parents, brief remarks at the beginning of various

> The universe is made of stories, not atoms.
>
> —Muriel Rukeyser

meetings, or explanations provided that establish a context and rationale for professional learning.

> Progress cannot happen without a good narrative.
>
> —Paul Danos

Stories provide a powerful means by which a theory of action can be simply explained and put in human terms. They can help educators, parents, and community members understand why change is important or why particular approaches were selected.

Stories can provide a plotline and characters with whom listeners can relate. Leaders can use stories about school traditions or individual students, for example, to articulate the school's goals and to link the old with the new. Stories provide a means by which leaders can explain or reinterpret the past, use the past as a stimulus for new action, and illuminate a path for the future. Such stories may be large in scope, or broken into smaller pieces to illustrate particular ideas or perspectives.

> I decided we would tell stories in our company. We'd tell stories about our goals and objectives, stories that would explain our core values and our vision of the future, and stories that would celebrate our victories. We'd even share a few stories that would underscore what should be done.
>
> —David Armstrong

Examine Your Assumptions

Write your assumptions regarding the value of theories of action in understanding and articulating a school's approach to improvement, stating them as succinctly and powerfully as possible. For instance, you may believe that "A theory of action complicates and impedes improvement because it's clear to everyone what has to be done and why it must be done." Share your assumptions with colleagues in the spirit of dialogue.

_____

_____

_____

_____

_____

_____

_____

_____

_____

_____

_____

DEEPEN YOUR UNDERSTANDING

To better understand the power of stories to shape behavior, discuss the influence stories have had on your motivation and action (these stories may have had either a positive or negative effect), particularly stories linked to school traditions and students. For example, you might recall stories that are frequently told in your school or district, stories told in your own family regarding various relatives, or stories that coaches, religious leaders, or political figures have told that influenced your thinking and actions.

_____

_____

_____

_____

_____

_____

_____

_____

ENGAGE IN NEXT ACTION THINKING

Specify actions you will take to clarify and communicate the theory (or theories) of action that guides your work as an educational leader (particularly those connected to major school improvement initiatives) and by what date you will take those actions.

CHAPTER 10

Gain Clarity Through Writing, Speaking, and Reflecting on Action

[C]larity and focus describe the most basic predisposition of authentic leaders: they know what they want, and they pursue it. . . . [T]hey prefer directness and specificity in their dealings with constituents about these goals, and they exemplify their commitment in their behavior.

—Robert Evans

Creating your future involves a continuous cycle of reflection and action. By taking action, you find out which aspects of your vision, goals, and plans are workable and which can be refined.

—Dave Ellis

My assumptions: Clarity of thought is a powerful enabling force. Writing, speaking, and reflecting on our actions are potent means for achieving clarity. In addition, speaking to a committed listener bestows clarity as it assists us in cutting through the fog-like nature of thoughts that often occupy our minds.

While there are many ways to clarify our thinking, in this chapter I recommend three in particular: writing, speaking, and reflecting on our actions. Combining two or three of these processes adds additional benefit. These methods help us better understand and express our purposes, values, intentions, assumptions, and theories of action for the purpose of creating the results we most desire.

Writing is a way of freezing our thinking, of slowing down the thoughts that pass through our consciousness at lightning speed, so we can examine our views and alter them if appropriate. Writing enables us to note inconsistencies, logical flaws, and areas that would benefit from additional clarity. I recommend writing progressively shorter and shorter drafts to crystallize and suc-cinctly express key intentions and beliefs so they can be powerfully stated in a sentence or two.

> An individual's consciousness forms only in literacy. . . . Reading and writing radically alter perception.
>
> —Barry Sanders

Speaking—even out loud to ourselves or into a voice recorder—also aids understanding and clarity. I often am not sure what I think about a subject until I have heard myself speak about it. After talking about a subject I may think to myself, "Yes, that's exactly right" or "That's not it at all" or "This part of what I said is clear but this other part is still confusing to me." And then I modify my speaking to reflect my new understanding.

Speaking as a means of clarification is significantly enhanced when we do so in the presence of a committed listener who simply hears us without judgment or his or her own agenda. Feeling truly heard and accepted by another person is a pow-erful experience, and clarity regarding our purposes, values, fundamental choices, intentions, theories of action, and assumptions is increased when we speak about these things to some-

> People learn best through active involvement and through thinking about and becoming articulate about what they have learned.
>
> —Ann Lieberman

one who encourages the full expression of our thinking in a nondi-rective, nonjudgmental way. Being in the presence of someone who has no purpose other than to absorb our thoughts and feelings and to deeply understand our meaning is a rare and often unforgettable event.

I encourage you to seek out individuals who will listen carefully, who will honor your intentions, and who will speak only for the pur-pose of clarifying something that is not understood or to encourage you to continue speaking. I cannot overemphasize the importance of open-ended, nonjudgmental listening as a way to clarify your pur-poses, values, and assumptions; add specificity to your goals; and to identify alternative ways to achieve those goals. I will have more to say on this subject in Chapter 11.

Another way to gain clarity is to try a promising behavior or practice and to reflect on its effectiveness. Sometimes it is important to move off the fence of indecision and make a tentative commitment to a course of action. And it is equally important that we pause frequently to see if it is producing the results we desire, or at least an initial approximation of those results. Writing and speaking are wonderful means for such reflection because they externalize our views so we can truly encounter them.

EXAMINE YOUR ASSUMPTIONS

Write your assumptions regarding clarity of thought as an enabling force for leaders, stating them as succinctly and powerfully as possible. For instance, you may believe "It's not my job to be clear. I say whatever is on my mind and it is the responsibility of others to make sense of it." Share your assumptions with colleagues in the spirit of dialogue.

_____

_____

_____

_____

_____

_____

DEEPEN YOUR UNDERSTANDING

Describe the methods you find most effective in clarifying your thinking. Discuss the benefits you receive from that clarity. For example, consider ways in which you use writing (for instance, journal keeping), discussion with others, interacting with ideas of experts through reading, or other approaches to clarify your views.

_____

_____

_____

_____

_____

_____

_____

ENGAGE IN NEXT ACTION THINKING

Specify actions you will take to clarify your views on important subjects that are now at hand and by what date you will take those actions.

_____

_____

_____

_____

_____

_____

CHAPTER 11

Provide Teachable Points of View

I need to become a well-educated person, as opposed to a well-trained person. This means reflecting upon and deepening my own ideas, and giving greater value to my own thinking. . . . We each have our own theories and models about the world and what it means to be human. We need to deepen our understanding of what we believe.

—Peter Block

You are more likely to succeed if you concentrate on transforming your mental framework, rather than on memorizing mechanics.

—Rayona Sharpnack

> **My assumptions: Teachable points of view (TPOVs) are a powerful means through which leaders can develop shared understanding throughout organizations, develop leadership in others, strengthen relationships, and produce results. Effective TPOVs are expressed with clarity in simple, accessible language.**

I n *The Cycle of Leadership: How Great Leaders Teach Their Companies to Win,* Noel Tichy (2002) recommended that leaders lead teaching organizations formed around virtuous teaching cycles, in which "a leader commits to teaching, creates the conditions for being taught him or herself, and helps the students have the self confidence to engage and teach as well" (p. 21).

Leaders begin virtuous teaching cycles when they craft their teachable points of view (TPOVs). A TPOV, according to Tichy (2002), is "a cohesive set of ideas and concepts that a person is able to articulate clearly to others" (p. 78). A TPOV reveals clarity of thought regarding ideas and values and is a tool that enables leaders to communicate those ideas and values to others.

> People with clear minds are like magnets.
>
> —Wilma Mankiller

Some possible topics for leaders' TPOVs include the nature of human learning and the type of teaching that promotes it, the meaning and value of professional learning communities, how assessment can contribute to student learning, and the role of parents and other community members in improving teaching and learning.

> New patterns of behavior usually only occur when I, the change agent, have a new viewpoint and a new purpose.
>
> —Robert Quinn

"The very act of creating a Teachable Point of View makes people better leaders," Tichy (2002) wrote. "[L]eaders come to understand their underlying assumptions about themselves, their organization and business in general. When implicit knowledge becomes explicit, it can then be questioned, refined and honed, which benefits both the leaders and the organizations" (p. 97). And the creation of TPOVs and virtuous teaching cycles is central to one of a leader's most important tasks, Tichy points out—developing leaders throughout the organization.

But developing a TPOV is not a simple or easy process, Tichy (2002) recognized. "It requires first doing the intellectual work of figuring out what our point of view is, and then the creative work of putting it into a form that makes it accessible and interesting to others. . . . We live our lives and do our jobs based on a huge internal database of assumptions and ideas, but we usually aren't very aware of what they are or how they shape our behavior" (p. 100).

Tichy (2002) strongly recommended "writing as an essential part of the process of developing a TPOV" (p. 103). In addition, he recommends reflecting, getting feedback from others, and revising. "The process of articulating one's Teachable Point of View is not a one-time event. It is an ongoing, iterative and interactive process," Tichy wrote (p. 103). Tichy (2002) underscored:

Coming up with the initial TPOV really is hard work. . . . It starts with the leader taking a mental inventory of the stuff inside his or her head. It requires a total commitment of head, heart and guts. The head part is the intellectual work of taking decades of implicit internal knowledge and making it explicit. It means examining your own thought processes and behavior to figure out why you do the things you do. It means framing the various ideas and beliefs that underlie your actions, and then tying them together into a cohesive whole. . . . The heart part is generating the enormous amount of emotional energy required to the job thought. . . . And the guts are about opening yourself up and letting others see what really is, or isn't, inside of you. (pp. 101–102)

Examine Your Assumptions

Write your assumptions regarding the value of leaders' TPOVs, stating them as succinctly and powerfully as possible. For instance, you may believe that leaders don't have sufficient time to develop TPOVs, especially in writing, and that this task is the job of other specialists in the organization. Share your assumptions with colleagues in the spirit of dialogue.

_____

_____

_____

_____

_____

_____

Deepen Your Understanding

Describe a time when you felt clear about what you thought about a particular educational issue and how your clarity affected the thinking and actions of others. For instance, as a result of experience, reading, study, and discussion, you may have acquired a depth and breadth of understanding about ways to successfully teach all students that you were able to express clearly and effectively to your colleagues.

_____

_____

_____

_____

_____

_____

Engage in Next Action Thinking

Identify a topic of importance to you or your organization. Set aside a time to clarify your views on this subject in writing, perhaps redrafting your view several times to gain clarity. Specify a date by which you will have developed a first iteration of this TPOV and the individuals or groups with whom you will interact regarding your view.

_____

_____

_____

_____

_____

_____

Reference

Tichy, N. (2002). _The cycle of leadership: How great leaders teach their companies to win._ New York: HarperCollins.

PART II

Transformation Through Interpersonal Influence

Change the world—one conversation at a time. . . . It is not enough to be willing to speak. The time has come for you to speak. . . . Your time of holding back, of guarding your private thoughts, is over. Your function in life is to make a declarative statement.

—Susan Scott

Well-expressed ideas and observations can shift consciousness and change life's prospects.

—John R. O'Neil

The language leaders use and the ways in which they interact with others can empower or disempower, enable or disable, increase commitment or intensify resistance, and inspire passion and creativity or promote resignation and passivity. Here's an example: One evening a few years back I sat for dinner with several educational leaders who had asked me to speak the next day about professional learning to a group of area educators. In between their exchanges of information about upcoming events or projects in which they were engaged, individuals would speak at some length with anger and frustration about decisions by the state legislature, the governor, or the state education agency. As dinner progressed, one person's observations seemed only to intensify the frustration of the next speaker. Without quite being aware why, I awoke the next morning feeling discouraged and resigned about any sort of improvement in teaching and learning, let alone the type of dramatic changes I would advocate that day. As I thought back on the previous evening's conversation, I realized the language of complaint and resignation is indeed contagious and can deaden the human spirit and lead to organizational atrophy.

> **A basic premise of this book is that high-quality relationships built upon clarity, directness, and integrity compel change and produce results. To that end, the chapters in this section address the importance of candor, of making and keeping promises, of committed listening, of dialogue, of silence, and of making specific, actionable requests, among other topics.**

When educators speak with clarity, possibility, and accountability, and when they interact with others in respectful and mutually satisfying ways, they empower themselves and their organizations to produce extraordinary results. Such interactions add purpose, joy, and energy to our lives and the lives of those with whom we relate and increase the organization's capacity to engage in demanding, complex tasks and to sustain that effort over time.

CHAPTER 12

Tell Your Truth

What you perceive, your observations, feelings, interpretations, are all your truth. Your truth is important. Yet it is not The Truth. . . . When you accept responsibility for your thinking, you can speak without pushing your truth at the other person and minimize defensive responses. Chances are, people will listen more closely to what you say if you first acknowledge that it is your perception and may not be shared by anyone else.

—Linda Ellinor & Glenna Gerard

I wonder how many children's lives might be saved if we educators disclosed what we know to each other.

—Roland Barth

> **My assumptions: We generate energy to create the results we desire when we consistently speak our truth forthrightly and with compassion. While telling our truth may be difficult in the short term, other people have the capacity to receive and benefit from it.**

The perspective of this chapter can be put quite simply: Be candid. Tell "your truth." And, if necessary, tell it again and again to improve relationships and achieve intended results. Candid communication may be called "uncompromising straight talk," "courageous conversation," "entering the danger," or "fierce conversation." Whatever term is used, it means nonjudgmentally describing what we observe from our vantage point, stating our assumptions, and making clear, actionable requests for what we want. While it is common to feel fear or anxiety when expressing our views, hence "entering the danger," withholding them is often the difference between actions that benefit students and those that do not. When we express this truth, we feel energized, vital, and more effective.

> Words are a form of action, capable of influencing change.
>
> —Ingrid Bengis

Avoiding telling the truth in schools is so pervasive in many schools that educators have coined a term to describe it—"parking lot meetings." Such truth-telling occurs when individuals gather in parking lots, hallways, or bathrooms during or after meetings to say what is really on their minds. As a result, many schools are "pseudo-communities" based on "contrived collegiality" rather than places that foster authentic exchange of views for the benefit of students.

Few claims are based in "absolute truth" (truth with a capital "T"). Rather, human beings formulate "their truth" (truth with a lowercase "t") from experiences and assumptions that have shaped their perception of "reality."

Summoning courage to offer our truth enables us as leaders, no matter what our formal position in the organization, to achieve results that are aligned with our values, purposes, and intentions. In addition, truth-telling enlivens our relationships and adds vitality to our work. It is an antidote to the boredom that too frequently permeates meetings and other professional interactions and the "slow death spiral" that too many educators experience in their work lives.

We have many reasons for withholding our truth in professional settings, some of which are quite valid. Few individuals are rewarded for sharing comments that increase anxiety or conflict and that introduce complications and messiness where once there was clarity and certainty. Having anger directed at us because of our views can be unpleasant. And feeling ostracized by colleagues for taking unpopular positions is often painful.

> Tell the truth about what you want in life and what you're willing to do to get it. Being candid releases the energy that's bound up in hiding the truth from others and ourselves.
>
> —Dave Ellis

Educational leaders want their schools to be well regarded, so there is a natural tendency to refrain from saying things that may place themselves or their organization in an unflattering light. In addition, speaking our truth may not alter the outcome, and in a few situations, it may even put our career prospects or jobs at risk. Superintendents have lost their jobs because they told the truth about a problem and the barriers that impeded its resolution.

Telling the truth, even with data at your side, about achievement problems related to race, social class, and gender is fraught with risks. In these situations, I encourage you to carefully consider the costs and benefits of various courses of action; as in all such situations, there typically is no single correct way to proceed.

> I believe the health of an organization is inversely proportional to the number of its nondiscussables: the fewer the nondiscussables, the healthier the culture; the more the nondiscussables, the sicker it is.
>
> —Roland Barth

Given those caveats, truth-telling can nonetheless help us gain clarity about our views, be an important source of learning for others, and deepen relationships with colleagues, an important aspect of job satisfaction and the retention of teachers in their schools. Telling our truth may also lead to "breakthroughs" for others. When our truth resonates with the truth that others experience, it can have a very powerful effect on a group's intentions and actions. In addition, withholding our perspective, particularly our emotions, is a barrier to tapping our inherent creative and problem-solving abilities.

> The great sadness of denying truth is that we all become accomplices in our own spiritual demise.
>
> —Max DePree

Prefacing "our truth" with "this is what I hold to be true" or "this is how I see it" or a similar phrase recognizes the legitimacy of others' points of view. Inviting others to share their views in the accepting and inquiring spirit of dialogue reduces defensiveness, improves relationships, and often leads to new understanding and clarity regarding next steps. More will be said about dialogue in Chapter 10.

EXAMINE YOUR ASSUMPTIONS

Write your assumptions regarding professional candor, stating them as succinctly and powerfully as possible. For instance, you may believe "Candor seldom produces desirable results and is usually not worth the risk." Share your assumptions with colleagues in the spirit of dialogue.

_____

_____

_____

_____

_____

_____

_____

_____

_____

_____

DEEPEN YOUR UNDERSTANDING

Recall times when you were candid with others and describe the effect on you (emotionally and physically) and on others. Discuss approaches to speaking candidly that increase the likelihood of a positive outcome.

_____

_____

_____

_____

_____

_____

_____

_____

ENGAGE IN NEXT ACTION THINKING

Identify a relatively low-risk situation in which you can state your views. Rehearse what you might say, including your observations and assumptions. Consider making a request if that is appropriate.

CHAPTER 13

Use Candor to Assess Current Reality

[T]here is something within us that responds deeply to people who level with us, who do not pamper us or offer compromises but, instead, describe reality so simply and compellingly that the truth seems inevitable, and we cannot help but recognize it.

—Susan Scott

Instead of withholding our thoughts and feelings, we can share them. We can tell the truth—not The Truth (as in assuming our ideas are always right) but our truth, the way we honestly think and feel. . . . Refusing to speak our minds often cheats others of an opportunity to look at a problem with a fresh pair of eyes.

—Dave Ellis

> **My assumptions: Candidly expressed communication, particularly when it takes the form of intentions, observations, assumptions, and requests, is a powerful means of assessing current reality.**

Drawing on the work of Robert Fritz (1989), I often use a simple formula to guide my thinking and action related to creating the results I most desire in my personal life and at work: Current Reality + Compelling, Stretching Aspiration + Powerful Strategies = Desired Results. The tension that exists between current reality and a compelling, stretching goal (see Chapter 3 for more about stretch goals) provides a tremendous motivating force in the achievement of important goals. Combined with powerful strategies (see Chapters 5 and 6 to consider why not all strategies are equal in their influence), this tension can lead to the achievement of important organizational goals.

> One of the most important—and most neglected—elements in the beginning of the interior life is the ability to respond to reality, to see the value and the beauty in ordinary things, to come alive to the splendour that is all around us.
>
> —Thomas Merton

Current reality can be assessed in a number of ways. For instance, various types of data and other evidence can be collected, disaggregated when appropriate, and analyzed. Because a great deal has been said and written elsewhere about data analysis, I focus in this chapter on interpersonal candor, an underused but effective tool for assessing current reality. For some people, *candor* is synonymous with *brutal honesty*, a no-holds-barred and often disrespectful expression of one's feelings about someone or something with little regard for the consequences. That is not what I am advocating here. For the purpose of this discussion, I define *candor* as a clear expression of what one observes, assumes, or wants.

My dictionary defines *observation* as "an act of recognizing a fact or occurrence" and "a record or description so obtained." Observations are distinct from inferences we draw based on observations. "I noticed that your eyes have been closed for the past couple of minutes" is an observation; concluding from that observation "you are bored" is an inference.

Assumptions are what we hold to be true about a particular subject or situation (see Chapters 13 and 14, where I discuss dialogue). Both observations and assumptions are offered in the spirit of dialogue as the speaker's perspective, "a truth" rather than "The Truth." Participants in this form of interaction do so with an open mind so that the views of others may affect their own thinking.

Requests are things we want others to do. They are framed so that they are within the circle of influence of those to whom they are directed and are made with an understanding that they may be declined without a negative consequence. (Demands include the possibility of a negative consequence if they are refused. Once agreed on, requests become promises that the requester

> The greatest mistake is trying to be more agreeable than you can be.
>
> —Walter Bagehot

can count on being fulfilled unless renegotiated. Chapters 18 and 19 offer more opportunities to explore these topics.)

Here's an example: "I've noticed that at each successive meeting of our committee fewer people are present. We began with 20 members, and 3 months later only 8 or 9 people are showing up at meetings (*observation*). I think the absences may have something to do with the confusion and frustration that some members have expressed about the purpose of this committee and whether anyone with higher authority will pay attention to what we decide (*assumption*). But that may not be the reason. I'd like us to devote the next meeting to a candid discussion about how people are feeling about their participation on this committee, and I'd like us to extend a special invitation to those who haven't participated in quite a while, letting them know that their views are very important to us (*request*). But others here today may have other observations and views, and I'd really like to hear them and have all of us learn from one another's perspectives" (*spirit of dialogue*).

EXAMINE YOUR ASSUMPTIONS

Write your assumptions regarding the value of candor in defining current reality, particularly as it is expressed in observations, assumptions, and requests. For instance, you may believe that getting along with others in organizations requires a certain amount of holding back and that candor can be an infectious agent that destroys relationships rather than strengthens them and improves organizational effectiveness. Share your assumptions with colleagues in the spirit of dialogue.

_____

_____

_____

_____

_____

_____

DEEPEN YOUR UNDERSTANDING

Discuss with others the extent to which you think your school or school system engages in candid conversations in the spirit of dialogue regarding what is observed and assumed. Also discuss the extent to which requests are made of others in contrast to the use of demands, directives, or indirect statements (e.g., "someone ought to do something about that problem").

_____

_____

_____

_____

_____

_____

ENGAGE IN NEXT ACTION THINKING

Make a commitment to yourself and to others to practice the skills of making observations and stating assumptions in the spirit of dialogue and in making requests. Ask for feedback on your performance.

_____

_____

_____

_____

_____

_____

REFERENCE

Fritz, R. (1989). *The path of least resistance*. New York: Fawcett Columbine.

CHAPTER 14

Use Genuine Dialogue

Out beyond the idea of right thinking and wrong thinking is a field. . . . I will meet you there.

—Jalaluddin Rumi

Engaging in dialogue once, twice, or a handful of times will yield more meaningful conversation around important questions. If practiced on a continuing basis, it can produce significant shifts in the culture of the group or organization.

—Linda Ellinor & Glenna Gerard

My assumptions: Our beliefs and those of others have a powerful effect on professional practice. Dialogue engages us in a thorough examination of our beliefs, deepens our understanding, and improves relationships.

Lectures, publications, and traditional training methods used to improve teaching and leadership are usually insufficient to affect practice unless they are preceded or accompanied by genuine dialogue. While acquiring knowledge and developing skills are important, some of the most profound changes in individuals occur at the level of beliefs and assumptions.

Each of us operates from a set of beliefs and images about how the world works that derive from our experiences. While often unknown to us, these "mental models" exert significant influence over our professional practices. Some of these implicit beliefs unknowingly impede progress toward our goals. A part of us—our intentions—wants to go in one direction. Another part of us—our beliefs—may act as a brake that slows our progress.

Dialogue is the process by which we make known to one another the assumptions that underlie our perspectives and the thought processes and information that shape those assumptions. These underlying factors may include, for instance, other layers of assumptions, learning gleaned from life experiences, or findings of scientific studies. Dialogue can build bridges of understanding, clarify areas of agreement and disagreement, promote deeper understanding of issues, and improve a group's

> It is hard to overemphasize the importance of an ongoing practice of dialogue to the maturing of conversations that will bear the fruits of learning and transformation.
>
> —Linda Ellinor & Glenna Gerard

capacity to make good decisions. In addition, when we remain open to the perspectives of others in the spirit of inquiry, we may change our views in ways that support our most important goals.

In *Dialogue: Rediscovering the Transforming Power of Conversation*, Linda Ellinor and Glenna Gerard (1998) list several qualities of genuine dialogue: suspension of judgment, release of our need for a specific outcome, an inquiry into and examination of underlying assumptions, authenticity, a slower pace of interaction with silence between speakers, and listening deeply to self and others for collective meaning. To those ends, they suggest focusing on shared meaning and learning, listening without resistance, respecting differences, suspending role and status distinctions, sharing responsibility and leadership, and speaking to the group as a whole (one-on-one conversations in front of a group lead to the disengagement of other group members).

> To achieve different results, we must take different actions. Because our actions are shaped by how we see the world, to do something different we must see something different. We must question the assumptions and mental models we use to see the world, frame our thinking, and determine action. Innovation depends on it.
>
> —M. Kathryn Clubb

Dialogue is distinct from discussion, debate, and argument. Advocacy for a point of view is not part of dialogue, nor is attempting to convince others that they are wrong. While each of these methods sometimes have their place, they often produce defensiveness, which is a barrier to the deep understanding and transformational learning that often accompanies dialogue. The assumptions we hold as unquestionable "Truth" often represent some of the most fruitful areas for dialogue because alterations in these assumptions can produce profound changes in our lives.

Examine Your Assumptions

Write your assumptions regarding the value of dialogue in affecting beliefs, deepening understanding, and improving relationships, stating them as succinctly and powerfully as possible. For instance, you may believe "Change involves changing what we do, and it's more important to talk about what those actions will be than it is to engage in dialogue about our assumptions." Share your assumptions with colleagues in the spirit of dialogue.

_____

_____

_____

_____

_____

_____

Deepen Your Understanding

Consider the professional discussions in which you regularly participate to determine which ones would most benefit from dialogue. Describe ways that participants could learn the skills of dialogue and the methods that could be used to prevent the conversation from unintentionally shifting to debate, argument, or action planning.

_____

_____

_____

_____

_____

Engage in Next Action Thinking

The development of the skills of dialogue requires intention, practice, feedback, and persistence.

- Practice empathy in all conversations. Offer "gestures of empathy" to demonstrate that you see the world from another's perspective when you feel at an impasse with someone.
- Identify underlying assumptions in what you read and in what others say. Reflect on your own assumptions about that particular topic and consider how you would express them.
- Practice being nonjudgmental regarding your assumptions and those of others. Hold your assumptions loosely rather than as "The Truth."

Specify which of these actions or others you will take and by what date.

_____

_____

_____

_____

_____

_____

_____

Reference

Ellinor, L., & Gerard, G. (1998). *Dialogue: Rediscovering the transforming power of conversation.* New York: John Wiley & Sons.

CHAPTER 15

Engage in Dialogue-like Conversations

If you advocate with the intention to persuade, control, or manipulate others, the group will instantly fall out of dialogue. Advocacy spoken with attitude of "I am right" squashes listening and triggers defensiveness, aggression, and/or withdrawal. In such advocacy, there is no invitation to hear and learn from differing perspectives. . . . We are all experts at advocating from an 'I am right' stance.

—Linda Ellinor & Glenna Gerard

Human conversation is the most ancient and easiest way to cultivate the conditions for change—personal change, community and organizational change, planetary change. If we can sit together and talk about what's important to us, we begin to come alive.

—Margaret Wheatley

> **My assumption: When people speak to one another regarding important educational subjects in ways that convey that they are open to being influenced and when they listen carefully to the assumptions and perspectives of others, relationships are strengthened, understanding is deepened, beliefs are altered, and decision making is improved.**

In far too many faculty meetings and professional development sessions, school leaders or staff development providers tell or direct rather than interact with teachers in ways that promote deep and meaningful learning and shared understanding of important subjects. As a result, a precious resource for professional learning and teamwork is squandered and an opportunity for addressing the most fundamental issues of teaching and learning is lost. The kind of dialogue-like interactions that Noel Tichy (2002) terms *interactive teaching* provide a powerful means through which educators can influence and deepen one another's understanding of important issues.

> Conversations have the capacity to promote reflection, to create and exchange craft knowledge, and to help improve the organization. Schools, I'm afraid, deal more in meetings—in talking at and being talked at—than in conversation.
>
> —Roland Barth

Chapter 11 discussed Noel Tichy's (2002) view that leaders help to create teaching organizations when they craft teachable points of view (TPOVs) as a means of communicating their ideas and values to others. Tichy recommended that leaders share their TPOVs through what he calls interactive teaching, a dialogue-like process that "occurs when the teacher respects the students and has a mind-set that they probably know things that he or she doesn't, and when the students have the mind-set that they have something to say and that the teacher would be interested in hearing it" (p. 70).

Tichy (2002) underscored that interactive teaching is not the same as selling or telling: "Many executives close off learning. In their day-to-day interactions with staff they are usually either issuing instructions or making judgments about the ideas or performance of others. . . . Even executives who participate as teachers in formal development programs are often little more than lecturers" (pp. 60–61).

To convey a TPOV, Tichy (2002) recommended weaving its elements into a story "that people can understand, relate to and remember" (p. 121). Tichy described three types of stories:

- Who am I? (explains the real-life experiences that have shaped the leader and his or her TPOV)
- Who are we? (describes the common experiences and beliefs of those in the organization)
- Where are we going? (describes what the organization is aiming to do and how it is going to do it)

"At the same time that leaders are creating and constantly improving their TPOVs, they must also craft them into stories that are not only intellectually clear, but emotionally engaging, so that other people will be eager and willing to participate in the Virtuous Teaching Cycle that will make everyone smarter and faster and more aligned," Tichy wrote (2002, p. 131). In these dialogue-like

> We need each other to test out ideas, to share what we're learning, to help us see in new ways, to listen to our stories. We need each other to forgive us when we fail, to trust us with their dreams, to offer their hope when we've lost our way.
>
> —Margaret Wheatley

interactions leaders speak their truth as formulated in their TPOVs, rather than "The Truth." They also convey a willingness to be influenced by the views of others by listening attentively to others' perspectives.

I use the term *dialogue-like* conversations because individuals sometimes mistakenly believe that true dialogue can occur only in particular settings in the presence of trained facilitators over a period of several hours or even days. In my experience, powerful dialogue-like interactions can be quite brief and can be motivated by the desire of two or more people to candidly and respectfully share their views. For instance, such interactions may occur in a school hallway when one person succinctly expresses his or her assumptions (what the person holds to be true) or perspectives related to a particular topic, while others listen attentively and as time permits share their views. Meetings are another commonly occurring context in which both brief and extended dialogues may take place as part of a larger agenda.

EXAMINE YOUR ASSUMPTIONS

Write your assumptions regarding the value of interactive teaching, stating them as succinctly and powerfully as possible. For instance, you may believe that interactive teaching is too time-consuming and that it is far more efficient and effective to tell teachers what to do because that is what they prefer. Share your assumptions with colleagues in the spirit of dialogue.

_____

_____

_____

_____

_____

_____

_____

DEEPEN YOUR UNDERSTANDING

Describe a time when you engaged in a dialogue-like conversation with others and the results that occurred from that interaction. For instance, at a school improvement planning meeting participants may have candidly and respectively shared their views on significant barriers to high levels of achievement for all students, listened carefully and thoughtfully to others, and were demonstrably changed by the thought-provoking interaction.

_____

_____

_____

_____

_____

_____

ENGAGE IN NEXT ACTION THINKING

Create a TPOV on the value of dialogue-like interactions. Use interactive teaching with others in your organization to explain your views regarding this concept and its potential benefits.

_____

_____

_____

_____

_____

_____

_____

REFERENCE

Tichy, N. (2002). *The cycle of leadership: How great leaders teach their companies to win.* New York: HarperCollins.

CHAPTER 16

Listen to Others in a Deep, Committed Way

It seems so simple, but to be able to deeply listen to another without trying to fix, but to just be there with them, it is transformational in itself.

—Linda Ellinor & Glenna Gerard

While no single conversation is guaranteed to transform a company, a relationship, or a life, any single conversation can. Speak and listen as if this is the most important conversation you will ever have with this person.

—Susan Scott

My assumptions: Committed listening transforms relationships and deepens learning. Its skillful use requires practice and discipline.

Dialogue and the other methods for transforming conversation discussed in this book have at their core a quality of listening that is rare in most human communication. This type of listening allows the speaker to determine the agenda for what is said, seeks to understand the speaker's views, is nonjudgmental, and honors the speaker's perspective. Because it is so rare and powerful, I believe it is one of the greatest gifts one human being can give another.

As someone with graduate degrees in counseling, I was taught "active listening"—to paraphrase the speaker's views and to reflect back his or her feelings. I asked questions that probed beneath the surface of what was said and assessed others' "needs" based on what they told me. Likewise, many of us have learned to demonstrate interest in what others are saying by asking questions, sharing our experiences related to what the speaker has said, and offering another perspective regarding the speaker's views.

In recent years, though, I have learned a different style of listening that I view as even more effective in helping others express their feelings and in clarifying their intentions and assumptions. Committed listening asks that I give my complete attention to what the speaker is saying by removing distractions that are occurring around me (for instance, other tasks that I may not have fully set aside) and within me (things I want to say that are prompted by what the speaker has said). As a committed listener:

> One of the greatest gifts you can give another human being is to care enough to listen to their story.
>
> —Richard Leider

- I listen carefully to what is said without interruption until the person is finished, refraining from comment, commiseration, and offering assistance. And when the person seems to be done, I inquire, "What else?" to make certain he or she has spoken fully on the subject at hand.
- I convey nonverbally my full attention and interest in what is being said.
- I minimize my use of statements or questions that direct the conversations or subtly convey a point of view. I have learned to trust that people will reveal to me as little or as much as is appropriate at the moment. Even clarifying questions may take the conversation in a different direction than the one of greatest value to the speaker, so I use them sparingly. Likewise, knowing that I will say very little means that I will not use part of my attention to formulate a story I would like to tell about the subject at hand or to offer my interpretation of events.
- I genuinely honor the speaker's views even though they may not be my own. I typically make only a brief statement that conveys my understanding and nonjudgmental acceptance of what was said. Honoring a speaker's view is not the same as agreeing with what was said; disagreements about

> Listening is the doorway through which we allow the world to enter. How we listen, to what and to whom we listen, and the assumptions we listen through all frame our perceptions of reality. Listening may be the single most powerful act we perform; we listen and create reality based on what we hear in each moment.
>
> —Linda Ellinor & Glenna Gerard

factual issues or differing views may be expressed later after the person has had an opportunity to speak his or her mind without interruption or can be deferred to another occasion. It is my experience that change is accelerated when someone feels the unconditional regard of another and as conversations focus on intention rather than contention. Contrarily, criticism promotes defensiveness, which in turn helps preserve the status quo.

> The people I have met who are most effective at changing the world have two qualities. On the one hand, they are extraordinarily committed, body and soul, to the change they want to see in the work, to a goal larger than themselves. On the other hand, they are extraordinarily open to listening to what is happening in the world, in others, and in themselves.
>
> —Adam Kahane

- I realize that when I find myself arguing with the person about our respective points of view I have slipped from committed listening to a form of interaction that is far more likely to produce heat than light. I then turn from sending communication and begin receiving again.
- I refrain from analyzing what has been said and why it is being said so that my mind is fully engaged with and respectful of the person's perspective.

While committed listening may sound simple, it is a demanding skill that requires practice and discipline in its execution. Without constant vigilance, it is easy to backslide into inattention, to redirect the speaker to better serve our interests, or to fall into argument or debate rather than provide genuine acceptance.

EXAMINE YOUR ASSUMPTIONS

Write your assumptions regarding the value of committed listening in high-quality relationships. For instance, you may believe "While listening is important, there simply isn't time in schools to give sustained attention to anyone." Share your assumptions with colleagues in the spirit of dialogue.

_____

_____

_____

_____

_____

_____

_____

_____

_____

DEEPEN YOUR UNDERSTANDING

Recall times when you were the recipient of exceptionally high-quality listening. Discuss the attributes of the interaction that you believe made it so memorable.

_____

_____

_____

_____

_____

_____

_____

_____

ENGAGE IN NEXT ACTION THINKING

Practice listening with your full attention to another person who is speaking about something of importance to him or her. Refrain from interrupting or asking questions. Convey your close attention through your body language and overall demeanor. Specify with whom you will do so and by what date.

_____

_____

_____

_____

_____

_____

_____

_____

CHAPTER 17

Use Stillness and Silence as Learning Tools

One must not be afraid of a little silence. Some find silence awkward or oppressive. But a relaxed approach to dialogue will include the welcoming of some silence. . . . [I]t is sometimes important to ask. . . . In saying what I have in mind, will I really improve on the silence?

—Robert Greenleaf

Without stillness there can be no knowing.

—Sig Olson

> **My assumptions: Silence alters our perceptions and offers access to types of knowledge that are not available through other means. Such forms of knowledge are often critically important to informed and nuanced professional judgment and action in a variety of settings.**

Most educators report that their lives are too full. They move from activity to activity, place to place, without pause or opportunity for rest, restoration, or reflection. As a result, their lives are too often driven by the trivial and urgent rather than those things that are most important to themselves and their organizations. Such frenetic activity is often a barrier to learning, planning, and decision making.

From my perspective, a central challenge of professional life in these busy times is the creation of a sense of spaciousness that provides room for what is most important for us and our organizations. From this spaciousness flows an understanding that we have enough time to learn the most important things and to act in ways that can make a great deal of difference to us and to others with whom we work.

The key to spaciousness and a feeling of "enough," I believe, is a recognition of the value of going slow. Author Parker Palmer tells a story about a veteran heart surgeon teaching neophyte surgeons a challenging procedure in which they have only 60 seconds to complete a procedure during which a patient's life hangs in the balance. His advice: "Go slow at the beginning." So, too,

> You do not need to leave your room. Remain sitting at your table and listen. Do not even listen, simply wait. Do not even wait, be quite still and solitary. The world will freely offer itself to you . . .
>
> —Franz Kafka

it is important to slow down to gain clarity and direction when our culture and the adrenaline flowing through our bodies tell us that success requires moving ever faster.

Stillness and silence are potent and underused learning tools. They enable us to bring ourselves fully into the

> In the attitude of silence the soul finds the path in a clearer light, and what is elusive and deceptive resolves itself into crystal clearness.
>
> —Mahatma Gandhi

moment, whether that moment is a meeting or a learning experience, and to create the boundaries of a "container" in which some of our most important thinking can emerge. Because learning can only occur in the present moment, being fully present in that moment is a prerequisite to the type of learning that truly affects educators' habits of mind and practice.

Silence and stillness offer a source of knowing and understanding that is only accessible through that means. For instance, silence that precedes and follows discussion provides a boundary and a space to contain the learning and decision making. In such situations, we are freed from an obligation to respond, analyze, or comment and we experience others' speaking differently. Silence also offers access to the clarity and power of our own "voice"—which is the wellspring of our authenticity—because silence connects us to our deepest values and aspirations. Authenticity, in turn, is one of our most important sources of influence as leaders.

While speaking of her classroom, middle school teacher Catherine Gerber (2003) could just as well have been writing about many school meetings or traditional staff development sessions:

> I realized that what we needed was not more words but to stop for a while. We needed no more information; we

> He who does not know how to be silent will not know how to speak.
>
> —Ausonius

were swimming in it. . . . Being quiet together is a profound acknowledgement of the interior life of each of us. It provides space to breathe, to remember, to question, to feel compassion, to connect to each other and ourselves. (p. 102)

About applying the use of silence to her classroom, high school English teacher Lucile Burt (2003) made the following comment:

In my classroom, I have begun the practice of starting each class with silence. In the noise and busy-ness of the school day, I tell my students, we need time to stop and call our attention home in order to be ready for our work together. I began this practice of silence with trepidation, in fear of adolescent ridicule. . . . I knew I needed something to lift, to carry me out of the feeling of racing from one class to the next. The silent time allowed me to start "here, right in this room." Surprisingly, after initial discomfort, the students report the same feeling of calm readiness for the work at hand. (p. 110)

Stillness and silence in school settings might be used in the following ways:

- As a boundary marker that separates the fast-paced day from faculty or committee meetings or from learning experiences in which a slower, more deliberative pace will improve decision making and learning
- At contentious moments in meetings in which a period of silence may calm emotions and provide participants with time to reflect on what has been said and on their current points of view
- As a symbol and a reminder of the leaders' belief that important sources of knowledge, wisdom, and inspiration lie within individuals and the group

EXAMINE YOUR ASSUMPTIONS

Write your assumptions regarding the value of stillness and silence in learning and decision-making settings. For instance, you may believe that silence is uncomfortable, and uncomfortable people find it difficult to learn and make sound decisions. Share your assumptions with colleagues in the spirit of dialogue.

_____

_____

_____

_____

_____

_____

DEEPEN YOUR UNDERSTANDING

Describe a time when you became still and silent—for just a few minutes or for an extended period of time—and the benefits you derived from the experience.

_____

_____

_____

_____

_____

_____

ENGAGE IN NEXT ACTION THINKING

List situations in which you might apply stillness and silence to promote reflection, deepen learning, or improve decision making.

_____

_____

_____

_____

_____

_____

_____

REFERENCES

Burt, L. (2003). Essay. In S. M. Intrator & M. Scribner (Eds.), *Teaching with fire: Poetry that sustains the courage to teach* (pp. 110–111). San Francisco: Jossey-Bass.

Gerber, C. (2003). Essay. In S. M. Intrator & M. Scribner (Eds.), *Teaching with fire: Poetry that sustains the courage to teach* (pp. 102–103). San Francisco: Jossey-Bass.

CHAPTER 18

Make Requests to Initiate Action and Create Results

Self-responsible human beings are "request machines." They know that one way to get what they want is to ask for it.

—Dave Ellis

We must change the way we speak, the way we ask, the way we listen.

—Susan Scott

My assumptions: We are more likely to get what we want when we ask for it clearly and directly. Requests produce results when they are specific, are actionable, and have a deadline by which they will be honored.

Clarity regarding intentions (what we want to create) provides focus and energy for creating the results we desire. Clearly expressed intentions guide individual and collective action. But simply stating a desire for a particular outcome is not the same as asking one or more people to take specific actions related to that intention. We are far more likely to get things we want if we clearly and directly ask for them, and people are more likely to be motivated to give us what we want if they perceive it as a request (it's okay to say "no") rather than a demand (saying "no" leads to a negative consequence). Confusing requests and demands can strain relationships and inhibit the achievement of results.

A request is a statement of what we want someone to do that is actionable on his or her part and allows the individual to turn down the request without a negative consequence. Individuals may accept, decline, or defer a decision until a specified time. While the word "request" may or may not be used, it is important the recipient of the request understand that a response is sought and that agreeing to the request is considered a promise between the two parties.

> If you're leading without authority, other people's attention spans are going to be short whenever you try to communicate with them. Forget two-hour speeches—most people aren't willing to give you more than 30 seconds! So you have to use their attention wisely. You have to make your interventions short, simple, intelligible, and relevant.
>
> —Ronald Heifetz

Think of "stretch goals" or other large-scale intentions as bundles of requests that may eventually be made at different levels of complexity and specificity to various individuals. For instance, a superintendent may want quality professional learning to be part of teachers' daily work life within three years. As a result, she might ask principals to read the *National Staff Development Council's Standards for Staff Development* and be prepared to discuss its implications at the next principals' meeting. (If it truly is a request, an individual may decline.) The superintendent might also ask the district's assistant superintendent

> You have to know how to have what I call "conversations for action." Everybody spends time in meetings where there's a lot of talk and not a lot of action. That's because we don't identify which kinds of conversations result in performance.
>
> —Rayona Sharpnack

for instruction to work with principals and teacher leaders to design school schedules so that every teacher will be part of a team that meets several times a week. During team meetings, teachers will work together to improve their lessons, to help one another more deeply understand the content they are teaching, and to examine student work and other evidence to determine the effectiveness

of their lessons. The assistant superintendent might, in turn, make requests of several teachers to attend a workshop offered by the local university on the use of protocols for examining student work and to present their views on this method to a districtwide committee.

Requests provide a helpful alternative to giving advice and using obligatory language. Rather than telling others what they *should* do, *must* do, or *need* to do (all of which can produce defensive responses and dampen motivation), leaders can state their intentions and make requests. We may also say our assumptions about the subject under discussion and invite the other person to do the same in the spirit of dialogue. Chapter 15 discusses the drawbacks of obligatory language.

Persistence in making requests is often important. In some circumstances, it may be necessary to ask for what we want several times over a period of weeks, months, or even years before a request is granted. And even if the request is never granted, persistence may represent an important way to stand up for one's values and views and stimulate in others important professional learning.

EXAMINE YOUR ASSUMPTIONS

Write your assumptions regarding the value of making requests as a tool for realizing your goals. For instance, you may believe "If something is important, people should know what to do. Therefore, asking them to do it is unnecessary." Share your assumptions with colleagues in the spirit of dialogue.

_____

_____

_____

_____

_____

_____

_____

DEEPEN YOUR UNDERSTANDING

Describe times when you or others have confused requests with demands and the consequences of that confusion. Discuss ways that you can make requests without producing unintended negative consequences.

_____

_____

_____

_____

_____

_____

_____

Engage in Next Action Thinking

Practice identifying requests that will contribute to achieving what you desire. Write out one or more requests, making certain they are indeed requests (not demands) and that they are actionable by the person to whom you are making the request.

_____

_____

_____

_____

_____

_____

_____

CHAPTER 19

Make and Keep Promises

We define integrity—a key ingredient in character and a primary spiritual muscle—as doing what you say you are going to do when you say you are going to do it.

—Jim Loehr & Tony Schwartz

Only one thing is more toxic and destructive than a promise made and not kept: a pattern of promises made and not kept.

—Roland Barth

> **My assumptions: Promises are the starting points of action. They keep us on track for realizing our intentions. Making and keeping promises demonstrates integrity, promotes trust, and gets important work done. Internal accountability to one another—rather than external accountability through state testing or other methods—is the most powerful source of continuous improvement in teaching and learning.**

Promises made and kept are the highest representations of our integrity—they are an affirmation of our desire to behave consistently with our stated values and purposes. Without commitment to sustained, purposeful action and accountability for those actions, schools are unlikely to achieve their intended outcomes. Because promises stimulate action, organizations realize more of their intentions when individuals within them make and keep promises and expect others to do the same. Consequently, organizations are ultimately only as effective as the promises made and kept by the individuals within them.

When promises are not explicitly stated, much of their value may be lost. A *New Yorker* cartoon (Jan. 7, 2002, p. 55) shows two men sitting at a bar. One says to the other: "Doris and I have an unspoken agreement, but she won't tell me what it is." Many people have unspoken agreements that one or more of the parties may not know exists. And when that happens, misunderstanding and even complete breakdowns in relationships can result.

> Our promises create our lives. Our promises give life to our purposes and goals. Our promises move us into action. . . . Life works to the degree we keep our promises.
>
> —Dave Ellis

Another way of thinking about the significance of promises is to consider the promises we make to ourselves as well as those made to others. When we make promises to ourselves—for instance, as leaders to spend more time in schools and classrooms—but fail to keep them, our own sense of personal efficacy is on the line even though we may be the only one who knows of the promise. And when we consistently let ourselves down in this way, a sense of resignation is almost certain to follow.

Knowing how to move into action and maintain momentum is a fundamental aspect of promise-keeping. In *Getting Things Done: The Art of Stress-Free Productivity,* David Allen (2001) stresses the importance of clearly defined outcomes and the value of knowing the next actions for moving them forward. "Next actions" are promises individuals make to others about what they agree to accomplish by a particular time. Without such a focus and a system of internal accountability for sustaining attention on goals and actions, organizations are far less likely to achieve their intended outcomes.

> I used to make a lot of them (agreements), just to win people's approval. When I realized the price I was paying on the back end for not keeping those agreements, I became a lot more conscious about the ones I made.
>
> —David Allen

A simple and common example of the value of making and keeping promises is attending meetings we have agreed to attend and, when we are responsible for meetings, beginning and ending them on time. When individuals hold their participation and the established beginning and ending times as promises, meetings are more productive and help establish a climate of responsibility throughout the organization.

A November 2001 *Fast Company* article about IBM's PC division head Bob Moffat provides an illustration of the value of "calendar integrity": "Moffat always shows up on time for meetings, a sign of accountability and respect for his colleagues that is almost unheard of at his level," the article points out. "Says one senior manager: 'We have a name for it here. It's called calendar integrity'"(Fishman, 2001, p. 96).

Because in many groups providing an excuse for not fulfilling a promise is regarded as the equivalent of having kept the promise, it is important to establish group agreements about promises—the protocol that will be followed when problems arise in the completion of a task that may mean that a promise will not be kept. For instance, district curriculum and instruction staff members might agree that promises are expected to be kept in the manner in which they are specified, and that if the person who has made the promise becomes aware of a problem, he or she will immediately notify others and renegotiate the agreement. Consistent breakdowns of promise-keeping by one or more people may signal that it is time to discuss the problem with individuals who are not honoring their agreements or to review group agreements and remind everyone why promise-keeping is important.

EXAMINE YOUR ASSUMPTIONS

Write your assumptions regarding the value of making and keeping promises, stating them as succinctly and powerfully as possible. For instance, you may believe "Given the number of balls that school leaders are asked to constantly juggle, it is unfair to expect people to honor their commitments or to even take the time to renegotiate them." Share your assumptions with colleagues in the spirit of dialogue.

_____

_____

_____

_____

_____

_____

DEEPEN YOUR UNDERSTANDING

Discuss the extent to which both promise-making and promise-keeping are norms in your organization. For example, consider whether individuals are expected to arrive on time for meetings and ways in which tardiness is addressed by leaders. If appropriate, consider ways that promise-making and promise-keeping might be addressed.

_____

_____

_____

_____

_____

_____

ENGAGE IN NEXT ACTION THINKING

Create protocols within your work group for what will be done if unanticipated problems arise after an agreement is made. Specify by what date the protocol will be drafted.

_____

_____

_____

_____

_____

_____

REFERENCES

Allen, D. (2001). *Getting things done: The art of stress-free productivity.* New York: Viking.

Fishman, C. (2001, November). Leader—Bob Moffat. *Fast Company, 52,* 96.

The New Yorker. (2002, January 7). Cartoon. 55.

CHAPTER 20

Reduce Question Asking, Increase Declarative Statements

It is not enough to be willing to speak. The time has come for you to speak. . . . Your time of holding back, of guarding your private thoughts, is over. Your function in life is to make a declarative statement.

—Susan Scott

A chief event in life is the day in which we have encountered a mind that startled us.

—Ralph Waldo Emerson

> **My assumptions: Questions are often an indirect and less efficient method of stating assumptions and intentions, making requests, and deepening understanding. In addition, questions that are knowingly or unknowingly intended to elicit a particular answer often induce anxiety or defensiveness.**

A teacher friend says she sometimes suffers from delusions of clarity. I have no such delusion as I approach the content of this chapter. When I interact with others about these ideas in face-to-face settings, it is quickly evident that my ideas about question-asking are confusing because they contradict recommendations made in numerous articles, courses, and workshops on teaching and leadership. We have been taught that effective leaders know how to use well-timed, thoughtfully articulated questions and that teachers' questioning strategies can stimulate students' interest, deepen understanding, and develop critical thinking skills.

Acknowledging that perspective, I ask you to approach this topic with an open mind and to thoughtfully consider situations in which declarative statements may better serve your purposes. I also ask you to consider how commonly used terms that connote questions, such as "inquiry" and "ask," may take on other meanings when viewed through the perspective of this chapter. For instance, the inquiry process may begin with an assertion or observation that startles us rather than with a question, and "ask" may take the form of a declarative statement that makes a request (for instance, the first two sentences in this paragraph). With that as context, I offer you the following reasons for reducing the number of questions you ask as a way to increase your interpersonal influence.

Educators sometimes disguise and dilute their points of view by asking questions rather than stating their observations, assumptions, intentions, and requests in simple, declarative sentences. While questions have merit when they are a method of genuine inquiry into the unknown, the unthinking use of questions is often a barrier to effective communication and deeper understanding.

Questions can dilute conversations in a number of ways. I have observed that people are often more comfortable asking a question than making a direct statement of their views, even when their perspective is evident in the wording of their questions. I have attended many meetings in which unanswered questions were the dominant form of interaction. One question was followed by another and then another without anyone succinctly stating their perspective on the subject. There is safety in such confusion because questions can provide immunity from the criticism that speakers fear will follow their declarative statements.

Another problem is that questions are often asked by those with more power to those with less power—for example, parents to children, teachers to students, and bosses to subordinates. Individuals in these circumstances often report that they felt interrogated and that it was not acceptable to pose their own questions. Because answering the questions of more powerful individuals usually is not optional, such interactions often provoke defensiveness and anxiety rather than an honest exchange of views regarding the subject.

A third problem is that questions are often nothing more than concealed, indirect statements of the speaker's point of view or disguised requests for a particular action. For instance, "Don't you think . . . ?" "Have you ever considered . . . ?" "Why don't you try . . . ?" begin with an indirect statement of the speaker's point of view. Turning such questions into statements or requests

("I think . . . " "I assume . . ." and "I'm asking you to . . .") is more honest, direct, and likely to receive the desired response. Such an approach also moves the conversation into a more fertile exchange of perspectives and assumptions, which in turn deepens understanding and promotes transformational learning.

> We all have multiple sets of assumptions that act as lenses or filters for our perceptions. . . . The next time you find yourself with a vastly different interpretation of events than a colleague . . . reveal your own thinking process and ask about the other person's.
>
> —Linda Ellinor & Glenna Gerard

While some questions appear on the surface to be open-ended, it quickly becomes evident that the speaker is fishing for the "correct answer." These questions imply that there is a single correct answer or solution to the problem and the speaker knows the answer. A particularly damaging outcome of this type of interaction is that those to whom the questions are directed may shut down their minds and become resigned and dependent.

Yet another problem is when someone in the role of listener asks questions that divert a conversation away from the topics of most value to the speaker. At one level, the questions may seem to demonstrate interest in the speaker's views; at another level, they are an expression of what the question-asker wants to know, which may or may not be what the speaker wishes to say.

Most of these problems can be overcome, I believe, when speakers directly state their observations and assumptions and invite others to respond in the spirit of dialogue. Such dialogue, of course, is based on equality of status and a lack of coercion. In addition, I believe that it is more fruitful for speakers who want others to take a particular action to make requests rather than to conceal their purpose within questions. It is far more effective—and more honest—to ask for behavior in the form of a request than to ask a question that may or may not reveal the speaker's real intentions.

> We find comfort from those who agree with us, growth from those who do not.
>
> —Anon.

EXAMINE YOUR ASSUMPTIONS

Write your assumptions regarding the value and place of question-asking in deepening understanding, affecting beliefs, and producing results, stating them as succinctly and powerfully as possible. For instance, you may believe "Questions are a particularly effective way of interacting because they provide the freedom and opportunity to inquire together into complex problems." Share your assumptions with colleagues in the spirit of dialogue.

_____

_____

_____

_____

_____

_____

DEEPEN YOUR UNDERSTANDING

Describe times when questions you have asked or that were asked of you were indirect expressions of assumptions or disguised requests for agreement or action. For example, recall questions you or others have asked that begin with phrases such as "Wouldn't you agree . . . ?" or "Don't you think . . . ?" Consider ways you could reframe questions into a statement of intention, assumption, or request. Ask others for feedback regarding the clarity of your reframed statements.

_____

_____

_____

_____

_____

ENGAGE IN NEXT ACTION THINKING

Monitor your use of questions and develop a new habit of conversation that is less dependent on questions and more oriented to direct expressions of observations, intentions, assumptions, and requests. Specify when you will begin and what methods you will use to monitor this change in your behavior.

_____

_____

_____

_____

_____

_____

_____

CHAPTER 21

Minimize the
Language of Obligation

A common strategy in life is to take something that matters to you and translate it into a sense of obligation, so that you manipulate yourself into doing what you want to do anyway. . . . When your actions are based on obligation, it is very hard to determine what truly matters to you.

—Robert Fritz

We persuade, cajole, manipulate, and issue directives. Nothing changes.

—Susan Scott

> **My assumptions: Language forms affect energy and guide action. The language of obligation diminishes motivation and increases dependency. Language that asserts our observations, assumptions, intentions, and requests is more direct and honest and increases energy to sustain effort over time.**

While "obligatory language"—words such as *should, ought, must,* and *need*—are common in everyday communication, the sense of obligation they convey often takes its toll on our individual and collective sense of energy, commitment, and responsibility. Obligatory language seldom reveals the intentions, assumptions, or reasoning upon which the obligation is based and directs us to unquestioningly act in accordance with someone else's rules or standards rather than our own.

Sometimes the observations, intentions, and assumptions that stand behind obligatory language are even unknown to the speaker who "inherited" them unquestioningly from others. Because the human mind has a tendency to turn desire, once experienced, into obligation (at first I did it because I wanted to and I enjoyed it; now I do it because I *should* do it), we can inadvertently diminish our passion and capacity to invent the means by which we will achieve our goals and to pursue those means over time.

> You can trust your desires. . . . [W]e can let go of struggle and self-discipline. We can get what we want by following our passions—not by following other people's desires, doing what we "should" do, doing what we have always done in the past, or following any other external pressures. Instead, we can trust our desires.
>
> —Dave Ellis

Obligatory language by its very nature implies certainty, a belief that there is only one right way to approach a given situation. It is often spoken in a manner that implies "truth" with a capital "T" rather than as an assumption spoken to stimulate dialogue or invention. "Shoulds" typically withhold the observations, assumptions, intentions, and requests that if directly expressed would enable the recipient to enter into the kind of conversation advocated in this book and to decide on an appropriate course of action. Because "shoulds" are seldom expressed as requests, which a person may decline without negative consequences, obligatory language diminishes an individual's sense of personal power and resourcefulness.

Obligatory language imposes the speaker's point of view or intention upon others as if there is no viable alternative. Sometimes its authority comes from an unquestioned nameless source ("They say you should . . ."). In addition, the speaker's desire to control may be so strong that he or she does not desire a dialogue nor want to make a request because of the risk that it may be denied. Consequently, obligatory language is often in reality a demand for which the speaker does not wish to assume responsibility.

> Obligation is a flimsy base for creativity, way down the list behind passion, courage, instinct, and the desire to do something great.
>
> —Twyla Tharp

When we accept the obligations imposed by others as our own, we live in obedience to solutions someone else has invented to problems that we may or may not perceive as our own. Recipients of obligatory language often sense at some level that their prerogatives for self-determination are being usurped by the speaker. While the speaker may view such language as an expression of friendship and caring—or perhaps even of a more highly developed expertise or wisdom—recipients are more often inclined to experience it as controlling, meddling, or micromanaging. Of even greater consequence, I believe, is when recipients of such high-pressured advice interpret it as a reflection of their inability to successfully conduct their own lives and surrender their capacity for self-management, increasingly turning to others for direction.

When used by "outsiders" (those who work in district offices, consultants, professors, and so on) who are attempting to affect school practices, obligatory language often leads teachers and principals to become dependent on "expert" advice (which is often spoken in obligatory terms), which in turn contributes to the resignation and dependency that many educators experience in their professional lives. And when teachers and principals use obligatory language to describe their motivation ("We should do . . ." rather than "We want to do . . ."), their sense of commitment and responsibility is diminished. In either case, the obligatory language of outsiders fosters dependency and reduces commitment.

Examine Your Assumptions

Write your assumptions regarding the use and effects of obligatory language, stating them as succinctly and powerfully as possible. For instance, you may believe "Obligatory language is an effective and efficient method to get people to do what we want and consequently is a valuable skill for producing results." Share your assumptions with colleagues in the spirit of dialogue.

_____

_____

_____

_____

_____

DEEPEN YOUR UNDERSTANDING

Describe the effects on you when others tell you that you "must" or "need" to do something. For example, recall the common reaction of feeling disrespected or defensive in such situations. Practice identifying the intentions, assumptions, and requests that stand behind your obligatory language and that of others.

_____

_____

_____

_____

_____

_____

ENGAGE IN NEXT ACTION THINKING

Become conscious about your use of obligatory language. Ask someone to let you know when you are using it. Develop the habit of substituting statements of observation, intentions, assumptions, and requests for obligatory language, using these statements as a springboard for dialogue. Pay attention to the results of this new habit. Specify exactly what actions you will take and by what date you will take those actions.

_____

_____

_____

_____

_____

_____

CHAPTER 22

Decrease the Use of Cause-Effect Language

In our minds, we think very simply in terms of cause. We think that one cause is enough to bring about what is there. With the practice of looking deeply, we find out that one cause can never be enough in order to bring about an effect.

—Thich Nhat Hanh

There is magic in being in the present in your life. I'm always amazed at the power of clear observation simply about what's going on, what's true.

—David Allen

> **My assumptions: The habitual use of cause-effect language to describe the influence that others have on our feelings and actions diminishes our sense of efficacy and our ability to produce the results we desire.**

Most of us use cause-effect language with little awareness of the effects it has on our sense of personal and professional efficacy and on the efficacy of others. For instance, we may say, "The principal upset me by what he said in the meeting today about how our school is not being successful with all its students." When we use language that attributes the source of our feelings and actions to others, we give others tremendous power over our lives and we lose a portion of our freedom. Consequently, such attributions often lead to feelings of powerlessness and resignation and diminish our capacity to produce the results we desire.

Because most of our feelings and reactions are a result of many factors, attributing causation to one particular thing is usually very difficult. Some social scientists use the term "overdetermined" to describe the complex set of factors that contribute to a particular result. When we say, "What you just said makes me angry," we are claiming the speaker's words are the sole and most important source of our feelings. While in some instances that may be true and while the person's words undoubtedly played a part in our reaction, any number of factors may also have affected our response. Our reaction to the principal's comments at a meeting, for instance, may be affected by significant but less proximal events that were not evident to us at the moment—a poor night's sleep, a family argument from the evening before, or even a tone of voice that reminds us of how a parent spoke to us as a child.

The most effective and accurate way to depict our feelings and reactions, I believe, is to simply report them without attribution of cause. Instead of saying "The principal made me angry," we might say "I am angry and I find myself obsessing about the principal's comment that if teachers really cared about kids we'd be more open to new ideas."

Once acknowledged, we may choose to use our feelings to gain clarity regarding our observations, assumptions, and requests related to the situation. We might say to the principal, "Your view seems to be that teachers' resistance to new ideas is the major source of problems in this school *(Observation)*. I believe most teachers in this school want to do an outstanding job for kids *(Assumption)*. I'd like the entire faculty to have a genuine dialogue about their views on this subject, and I'm asking you to provide a generous amount of time for it at our next faculty meeting" *(Request)*.

EXAMINE YOUR ASSUMPTIONS

Write your assumptions regarding the effects of cause-effect language on personal and professional efficacy, stating them as succinctly and powerfully as possible. For instance, you may believe "A person's feelings and reactions are determined by what happens to that person. Because he or she really has no choice in the matter, cause-effect language is an accurate depiction of reality." Share your assumptions with colleagues in the spirit of dialogue.

_____

_____

_____

_____

_____

_____

_____

_____

_____

DEEPEN YOUR UNDERSTANDING

Identify a recent situation in which you attributed your feelings or actions to others. For example, recall thinking or expressing phrases such as "Susan made me so mad during that meeting" or "The school board's decision last night really upset me." Describe ways you might have responded differently by reporting an observation, offering an assumption in the spirit of dialogue, and making a request.

_____

_____

_____

_____

_____

_____

_____

_____

_____

Engage in Next Action Thinking

Create a monitoring system to become conscious of your use of cause-effect language and to develop new habits of reporting your feelings, engaging in dialogue, and making requests. Specify what actions you will take and by what date you will take those actions.

CHAPTER 23

Stand Up for
Your Point of View

Speak your mind, even if your voice shakes.

—Bumper sticker

What enables choices is the courage of our own voice. And that voice takes place through what we do, what we say, and how we show up.

—Richard Leider

My assumptions: Educational leaders increase their inter- personal influence and ability to produce the results they desire when they clearly, succinctly, and persistently express their observations, intentions, and assumptions in the spirit of dialogue.

"Standing up" in conversations means expressing the unique perspective and assumptions that each of us add to a discussion and doing so persistently over time. Standing up means bringing the passion of your values, purpose, and intentions; the uniqueness of your observations; and the intellectual clarity of your assumptions to all of your interactions. It also means having confidence and pride in your point of view and the courage to speak your mind in important situations. Taking a stand is a significant way that leaders change the conversation in ways that perturb systems, provoke important professional learning, and produce the results they seek.

When leaders present new ideas or initiate professional learning, they traditionally do so in relatively standard ways—they offer research or other forms of information through presentations, books, or articles; they ask questions; and they sometimes engage others in activities such as small-group discussion to consider or apply what has been presented. I am proposing an alternative way of stimulating professional learning that is appropriate to many everyday settings: Whenever appropriate, leaders state their observations in a descriptive, nonjudgmental way; they explain their intentions regarding the subject and the assumptions that underlie them; and they ask for what they want. Along the way, they engage in dialogue to bring depth and clarity to the conversation.

> Those people who experience the greatest joy offer to the world their distinctiveness.
>
> —George Land & Beth Jarman

Stating our observations in descriptive, nonjudgmental terms may seem like a relatively easy thing to do, but it can be one of the most challenging skills presented in this book. Most of us have deeply ingrained habits of perception and speech that lead us to infer, assume, and speculate rather than simply note what our senses reveal to us.

For the most part, stating an observation means saying what we see and hear. It may also include a statement of what we are thinking or feeling, again reported in a nonjudgmental, factual manner. It is like holding up a mirror that reveals to others what we note around us or making ourselves transparent so our thoughts and feelings are known to those with whom we interact. We do not, however, speculate or infer meaning beyond the observation.

> Individuals face the same challenge as organizations. They must find what they deeply care about, what gives their life passionate meaning and then harness those things to a compelling purpose. Each of us has been gifted with our own remarkable way of expressing our humanity.
>
> —George Land & Beth Jarman

Here are two examples: Instead of saying "It's clear you really dislike what I just said," we might say, "I noticed that while I was speaking you turned your body to the side and closed your eyes." In making ourselves transparent, we might simply say "I am feeling really frustrated at the moment" or "I'm finding myself thinking that we have begun the process of solving a problem that we haven't yet clearly defined."

An advantage of stating observations over drawing inferences is that others are less likely to become defensive, particularly when we in turn invite the expression of their observations for the purpose of developing shared understanding. The person may respond, "Thanks for pointing that out and giving me the opportunity to say how I see things." At other times, our observations may simply be ignored. At still other times, in spite of our best efforts to the contrary, our observations may provoke defensiveness and anger. That is a time to practice the committed listening skills discussed in Chapter 13. It may be necessary to repeat this cycle—stating observations and assumptions, making requests, engaging in dialogue, listening in a committed way—with patience and persistence over many months before our views begin to gain traction.

> Live as if your life makes a difference. Offer your unique talents to realize the future purpose and possibilities of making the world a better place—in every situation.
>
> —George Land & Beth Jarman

For many of us, a lack of practice in clarifying and stating our observations and assumptions makes this unfamiliar and difficult. Exposing our perspective and thinking to the scrutiny of others can be intellectually demanding and even threatening. One way we avoid putting our views on the line is to quote experts as a method of stating our thoughts without taking the risk of claiming them as our own. We may say, for instance, "Michael Fullan thinks improvement efforts are often fragmented and incoherent" rather than "From my perspective, our improvement efforts are fragmented and incoherent." While we always want to credit others for their original ideas and the words they have written, there comes a point in our journey to effectiveness at which we own the idea, express it in our own unique way, and apply it concretely to the matter at hand. A direct expression of our views, I believe, is more persuasive than obliquely made assertions expressed through the words of others.

Examine Your Assumptions

Write your assumptions regarding the value of clarifying and standing up for one's views, stating them as succinctly and powerfully as possible. For instance, you may believe "Strongly and clearly expressing my views is a waste of time and risky because no one takes them seriously and they may offend people who can affect my job and career." Share your assumptions with colleagues in the spirit of dialogue.

_____

_____

_____

_____

_____

_____

_____

DEEPEN YOUR UNDERSTANDING

Describe times when you stood up for what you believed and the consequences of your actions. Discuss ways that you might have been more effective in expressing your views.

_____

_____

_____

_____

_____

_____

_____

_____

_____

ENGAGE IN NEXT ACTION THINKING

Identify situations in which standing up for your point of view will help you and others create desired results. Specify with whom and by when you will do so.

_____

_____

_____

_____

_____

_____

_____

_____

_____

PART III

Transformation Through a Culture That Promotes Professional Learning, Teamwork, and Continuous Improvement

Building an improved professional culture is possible by developing leaders' capacities to work with teacher teams on shared beliefs, academic focus, and productive professional relationships.

—John Saphier, Matt King, & John D'Auria

Leaders and groups who can cultivate the ability to stay open and vulnerable when they are most inclined to feel defensive and self-protective will be well poised to problem solve effectively.

—John Glaser

School culture includes the stories that people tell about the school, the emotions they feel when they walk into the building, the expectations teachers and students have for themselves and for each other, and the agreements they make regarding how they will interact with one another.

Leaders help determine the cultural tone of a school through the beliefs they hold, the words they speak, and the actions they take. The chapters in this section address various aspects of school culture that are within leaders' circles of influence.

Teaching and learning will be more effective, I believe, when leaders:

- Cultivate energy, passion, appreciation, celebration, and a sense of possibility
- Help teachers believe that what they do every day makes a difference
- Encourage examination of personal strengths and inner development
- Monitor and continuously improve the quality of relationships
- Address both the emotional and intellectual lives of teachers
- Distribute leadership widely throughout the school community

In such cultures, teachers are more likely to maintain high levels of enthusiasm and energy in their work, share successful practices, engage in individual and group reflection, and express themselves with candor. Their shared commitment to high levels of learning and performance for all teachers and students and the enthusiasm they bring to their work each day are hallmarks of productive and professionally satisfying work settings.

CHAPTER 24

Shape School Culture to Improve Teaching and Sustain Competent Teachers

Teacher isolation is so deeply ingrained in the traditional fabric of schools that leaders cannot simply invite teachers to create a collaborative culture. They must identify and implement specific, strategic interventions that help teachers work together rather than alone.

—Richard DuFour

You cannot order people to become cohesive. You cannot order great performance. You have to create the culture and climate that makes it possible. You have to build the bonds of trust.

—Michael Abrashoff

> **My assumptions: Skillful leadership by principals and teachers is essential if quality teaching is to occur in all classrooms. An essential part of such leadership is the creation of a performance-oriented culture that has professional learning and collaboration at its core.**

High-quality professional learning by all teachers is critically important if we want high-quality learning in all classrooms and if we want to sustain and retain competent teachers throughout their careers.

A primary task of school leaders is the gradual and sustained improvement of teaching in all classrooms by amplifying positive deviance throughout the school, closing the knowing-doing gap, appealing to emotion as well as intellect, and infusing external research and expertise when appropriate. Such activity and learning is ultimately based in and stimulated by a high-performance culture, which principals and teacher leaders are responsible for creating.

> [T]he old workshop delivery model for teachers must give way to vibrant and ongoing professional learning communities where teachers generate, as well as gain, knowledge.
>
> —Ann Lieberman & Diane Wood

A widely held view of instructional improvement is that good teaching is primarily an individual affair and that principals who view themselves as instructional leaders promote it by interacting one-on-one with each teacher to strengthen his or her efforts in the classroom. The principal is like the hub of a wheel with teachers at the end of each spoke. Communication about instruction moves back and forth along the spokes to the hub but not around the circumference of the wheel.

As other chapters in this book point out, some of the most important professional learning occurs in daily interactions among teachers when they work together to improve lessons, deepen understanding of the content they teach, analyze student work, examine various types of data on student performance, and solve the myriad of problems they face each day. From this perspective, sustained teacher-to-teacher communication about teaching and learning that is rich and deep in its content and processes is one of the most powerful

> Instead of inviting teachers to watch one another teach, to debate best classroom practices, and to pool resources, the school culture walls them off and parcels out their time. It actually promotes professional distance.
>
> —Mary Ann Smith

and underused sources of professional learning and instructional improvement. A principal's participation is valuable in improving instruction and student learning but it cannot be the primary form of learning-oriented interactions for teachers.

Because culture is the sum total of the beliefs of community members and their interactions, creating such a culture means establishing norms and practices that lead to trust and mutual respect, continuous improvement, team-focused collaboration, clarity of thought, candid expressions of views, and interpersonal accountability for the fulfillment of commitments. In such schools, teachers talk candidly using the type of skills recommended in this book about their views on student learning, teaching, and emotionally charged topics such as race and social class. These conditions seldom occur by chance, and, once they are in place, they are unlikely to be sustained without conscious attention to their maintenance.

> Vital organizations exude health and energy and enthusiasm. Like vital people, they are full of hope and anticipation for things to come.
>
> —Max DePree

School leaders' mental models and the cumulative effect of their actions have a large influence on the cultures within which teachers work. That means professional development for principals and teacher leaders not only prepares them to be instructional leaders who, for instance, know how to assess teaching and learning during classroom "walk-throughs," but also enables them to transform their organizations' cultures. Preparation programs and leadership development efforts are the logical places to teach these skills and provide one-on-one support as they are implemented in the schoolhouse.

> When people share a common vision, they can perform feats that would otherwise be impossible. . . . There is something in the human spirit that longs for participation with others, that wants to be involved in a collective endeavor.
>
> —Robert Fritz

The development of transformational leaders is qualitatively different from the information-sharing methods that are the staples of traditional forms of development. Among other things, leaders learn how to engage in the types of conversations recommended in this book for the purpose of deepening understanding, shifting beliefs and assumptions regarding teaching and learning, and promoting next action thinking and interpersonal accountability. These skills are best acquired when leaders personally and consistently *experience* these conversations as they interact with others throughout their development rather than simply *learn about* the attributes of such interactions.

EXAMINE YOUR ASSUMPTIONS

Write your assumptions regarding the significance of school culture in shaping the teaching that occurs within a school and the nature of the professional learning that is essential for school leaders to enable the creation of such schools, stating them as succinctly and powerfully as possible. For instance, you may believe "School culture is deeply ingrained and essentially fixed, and there is little that anyone, including school leaders, can do to alter it." Share your assumptions with colleagues in the spirit of dialogue.

_____

_____

_____

_____

_____

_____

DEEPEN YOUR UNDERSTANDING

Describe from your experience the attributes of a high-performance school culture. For example, reflect on the relationships or practices in your setting that promote excellence and those that are barriers to it. Compare your views with those expressed in this chapter.

_____

_____

_____

_____

_____

_____

ENGAGE IN NEXT ACTION THINKING

Specify the initial actions you will take to shift the culture of your school or school system in the direction of higher performance and by what dates you will take those actions.

_____

_____

_____

_____

_____

_____

_____

CHAPTER 25

Create Successful Schools

The human capacity to invent and create is universal. . . . Perhaps the most powerful example in my own work is how relatively easy it is to create successful organizational change if you start with the assumption that people, like all life, are creative and good at change.

—Margaret Wheatley

If you want to predict the future, create it! This is precisely what school people now have the opportunity—and the imperative—to do.

—Roland Barth

> **My assumptions: Engagement in creative work energizes and increases teachers' and administrators' commitment to continuous improvement. Educators' capacity to invent solutions to educational problems is a powerful, untapped resource for improvement.**

Educators do not typically think of themselves as creators or inventors of school reform. Creativity is usually associated with designing interesting lessons or classroom projects, not schoolwide improvement strategies. Consequently, the design of more effective schools is usually left to "experts" who determine better ways of teaching or organizing schools or to policy makers who use legislation to increase the use of "best practices."

Almost all schools can make significant improvements in teaching and learning, I believe, by more effectively sharing the effective practices that are already being used within them and by inventing additional ways to promote student learning that are unique to that school. (More will be said about this in Chapter 22.) After all, more often than not, the practices that reformers wish to spread among schools were initially invented by teachers and administrators who were creating innovative solutions to complex and important problems. In these schools, teachers' existing skills and creative capacity contributed to development of new practices and improved student learning.

> Inventing in the creative process is developing an original path between current reality and your vision. Convention is adopting a path others have already used and institutionalized. In school, we are usually taught the value of convention over invention.
>
> —Robert Fritz

At the same time, I want to underscore my belief that almost all schools can benefit from interacting with practitioners from other schools and from researchers or other sources of outside knowledge and skills. When teachers and principals initiate changes that encourage sharing effective practices and demonstrate their appreciation of the talents in their schools, teachers are more likely to reach out to other educators and to professional literature for energy and guidance.

> There's power in detail. When your destination is clear, you're more likely to arrive there. When your goals are loaded with specifics, you're more likely to know when you've met them.
>
> —Dave Ellis

My views about creativity have been heavily influenced by Robert Fritz (1989), whose ideas can be found in *The Path of Least Resistance*. Fritz believes the "structural tension" produced by the disparity between desired results and current reality precedes organizational creativity. Leaders can increase structural tension by developing a richly detailed vision of the desired results (for instance, being able to picture it as if it were being

> In order most productively to access the conscious and unconscious resource available to you, you must have a clear picture in your mind of what success would look like, sound, and feel like. . . . When you focus on something . . . that focus instantly creates ideas and thought patterns you wouldn't have had otherwise.
>
> —David Allen

enacted in a movie or described in a press release) and by grounding discussions of current reality in data and other forms of evidence.

Organizations, Fritz says, resolve this tension and move forward when they act to close the gap. Fritz recommends action plans that are simple to describe and to follow. Schools then use data to assess progress (the new current reality) and design new action plans. Each creative act and the success it generates produce professional learning and energy, which breeds more creativity, learning, energy, and success.

> Our greatest joy no matter what our role comes from creating. In that process people become aware that they are able to do things they once thought were impossible. They have empowered themselves, which in turn empowers those with whom they interact.
>
> —Robert Quinn

Educators diminish organizational creativity when they have low expectations for students or themselves. It is also diminished when educators distort current reality through denial and minimizing and when they select strategies based on wishful thinking rather than a rigorous assessment of the strategies' ability to produce the desired result. All three problems find their way into school improvement planning: schools select modest outcomes because the faculty does not believe it can achieve more ambitious goals, planners define current reality through opinions and anecdotes rather than rigorous analysis of data, and schools select improvement strategies without thorough, tough-minded discussions about how to produce the intended outcome.

> To artists, limitations are not liabilities, they are opportunities to find fresh, inventive solutions, to clarify key questions, to prioritize and to go deeper. . . . Creativity is sparked by boundaries.
>
> —Eric Booth

Creativity of the type described here involves far more than teachers and administrators spending an hour or two writing a vision statement and brainstorming strategies. Creating schools that have at their core high levels of student and adult learning and meaningful connections among members of the school community requires the continuous development and use of professional knowledge and judgment. It also requires sustained study of professional literature, dialogue, and debate based on a candid exchange of views regarding vision, current reality, and strategies. The best way to develop these skills is by using them and by reflecting on the results. Sometimes that reflection may include soliciting feedback from skillful individuals outside the school who can provide an unbiased and useful perspective. No matter what approaches are used, skillful leadership by principals and teachers is essential if schools are to tap the creativity potential that resides within them.

> The act of creating can bring out the best in people, because it is the natural motivator. No pep talk in the world, no matter how inspired, can touch the power of the involvement that creating generates.
>
> —Robert Fritz

EXAMINE YOUR ASSUMPTIONS

Write your assumptions regarding the role of creativity in designing schoolwide improvement efforts, stating them as succinctly and powerfully as possible. For instance, you may believe, "Teachers do not have the knowledge, skill, or interest to design effective improvement efforts, and even if they did, there is no reason to reinvent the wheel when a school can simply replicate what others have done." Share your assumptions with colleagues in the spirit of dialogue.

_____

_____

_____

_____

_____

_____

DEEPEN YOUR UNDERSTANDING

Describe a time when you participated with others in creating a valued outcome and how it was the same or different from the approach recommended by Robert Fritz. For example, you might recall the process you followed in developing a new lesson, course, program, or initiative in your school or district. Discuss the success of your creative endeavor and how you felt during and after the process.

_____

_____

_____

_____

_____

_____

Engage in Next Action Thinking

Practice using structural tension to produce a result you desire in your work. It may be helpful to choose a short-term goal that can be achieved in a few days. Describe in detail both the desired results and current reality. Specify actions you will take to decrease the gap between your vision and current reality and by when you will take those actions.

_____

_____

_____

_____

_____

_____

Reference

Fritz, R. (1989). *The path of least resistance.* New York: Fawcett Columbine.

CHAPTER 26

Promote Breakthrough Thinking

If you want to achieve the significant change that you and others need, you must achieve a paradigm shift in thinking.

—Gerald Nadler & Shozo Hibino

Breakthrough innovations depend on ordinary people, bridging their expertise and building communities around their insights.

—Kathleen Eisenhardt

> **My assumptions: Breakthrough thinking is a powerful source of energy and innovation. Breakthroughs can be cultivated through dialogue and other forms of interaction that recognize and appreciate diverse experiences and perspectives.**

"Breakthrough thinking" is a change in view regarding a particular subject after which everything related to that subject is viewed in a fresh and more empowering way. David Perkins (2000) in *The Eureka Effect: The Art and Logic of Breakthrough Thinking* says breakthrough thinking is creativity that makes a decisive break with the past in a way that is transformative rather than incremental.

As mentioned in this book's introductory chapter, in *The Right Words at the Right Time*, Marlo Thomas (2002) offers director Mike Nichols's description of breakthroughs in his life: "Two or three times in my life I have read or heard something that seemed in a moment to change me so palpably that I actually heard or felt a click, a sound, tumblers falling into place. . . . [I]t is simply the experience of becoming somebody slightly different, somebody new, the next you" (p. 238).

Thomas also provides Paul McCartney's account of the origins of his well-known song "Let It Be," which he wrote in 1968 during a troubled time in his life. One night his mother, Mary, who had died many years before, came to him in a dream and said to him "very gently, very reassuringly, 'Let it be.' It was lovely," McCartney wrote of the experience. "I woke up with a great feeling. It was really like she had visited me at this very difficult point in my life and gave me this message: Be gentle, don't fight things, just try and go with the flow and it will all work out" (p. 218).

> [A] breakthrough idea seldom occurs instantaneously as a bolt out of the blue. Breakthrough ideas occur when the mind has been prepared, stimulated, and opened to the possibilities.
>
> —Gerald Nadler & Shozo Hibino

Breakthroughs may seem to occur in an instant with what Perkins calls a "cognitive snap," although preparation for them often takes a very long time and occurs after an accumulation of experience and knowledge. For instance, a superintendent tells about hearing statistics regarding the large number of young men of color in prison and has a breakthrough thought that learning to read is a matter of life and death for many students. Teachers describe epiphanies that occurred when students learned things the teachers did not believe they could learn, seemingly realizing in that instant that their students were capable of more than they had previously thought.

> [T]o solve the problems we confront, and for the human species to advance—quite possibly to survive—we are now called upon fundamentally and radically to change our minds, to change our way of thinking and seeing, to bridge the gap between our knowledge and our values.
>
> —Gerald Nadler & Shozo Hibino

Breakthroughs may have many sources. Andrew Hargadon (2003) in *How Breakthroughs Happen: The Surprising Truth About How Companies Innovate* cites the value of networks or "collectives" to provide a range of perspective and ideas and to offer emotional support to innovators whose work goes against the established ways of doing things. "[C]ollectives encourage individuals to think different, together," Hargadon writes. "When you work with others who are visibly engaged in and passionate about the work, you feel better about it yourself" (p. 107). He quotes a manager of an engineering group who said, "There are cases where the person who has the knowledge is sitting right next to you and it goes unnoticed and you plow a lot of ground you didn't necessarily have to" (p. 165).

> I don't have any ambitions other than to change the way people think.
>
> —Clay Christensen

A potent form of preparation for breakthroughs, from my experience, is dialogue with others whose authentic views offer a stark contradiction to some of our most strongly held perspectives, explanations, and assumptions. Another form of preparation is the intellectual engagement involved in developing a clearly articulated purpose and a richly detailed vision. Consequently, leaders who assist staff members in gaining clarity about their purposes and vision of what they wish to create and who frequently engage them in dialogue lay the foundation for breakthrough thinking and innovation.

EXAMINE YOUR ASSUMPTIONS

Write your assumptions regarding breakthrough thinking, stating them as succinctly and powerfully as possible. For instance, you may believe that "Breakthrough thinking is so random and rare it really doesn't have any rel-

> There is nothing more powerful than an idea whose time has come.
>
> —Victor Hugo

evance to the daily work of improving teaching and learning." Share your assumptions with colleagues in the spirit of dialogue.

_____

_____

_____

_____

_____

_____

DEEPEN YOUR UNDERSTANDING

Describe breakthroughs you have experienced, the events or experiences that led to the breakthroughs, and the effects they had on your personal or professional life. For example, you may recall "aha" moments or epiphanies related to a challenging subject that you were studying, a new way of teaching a difficult concept, or sudden insight into a student's view of a lesson or classroom behavioral problem. Discuss ways that breakthroughs might be stimulated in your school or organization.

_____

_____

_____

_____

_____

_____

ENGAGE IN NEXT ACTION THINKING

Specify actions you will take to stimulate individual or collective breakthrough thinking and by what date.

_____

_____

_____

_____

_____

_____

REFERENCES

Hargadon, A. (2003). *How breakthroughs happen: The surprising truth about how companies innovate.* Boston: Harvard Business School Press.

Perkins, D. (2000). *The eureka effect: The art and logic of breakthrough thinking.* New York: W. W. Norton.

Thomas, M. (2002). *The right words at the right time.* New York: Atria Books.

CHAPTER 27

Attend to Leaders' Inner Development

Integrity is the ability to listen to a place inside oneself that doesn't change, even though the life that carries it may change.

—Rabbi Jonathan Omer-Man

[T]he importance of integrity can't be overstated. Another word for integrity is "authentic." Students know right away when they are being led and listened to by an authentic human being.

—Marcy Jackson & Rick Jackson

> **My assumptions: A leader's identity, integrity, and inner wisdom are important sources of direction and influence in the school community. Leaders can cultivate these qualities and in doing so enrich their own professional lives and add significant value to the organizations they lead.**

Successful school leadership is formed around many things—a deep understanding of subjects relevant to one's work, skillfulness in leading various aspects of instructional improvement, and the emotional and relationship demands of an intensively people-oriented job. But at its best such leadership is also a "way of being" in one's work that is as much or more about leaders' identity and integrity as it is about their knowledge and skills.

> Every person has access to an inner source of truth, a source of strength and guidance.
>
> —Sally Hare

Students and teachers, according to this view, want to know whether leaders are "real" and can be trusted. They size up leaders' genuineness and look to see, for instance, if leaders are truly compassionate, not simply applying a conversation formula that that they were taught to demonstrate "caring."

> The point is to become yourself, and to use yourself completely—all your gifts, skills, and energies—to make your vision manifest.
>
> —Warren Bennis

To describe the "inside," authorities use terms such as identity, integrity, purpose, meaning, values, passion, wholeness, soul, and inner voice. They emphasize leaders' self-knowledge, the importance of community in nurturing and supporting that knowledge, and the role of courage in reconciling leaders' inner and outer worlds.

An inside-out view of leadership recognizes the reciprocal influence between what is inside leaders and what occurs around them. In *A Hidden Wholeness*, Palmer (2004) wrote:

> Human beings, by changing the inner attitudes of their minds, can change the outer aspects of their lives.
>
> —William James

> If *you* are in the room, your *values* are in there too—if you do not believe that, you have not been paying attention. . . . What are we sending from within ourselves out into the world, and what impact is it having "out there"? What is the world sending back at us, and what impact is it having "in here"? . . . [W]e have the power to choose, moment by moment, between that which gives life and that which deals death. (p. 48)

Thomas Beech (in Intrador, 2005) described it this way: "Every person is grounded with an inner source of truth. . . . Our inner life of mind and spirit is interrelated with our outer life of action and service" (p. 87).

Leaders can cultivate their inner lives by:

- *Identifying their values and strengths.* Many school leaders report that it has been years since they thought seriously about the values that guide their lives and work. Making a list of such values may take only a few minutes, but the process may prove invaluable in guiding important decisions. Likewise, leaders and their organizations benefit when leaders consciously think about and embrace the strengths they bring to their work and consider ways they might apply them more deliberately. (See Chapter 29.)

- *Listening deeply to themselves.* Leaders and their organizations also benefit when leaders create spaces in their lives in which they may receive the wisdom and understanding that can best be heard in solitude, silence, and reflective activities. Journal writing, quiet walks in nature, and meditation are just a few examples of such activities.

- *Listening to others.* One of the greatest gifts we can give to another is committed listening, in which we absorb what the person has to say without distraction, judgment, or a desire to fix or save the speaker (see Chapter 16). When we do, we cultivate and deepen our appreciation of the human condition, a wellspring from which our wisdom grows.

- *Speaking their truths.* A leader's authenticity is a potent source of influence, and honesty is at the heart of authenticity. Leaders' inner wisdom is diminished when it is not shared. (See Chapters 12, 13, and 23.) On this subject Palmer (2004) wrote, "[W]e grant authority to people we perceive as 'authoring' their own words and actions, people who do not speak from a script or behave in preprogrammed ways" (pp. 76–77).

- *Living an examined life.* Taken together, these suggestions describe "the examined life." The dialogue between the inner and outer aspects of leaders' lives is a source of profound professional learning and guidance that enriches their work and the work of the schools they lead.

EXAMINE YOUR ASSUMPTIONS

Write your assumptions regarding the significance of leaders paying attention to their inner lives. For instance, you may believe that strong leadership is displayed in actions and that leaders' inner lives have little to do with the results their organizations produce. Share your assumptions with colleagues in the spirit of dialogue.

_____

_____

_____

_____

_____

_____

_____

DEEPEN YOUR UNDERSTANDING

Describe a time when inner clarity and strength affected your actions and served as a source of courage during a difficult period.

_____

_____

_____

_____

_____

_____

ENGAGE IN NEXT ACTION THINKING

List actions you might take to cultivate your inner life and to use it as a source of knowing and guidance.

_____

_____

_____

_____

_____

_____

_____

REFERENCES

Intrador, S. (Ed.). (2005). *Living the questions: Essays inspired by the work and life of Parker J. Palmer.* San Francisco: Jossey-Bass.

Palmer, P. (2004). *A hidden wholeness: The journey toward an undivided life.* San Francisco: Wiley.

Chapter 28

Recognize Our Best Selves

I do not believe that you should devote overly much effort to correcting your weaknesses. Rather, I believe that the highest success in living and the deepest emotional satisfaction comes from building and using your signature strengths.

—Marti Seligman

No institution can possibly survive if it needs geniuses or supermen to manage it. It must be organized in such a way as to be able to get along under a leadership composed of average human beings.

—Peter Drucker

> **My assumptions: Extraordinary performance and continued growth occur when leaders pay attention to their "best selves" and to the best selves of those they lead.**

Leaders dramatically increase their effectiveness, generate energy, and create a sense of possibility throughout their organizations when they adopt a positive rather than a deficit view toward themselves and toward the capacity of others to do outstanding work.

That's one conclusion of a group of scholars who study Positive Organizational Scholarship. In a *JSD* interview, Jane Dutton (Sparks, 2004) said:

Positive Organizational Scholarship seeks to understand extra-ordinariness in individuals, groups, and organizations. It is a

> In a real sense all life is interrelated. All persons are caught in an inescapable network of mutuality, tied in a single garment of destiny. Whatever affects one directly affects all indirectly. I can never be what I ought to be until you are what you ought to be, and you can never be what you ought to be until I am what I ought to be. This is the inter-related structure of reality.
>
> —Martin Luther King, Jr.

field of study arising in business, psychology, social work, sociology, and medicine. . . . We believe that exposure to these positive examples will change peoples' sense of possibility for themselves and the groups of which they are a part. . . . One of the things that we have learned is that even a slight shift towards the positive can create powerful new insights into what's possible for an individual, a group, or the organization. (p. 42)

As an example, Dutton described the Reflected Best Self Assessment as a tool that enables individuals to "shift towards the positive" by developing a deeper understanding of what they are like at their best:

Our students [at the University of Michigan School of Business] ask 20 people in their lives—friends, family members, work colleagues—to tell them three stories about how the student has added value. Because the query is open ended, these 20 people may respond in any way that is appropriate to that particular relationship. We ask students to use these 60 stories as the basis for a reflected best self portrait, a written statement of who they are at their best. We then ask them to set goals to make changes in their lives based on what they have learned about their reflected best selves. (Sparks, 2004, p. 42)

> I was always looking outside myself for strength and confidence, but it comes from within.
>
> —Anna Freud

Dutton (Sparks, 2004) said this process transforms people. "Students tell us that they receive stories about events that they did not know were significant to the people from whom they requested feedback. They also tell us that they experience a deep affirmation of their unique greatness and that they see themselves as being much more efficacious" (p. 42). Dutton added:

Students tell us that they often end up giving back to the person the same type of information they initially sought. This process enlarges people's sense of the positive difference they can make in the lives of others in both intended and unintended ways. Participants come away from this experience with an expanded sense of possibility and a great deal of hope." (Sparks, 2004, p. 42)

"An expanded sense of possibility and a great deal of hope" are important attributes for school leaders to cultivate among staff members. These qualities are within leaders' circles of influence and lie at the heart of cultural change and the generation of energy to sustain long-term improvement efforts. The process of identifying, appreciating, and fostering the best selves of everyone within schools begins with leaders and expands in ever-increasing circles among staff members and students.

EXAMINE YOUR ASSUMPTIONS

Write your assumptions regarding the value of leaders reflecting in their best selves. For instance, you may believe that real growth for leaders occurs when they first identify the deficits of staff members and then focus their energies on remediating them. Express your views in writing.

DEEPEN YOUR UNDERSTANDING

Conduct the Reflected Best Self Assessment using the process outlined by Jane Dutton to develop a deeper awareness of what you are like at your best.

_____

_____

_____

_____

_____

_____

_____

ENGAGE IN NEXT ACTION THINKING

Speak with staff members regarding the value of the Reflected Best
Self Assessment and ask them to engage in such a process within their
networks and to set goals based on their reflected best selves.

_____

_____

_____

_____

_____

_____

REFERENCE

Sparks, D. (2004). Look for ways to ignite the energy within. *JSD, 25*(3),
38–42.

CHAPTER 29

Increase the Use of Signature Strengths

A musician must make music, an artist must paint, a poet must write, if he is to be ultimately at peace with himself.

—Abraham Maslow

Let us think of education as the means of developing our greatest abilities, because in each of us there is a private hope and dream which, fulfilled, can be translated into benefit for everyone and greater strength for our nation.

—John F. Kennedy

> **My assumptions: Individuals are most productive and fulfilled when they consistently act on the basis of their most vital strengths.**

In many schools, a first step in improvement efforts—either for individuals or the organization—is the determination of deficits. "Weaknesses" are detected and "growth plans" are made and implemented to strengthen those areas. Although such an approach makes sense, it too often overlooks the strengths of individuals and of the school as a whole and fails to build on those qualities.

As I have expressed before, I believe in the ruthless assessment of current reality. That means that it's critically important that leaders use various means and sources of information to determine the organization's level of performance related to its most valued outcomes.

> Few men during their lifetime come anywhere near exhausting the resources dwelling within them. There are deep wells of strength that are never used.
>
> —Richard Byrd

But such honesty does not negate the value of recognizing and more consistently applying individual and organizational signature strengths as a means to greater effectiveness and personal fulfillment. "Signature strengths," Martin Seligman observed in *Authentic Happiness* (2002), are those that are "deeply characteristic of you." Signature strengths, he wrote, are those that "a person self consciously owns, celebrates, and (if he or she can arrange life successfully) exercises every day in work, love, play, and parenting" (p. 160). He also noted, "I do not believe that you should devote overly much effort to correcting your weaknesses. Rather, I believe that the highest success in living and the deepest emotional satisfaction comes from building and using your signature strengths" (p. 13).

> To give anything less than your best is to sacrifice the gift.
>
> —Steve Prefontaine

Seligman provides the "VIA Signature Strengths Questionnaire," an online assessment tool available at the Authentic Happiness Web site (http://www.authentichappiness. sas.upenn.edu/). This assessment can help you identify your signature strengths from among the 24 he includes in the survey. (Seligman estimates that completion of the survey takes about 25 minutes.) From my reading of Seligman's list, strengths many school leaders possess include love of learning, judgment/critical thinking, practical intelligence/street smarts, various types of emotional intelligence, perseverance, integrity, fairness, the ability to organize and implement activities, the use of discretion, future mindedness, humor, and enthusiasm, to name a few. In addition, Seligman says that one way signature strengths can be elicited—a method that could be used in various faculty groups—is to ask individuals to introduce themselves by telling a story about themselves that reveals a strength.

EXAMINE YOUR ASSUMPTIONS

Write your assumptions regarding the value of determining one's strengths and of more consistently applying them in one's life. For instance, you may believe that organizations improve when the individuals within them fearlessly face their weaknesses and create plans to address them. Share your assumptions with colleagues in the spirit of dialogue.

_____

_____

_____

_____

_____

_____

_____

DEEPEN YOUR UNDERSTANDING

Consider a time when you or a team of which you were a member acted on the basis of significant strengths. Write about the results your team produced and how you and others felt about the process.

_____

_____

_____

_____

_____

_____

_____

ENGAGE IN NEXT ACTION THINKING

Use the "VIA Signature Strengths Questionnaire" or other processes to identify key strengths. Establish one or more goals to apply those strengths more consistently in your work or personal life.

_____

_____

_____

_____

_____

_____

_____

_____

REFERENCE

Seligman, M. (2002). *Authentic happiness.* New York: Free Press.

CHAPTER 30

Enhance Your Personal Energy

Leaders in their everyday behaviors can make an enormous difference in activating and renewing the energy that people bring to their work.

—Jane Dutton

Great leaders . . . focus attention on developing their intellect, understanding and managing emotions, taking care of their bodies, and attending to the deep beliefs and dreams that feed their spirits.

—Richard Boyatzis & Annie McKee

My assumptions: Leaders' energy is a critically important leadership tool. Leaders may sustain and renew their energy through various approaches that are within their circles of influence.

If left unchecked, the demands of school and school system leadership can take their toll on personal health, emotional well-being, and relationships. Over time, the ever-increasing responsibilities of the job can take precedence and lives can become stressful and unbalanced and relationships strained. Therefore, it is critically important that leaders attend to their physical and emotional health and the quality of their most important relationships if they are to provide energetic and sustained service to their organizations. Fortunately, many energy-enhancing tools are within leaders' circles of influence, a subject Jim Loehr and Tony Schwartz (2003) addressed in *The Power of Full Engagement: Managing Energy, Not Time, Is the Key*

> Take rest; a field that has rested gives a bountiful crop.
>
> —Ovid

to High Performance and Personal Renewal. "Every one of our thoughts, emotions and behavior has an energy consequence, for better or for worse," they wrote (p. 4). "To be fully engaged, we must be physically energized, emotionally connected, mentally focused and spiritually aligned with a purpose beyond our immediate self-interest" (p. 5). To those ends, Loehr and Schwartz made the following recommendations:

- Eat energy-rich foods, such as low-fat proteins, and complex carbohydrates, such as grains and vegetables, rather than foods high in fats, sugar, and simple carbohydrates.
- Engage regularly in activities that are enjoyable, fulfilling, and affirming and make that time sacrosanct in your schedule.
- Stimulate creativity—an important source of energy—through periods of thinking and disengagement—"thinking and letting go, activity and rest. Both sides of the equation are necessary, but neither is sufficient by itself" (Loehr & Schwartz, 2003, p. 98).
- Connect to spiritual energy through the "courage and conviction to live by our values, even when doing so requires personal sacrifice and hardship" (Loehr & Schwartz, 2003, p. 110). The "muscles" of such engagement, Loehr and Schwartz said, are passion, commitment, integrity, and honesty. They defined *integrity* as "doing what you say you are going to do when you say you are going to do it" (p. 122). Regarding the spiritual importance of purpose, they added, "We become fully engaged only when we care deeply, when we feel that what we are doing really matters. Purpose is what lights us up" (p. 131).
- Take time periodically to gain clarity about values and purpose and to determine whether you are staying on track. "It is not coincident," Loehr and Schwartz (2003) wrote, "that every enduring spiritual tradition has emphasized practices such as prayer, retreat, contemplation and meditation—all means by which to quietly connect with and regularly revisit what matters most" (p. 140).
- Create positive rituals to develop "precise, consciously acquired behaviors that become automatic in our lives, fueled by a deep sense of purpose" (Loehr & Schwartz, 2003, p. 166). Such rituals are habits that, according to Loehr and Schwartz, "provide a stable framework in which creative breakthroughs

often occur" (p. 168). One such ritual recommended by the authors is brief recovery breaks—60 to 90 seconds of deep breathing, a few minutes of listening to a favorite song, a vigorous walk up and down several flights of stairs, 10 minutes of training with light weights, 10 minutes of meditation, or a light snack, such as a protein drink, a piece of fruit, or a handful of nuts to restore energy.

EXAMINE YOUR ASSUMPTIONS

Write your assumptions regarding the significance of leaders' energy in achieving organizational goals and the extent to which leaders have influence over energy renewal. For instance, you may believe that energy lies outside the influence of leaders because it is affected by many things over which leaders have no control. Share your assumptions with colleagues in the spirit of dialogue.

_____

_____

_____

_____

_____

_____

DEEPEN YOUR UNDERSTANDING

List activities and habits that deplete your energy and those that enhance it. In particular, discuss experiences you've had with activities like those suggested by Loehr and Schwartz and describe their effect on your physical, emotional, and spiritual energy.

_____

_____

_____

_____

_____

_____

_____

ENGAGE IN NEXT ACTION THINKING

Make a commitment to one or more daily actions that promote your physical, emotional, intellectual, or spiritual energy.

_____

_____

_____

_____

_____

_____

_____

REFERENCE

Loehr, J., & Schwartz, T. (2003). *The power of full engagement: Managing energy, not time, is the key to high performance and personal renewal.* New York: Free Press.

CHAPTER 31

Build Relationships to Sustain Positive Energy

Leaders are the stewards of organizational energy.

—Jim Loehr &Tony Schwartz

There is a clear relation between positive emotion at work, high productivity, and high loyalty.

—Martin Seligman

My assumptions: The quality of relationships within an organization can positively or negatively affect the level of energy the organization has available to achieve its goals. A primary responsibility of school leaders is creating and maintaining relationships that produce high levels of energy.

As I wrote in the last chapter, a significant part of school leaders' work is activating and sustaining a flow of energy in themselves so that they can do the interpersonally and intellectually demanding task of school reform over a period of many years. Another important part of leaders' work is activating and sustaining over time high levels of energy within the organization. To a large extent, this energy comes from high-quality relationships within a team or organization. About such relationships, Jane Dutton, in *Energize Your Workplace: How to Create and Sustain High-Quality Connections at Work* (2003), wrote, "[T]he energy and vitality of individuals and organizations alike depends on the quality of the connections among people in the organization" (p. 1).

> To make a system stronger, we need to create stronger relationships.
>
> —Margaret Wheatley

In a *JSD* interview, Dutton (Sparks, 2004) told me, "Leaders influence energy directly and indirectly. They directly affect it through their everyday exchanges with people. The way a superintendent engages with principals or teachers, for example, ignites or dampens their energy. This, in turn, sets the stage for respectful or disrespectful interactions among principals or between principals and teachers" (p. 39).

> The way a team plays as a whole determines its success. You may have the greatest bunch of individual stars in the world, but if they don't play together, the club won't be worth a dime.
>
> —Babe Ruth

Dutton (2003) stated that high-quality connections have at their core positive regard and trust and result in people feeling more engaged, more open, and more competent. When connections are absent, she noted, people's ability to learn, to show initiative, and to take risks drops. Dutton observed that "every interaction with others at work—big or small, brief or lengthy—has the potential to create or deplete vital energy" (p. 7).

In our *JSD* interview, Dutton (Sparks, 2004) said:

> The leaders we've talked with say that they began their careers thinking that leadership was about making broad and bold strategic strokes. And then a crisis—usually a personal crisis—in which they experience vulnerability guides them to try different ways of leading. They learn that it is the simple things, like being present or being more authentically who they are, that produces a long-lasting impact on their organizations. (p. 40)

> There are no leadership formulas for establishing such connections. They can take many forms. It may involve something as simple as looking someone in the eye, turning our body toward the person, or setting aside distractions so that we can give our full attention to someone. What's important is that we give ourselves license to be present, to bring ourselves emotionally and physically to the interaction. (p. 40)

When the space between people contains trust, engagement, and positive regard, the capacity for cognitive, emotional, and physiological changes is greater. Professional development leaders can increase learning by actively cultivating richer, more positive connections between people. That would have a higher yield of professional learning than the importation of experts who dispense lots of information. (p. 41)

EXAMINE YOUR ASSUMPTIONS

Write your assumptions regarding the link between the quality of relationships within organizations and the amount of energy organizations have to achieve their goals. In addition, write your assumptions regarding a leader's role in affecting the quality of relationships. For instance, you may believe that there is little or no connection between energy and the quality of relationships within organizations. Share your assumptions with colleagues in the spirit of dialogue.

_____

_____

_____

_____

_____

_____

DEEPEN YOUR UNDERSTANDING

Consider the attributes of relationships that energize you and those that diminish your energy. Be specific about the things that you or others did and the aspects of relationships that affect energy, particularly positive energy.

_____

_____

_____

_____

_____

_____

_____

Engage in Next Action Thinking

Identify a specific action or a set of actions intended to improve key relationships in your professional life. Make a commitment to that action either in writing or with another person.

_____

_____

_____

_____

_____

_____

_____

References

Dutton, J. (2003). *Energize your workplace: How to create and sustain high-quality connections at work.* San Francisco: Jossey-Bass.

Sparks, D. (2004). Look for ways to ignite the energy within. *JSD, 25*(3), 38–42.

CHAPTER 32

Address the Fundamental Barriers to Professional Learning and Teamwork in Schools

Our profession desperately needs school-based reformers. A school-based reformer is an educator who works in the school and is seldom heard to say, "They'll never let us," and seldom asks, "What am I supposed to do?"

—Roland Barth

The difference between what we are doing and what we're capable of doing would solve most of the world's problems.

—Mahatma Gandhi

My assumptions: The primary barriers to professional learning and teamwork in schools are lack of clarity, dependence, and resignation. Because to a large extent these barriers lie within leaders' circles of influence, leaders' beliefs, understanding, and actions can produce clarity, interdependence among members of the school community, and a sense of possibility and optimism about the future.

Author's Note: Portions of this chapter first appeared in "Leading for Transformation in Teaching, Learning, and Relationships," in *On Common Ground,* which was edited by Rick DuFour, Robert Eaker, and Rebecca DuFour and published by the National Educational Service in 2005.

Commonly cited barriers to professional learning and teamwork in schools are lack of money and time, recalcitrant teachers or teacher unions, and principals and district administrators who lack the desire or skills to lead such efforts. Such large and seemingly intractable barriers often leave educational leaders feeling helpless and hopeless.

> In the view of many observers, teachers' dissatisfaction is broad and deep but is closer to passive resignation than to active indignation, closer to dejection that deflates energy than to anger that inspires action. . . . There is much research to confirm the importance of a sense of efficacy—the sense of making a meaningful difference, of true accomplishment—in teachers' motivation and performance.
>
> —Robert Evans

Although each of these problems has some basis in reality, the primary barriers to professional learning communities, from my experience, are a lack of clarity regarding values, intentions, and beliefs; a dependence on those outside of schools for solutions to problems; and a sense of resignation that robs educators of the energy that is essential to the continuous improvement of teaching, learning, and relationships in schools.

Leaders' clarity is essential because individuals and organizations move toward that which they are clearest about. It is very difficult for leaders to lead in the creation of that which they cannot describe in some detail. Fortunately, leaders have the ability through processes such as writing and dialogue to clarify their values, intentions, and beliefs.

Dependence means that teachers and principals wait for others to direct their actions, a form of learned helplessness that is a by-product of school reform initiatives based on mandates and compliance. Although schools can benefit from synergistic relationships with district offices, universities, and other educational entities, for many schools the balance between internal and external sources of knowledge and action has become so skewed that those in schools no longer see themselves as initiators of action, generators of knowledge, or inventors of solutions to problems. Mike Schmoker (2004) lamented the culture of dependency in schools: "I routinely encounter teachers and administrators who are waiting, endlessly, needlessly, for the right research or staff development programs" (p. 87). In *The 8th Habit*, Steven Covey (2004) described the problem of dependence and its self-reinforcing cycle:

> The widespread reluctance to take initiative, to act independently, only fuels formal leaders' imperative to direct or manage their subordinates. This, they believe, is what they must

do in order to get followers to act. And this cycle quickly escalates into codependency. Each party's weakness reinforces and ultimately justifies the other's behavior. (p. 17)

Resignation is an intellectual and emotional state in which educators come to believe that their individual and collective actions cannot improve teaching and learning, particularly given the large and serious problems that affect the lives of many students and their families. "Low sense of efficacy" is a phrase that researchers use to describe this state. A profound consequence of this belief is that teachers and administrators act as if they have a very small, or perhaps even nonexistent, circles of influence related to student learning.

> If you want to build a ship, don't gather your people and ask them to provide wood, prepare tools, assign tasks. Call them together and raise in their minds the longing for the endless sea.
>
> —Antoine de Saint-Exupéry

The good news is that lack of clarity, dependence, and resignation are not genetically based but are learned, which in turn means that they can be replaced with new learning. Each of us as leaders can do something about these barriers, starting with ourselves. We extend our influence on teaching, learning, and relationships within schools when we expend effort to achieve clarity about our values, goals, and assumptions. We also extend our influence when we create goals with others, goals that are so large and compelling that their achievement requires interdependent action. In addition, we extend our influence when we counter resignation by enlarging our own sense of possibility and optimism through reading (e.g., reading biographies of individuals who overcame significant barriers in the pursuit of worthy goals), studying (particularly of research or other professional literature related to schools that have overcome significant barriers to improve student achievement), and participating in an ongoing community of supportive colleagues. My intention throughout this book has been to encourage exploration of such strategies.

EXAMINE YOUR ASSUMPTIONS

Write your assumptions regarding the primary barriers to professional learning and teamwork in schools. For instance, you may believe that until schools have the resources they require to do their challenging work, professional learning and teamwork will be an elusive luxury. Share your assumptions with colleagues in the spirit of dialogue.

_____

_____

_____

_____

_____

_____

DEEPEN YOUR UNDERSTANDING

Read biographies or research that explain how individuals and organizations overcame significant barriers to achieve worthy purposes.

_____

_____

_____

_____

_____

_____

ENGAGE IN NEXT ACTION THINKING

Design an action plan to counter the barriers described in this chapter. Begin with one of the barriers and identify specific steps you will take to address it. Share your plan with colleagues to increase your clarity and commitment to follow the plan you've created.

_____

_____

_____

_____

_____

_____

_____

REFERENCES

Covey, S. (2004). *The 8th habit: From effectiveness to greatness.* New York: Free Press.

Schmoker, M. (2004). Learning communities at the crossroads: Toward the best schools we've ever had. *Phi Delta Kappan, 86*(1), 84–88.

CHAPTER 33

Spread Positive Emotions Throughout the Organization

People take their emotional cues from the top.

— Daniel Goleman, Richard Boyatzis, & Annie McKee

In the real world, good doesn't replace evil. Evil doesn't replace good. But the energetic displaces the passive.

— Bill Bernbach

My assumptions: Leaders' emotions are contagious. Their emotions can spread to those around them in ways that can either improve or suppress organizational performance. Leaders' positive emotions are linked to their emotional intelligence, and leaders can deliberately develop this important capacity.

The emotional lives of leaders have a particularly powerful effect on those around them. Most of us can recall individuals in our personal and professional lives whose feelings were contagious. In some instances their enthusiasm, passion, energy, and commitment created similar qualities in us. In other situations, their resignation, anxiety, sadness, or anger infected others and led to a slow death spiral in themselves and their organizations.

In the preface to *Primal Leadership: Learning to Lead With Emotional Intelligence*, Daniel Goleman, Richard Boyatzis, and Annie McKee

(2002) wrote, "The fundamental task of leaders, we argue, is to prime good feelings in those they lead. That occurs when a leader creates resonance—a reservoir of positivity that frees the best in people. At its root, then, the primal job of leadership is emotional" (p. ix). Recognizing the irresistible spread of emotions and that people take emotional cues from their leaders, the authors claimed that a leader—even one with no formal leadership positions—exerts a "pal-pable force on the emotional brains of people around her" (p. 9). The authors used the term *resonance* to describe when "people's emotional centers are in synch in a positive way" (p. 33).

> We are co-creating the world every day, in everything we do—for better or for worse. If I walk into a classroom to teach from a place of fear or resentment, I am helping to co-create a world of fear and resentment. If I walk in with hope and a vision of possibility, I am helping to co-create quite a different thing.
>
> —Parker Palmer

Consequently, resonant leaders are upbeat and enthusiastic, according to Goleman, Boyatzis, and McKee (2002). These leaders are attuned to people's feelings and move them in a positive emotional direction. Discordant leaders, on the other hand, create groups in which participants feel "off key" and in which there is a surplus of anger, fear, distrust, and apathy, among other feelings. Given that "the main tasks of a leader are to generate excitement, optimism, and passion for the job ahead, as well as to cultivate an atmosphere of cooperation and trust" (Goleman et al., 2002, pp. 29–30), it is criti-cally important that a significant portion of leaders' learning focus on the four domains of emotional intelligence—self-awareness, self-management, social awareness, and relationship management.

According to Goleman et al. (2002), because of the brain's ability to stimulate new neural connections throughout life, leaders can develop their capacities in these domains by engaging in five discov-eries: (1) uncovering an ideal vision of yourself, (2) discovering who you really are, (3) developing an agenda for improving your abilities, (4) practicing new leadership skills, and (5) developing supportive and trusting relationships that make change possible. Such develop-ment, Goleman et al. pointed out, is self-directed—"intentionally developing or strengthening an aspect of who you are or who you want to be, or both" (p. 109).

The energy generated by leaders engaging a vision of their ideal self in the first discovery fuels the hard work of habit change that occurs later in the process, Goleman et al. (2002) claimed. To better understand the ideal self, Goleman et al. suggested free writing about your ideal life 15 years in the future—describing the types of activities in which you would engage in a typical day or week, your environment, and the kinds of people you'd be around.

To find your real self, Goleman et al. (2002) recommended taking an inventory of your talents and passions. They also recommended seeking out both positive and negative feedback by processes such as 360-degree evaluation: "By collecting information from many people—your boss, your peers, your subordinates—you benefit from multiple perspectives about how you act and how others see it" (p. 135).

The third discovery leads to a learning agenda with goals and action plans. The most powerful goals, according to Goleman et al. (2002), build on one's strengths. Learning plans with clear, specific goals and concrete, practical steps yield the most improvement. Learning is most likely to occur through a combination of concrete experiences, reflection, theory development regarding what was experienced (model building), and trial-and-error learning.

The fourth discovery reconfigures the brain through persistent practice of desired behaviors. Goleman et al. wrote, "[T]o master a leadership skill, you need to change the brain's default option by breaking old habits and learning new ones, which requires an extended period of practice to create the new neural pathway and then strengthen it" (p. 158). The authors added, "[I]t's possible to improve if you do three things: Bring bad habits into awareness, consciously practice a better way, and rehearse that new behavior at every opportunity until it becomes automatic" (p. 156). They acknowledged that a "new way of thinking, feeling, or acting feels unnatural at first, something like putting on someone else's clothes. . . . The key to learning new habits lies in practice to the point of mastery" (p. 157). The authors pointed out that mental rehearsal is another means to brain reconfiguration:

> [I]magining something in vivid detail can fire the same brain cells that are actually involved in that activity. . . . Experimenting with new behaviors, then, and seizing opportunities inside and outside of work to practice them—as well as using such methods as mental rehearsal—eventually triggers in one's brain the neural connections necessary for genuine change to occur. (p. 161)

The fifth discovery cultivates the power of "special relationships, those whose sole purpose is to help you along your path" (Goleman et al., 2002, p. 164). Goleman et al. view such relationships as crucial to an individual's continuing development as a leader. To that end, they recommend the use of mentors and coaches who can exert considerable influence in shaping a leader's abilities, particularly when the mentor or coach is one with whom you share your aspirations and learning agenda.

EXAMINE YOUR ASSUMPTIONS

Write your assumptions regarding the influence of leaders' emotions on organizational performance and whether leaders can enhance their emotional intelligence. For instance, you may believe that leaders' emotions have little effect on their organizations because most people don't have day-to-day contact with them. Furthermore, you may believe that leaders have little influence over their emotional states because there's not much they can do to influence their positive emotions. Share your assumptions with colleagues in the spirit of dialogue.

DEEPEN YOUR UNDERSTANDING

Describe a time when you were affected by either the positive or negative emotional state of a leader and the effect it had on you and on the organization. Also, reflect on a time when your emotions positively or negatively affected those around you. In addition, describe a time when you deliberately developed a new habit that improved your daily emotional state, the quality of your relationships with others, or both.

ENGAGE IN NEXT ACTION THINKING

Discuss with others in your school or school system the "emotional temperature" of your work setting and list actions that might be taken to move it in a positive direction. In addition, invite others who are likely to speak candidly with you about your overall emotional state to do so and to describe the effect your state has on them and on the organization. Use what you learn to apply the five discoveries in your life.

REFERENCE

Goleman, D., Boyatzis, R., & McKee, A. (2002). *Primal leadership: Learning to lead with emotional intelligence.* Boston: Harvard Business School Press.

CHAPTER 34

Address Anxiety in the Schoolhouse

Finding a corner of peace and quiet in the mind, a place of stillness, is absolutely essential for leaders.

—Richard Boyatzis & Annie McKee

The best leaders are not only highly motivated themselves, but able to somehow radiate that positivity, igniting and mobilizing positive attitudes in those around them.

—Daniel Goleman

> **My assumptions: Anxiety is an ever-present reality in many schools, and its effects can be contagious and toxic. If unrecognized and unaddressed, it can impede progress toward important goals and undermine relationships. Successful leaders recognize and address anxiety to ward off its ill effects on teaching, learning, and relationships.**

Many teachers and principals report increased anxiety due to the demands of teaching a more diverse student population to higher standards and the continuous improvements in teaching it requires. High-stakes testing exacerbates this challenge and the anxiety that accompanies it. District leaders also report various stresses as central staffs are reduced at a time when school requests for their services are growing.

All organizations have anxiety to one degree or another. Like other significant feelings, anxiety is contagious and seldom stays contained within one or two persons. Anxiety, of course, can alert a group

> The physical presence of a positive and calm leader during a crisis is particularly reassuring.
>
> —Richard Boyatzis & Annie McKee

to a problem and stimulate its solution. But as Harriet Lerner pointed out in *Fear and Other Uninvited Guests: Tackling the Anxiety, Fear, and Shame That Keep Us From Optimal Living and Loving* (2004), when the situation becomes overheated, it will more often than not lead to the wrong solution. "In anxious situations people rarely have bad intentions." But that doesn't prevent them from responding with "automatic patterned ways of managing anxiety" (p. 102).

"*All* anxious systems have certain traits and characteristics in common," Lerner wrote (2004, p. 93). She noted five common styles of anxiety management: overfunctioning, underfunctioning, blaming, distancing, and gossiping. Although each of these styles may bring some degree of comfort to the anxious individual, they may also generate even more anxiety in the system.

> Positive emotions such as compassion, confidence, and generosity have a decidedly constructive effect on neurological functioning, psychological well-being, physical health, and personal relationships.
>
> —Richard Boyatzis & Annie McKee

Overfunctioning school leaders make virtually everything their responsibility. Their anxiety leads them to believe they are the only ones who truly understand the situation and the only ones whose actions can be trusted to improve it. Consequently, they are less likely to delegate to others and are more likely to feel resentful because they are doing more than their fair share. Underfunctioning leaders' anxiety causes them to cease to perform key aspects of their job; they are more likely to underfunction if one or more persons in their work setting are overfunctioning. Finding fault through blaming—which is sometimes confused with honesty—promotes defensiveness or sets in motion a counterattack, neither of which contributes to productive problem solving. Emotional and physical distancing lead to a flatness of spirit, boredom, and what some observers call a "slow death spiral." Gossip means talking about people rather than to them. By its very nature, gossip leads to distrust and creates ever-shifting patterns of insiders and outsiders, all of which add to the current of anxiety in the organization.

Lerner (2004) cited the role of individual responsibility in managing anxiety in the system, a particularly important stance for leaders whose position and visibility amplify their emotional states throughout the organization. "The only part of the system you can change is your own reaction to anxiety," she argues. "You can learn to let other people's anxiety float by you, and to pass on less anxiety than you receive. When we can transmit less intensity than we receive in the systems we belong to, we are not only moving in the direction of calming things down. We are also doing what the world desperately needs: creating a more peaceable, open-hearted place to live" (p. 114).

Because calmness is as contagious as anxiety, leaders who learn to manage their own emotions are better able to dampen rather than amplify anxiety in their organizations (see Chapter 33 for more on this topic). They do so when they:

- *Have candid conversations with colleagues in the organization:* Leaders acknowledge rather than deny or minimize the presence of anxiety and its effects.
- *Clearly define their areas of responsibility:* Leaders carefully monitor their own performance to make certain that they are not overfunctioning or underfunctioning.
- *Monitor their emotional "default settings" in tense situations:* Doing so makes certain that leaders aren't reflexively blaming others and allows leaders to look for underlying causes and work on solving problems rather than finding fault.
- *Know their own feelings and engage in honest and open conversations with others:* Leaders do not emotionally or physically distance themselves from colleagues.
- *Talk directly to people rather than about them:* Leaders establish group agreements that acknowledge the insidious effects of gossip and that ask group members to refrain from gossip and to confront it whenever it occurs.

EXAMINE YOUR ASSUMPTIONS

Write your assumptions regarding a leader's role in recognizing and alleviating anxiety in the work setting. For instance, you may believe that anxiety is not only a fact of life but a valuable source of motivation and that effective leaders create anxiety rather than alleviate it. Share your assumptions with colleagues in the spirit of dialogue.

_____

_____

_____

_____

_____

DEEPEN YOUR UNDERSTANDING

Describe a time when you managed your anxiety so that it did not infect others or undermine relationships and organizational performance. List the methods you used to address your anxiety.

_____

_____

_____

_____

_____

_____

ENGAGE IN NEXT ACTION THINKING

Discuss with others the level of anxiety present in your work setting. If the anxiety is a source of concern, develop a plan to address it using some of the ideas provided earlier or other sources of information.

_____

_____

_____

_____

_____

_____

_____

REFERENCE

Lerner, H. (2004). *Fear and other uninvited guests: Tackling the anxiety, fear, and shame that keep us from optimal living and loving.* New York: HarperCollins.

CHAPTER 35

Appeal to the Heart as Well as the Head

The fallacy of rationalism is the assumption that the social world can be altered by logical argument. The problem, as George Bernard Shaw observed, is that "reformers have the idea that change can be achieved by brute sanity."

—Michael Fullan

People get the courage to try new things not because they are convinced to do so by a wealth of analytical evidence but because they feel something viscerally.

—Gary Hamel

> **My assumptions: Initiating and maintaining the momentum of significant change require experiences that appeal to the heart as well as the head. Intellectual engagement alone is usually insufficient to produce such changes.**

"People change what they do less because they are given analysis that shifts their *thinking* than because they are shown a truth that influences their *feelings*," John Kotter and Dan Cohen argue in *The Heart of Change: Real-Life Stories of How People Change Their Organizations* (2002, p. 1). Emotion underlies lasting change, Kotter and Cohen believe, and that emotion is generated more by vivid stories and images—even images that disturb rather than uplift—than it is by research and analysis that provide logical reasons for change. Things that people can see, hear, and touch generate energy that is often lacking from more formal intellectual processes, Kotter and

Cohen say. This emotion provides the passion and commitment that overcomes complacency and inertia and that enables individuals to change often difficult-to-break habits.

Pam Robbins, a consultant to schools, provides an example of such a process. In a letter to me, she wrote:

> [I]t's not a matter of having better information. . . . It's a matter of moral imagination, a wisdom of the heart.
>
> —Paul Ray & Sherry Ruth Anderson

Recently, I had the opportunity to represent NSDC in an on-site consultation with Los Angeles Unified School District D. The superintendent, Ronni Ephraim who had recently come to District D, met with all the administrators one morning to update them on the "State of the District." During the course of her remarks, she commended two administrators who had handled a very tragic situation—the loss of an elementary student in a car accident—with empathy, care and sensitivity.

As she continued with her remarks, Ephraim said that she wanted to leave the group with a "visual reminder" of the challenges facing every school. At that point, she asked two staff members to "unroll" a list of students who had not met proficiency in English language arts. The list was one-eighth of a mile long! It stretched four times across the ballroom in which we were seated. The group sat silently, in awe. The superintendent urged the audience not to think of the list

> Many so-called learning experiences don't provide opportunities for real thinking. Meetings are just thinly veiled attempts to persuade others . . . to agree with the teacher's . . . conclusions. Real thinking occurs only when everyone is engaged in exploring differing viewpoints.
>
> —Susan Scott

as a "group" of students, but rather as a series of individuals— each with their own needs, hopes, dreams, and aspirations. Ephraim added that a careful examination of the list would yield an awareness that many of the names represented African-American and Latino students. She noted that many of the same names could be found on the lists of non-proficient students in other disciplines as well.

I was deeply moved by this experience and observed that most of the administrators sitting around me were as well. Following the superintendent's remarks, I met with middle and high school principals. Our "visual reminder" became the foundation for examining the notion that schools that support the continuing development of students also support the continuing development of those who work with those students, as we addressed the topic of using meetings as learning-focused, capacity-building opportunities.

Research, data, and analysis have a role to play in improving teaching and learning. But without stories, images, and experiences that touch the heart, it is difficult to break through complacency and inertia to the sources of energy that are essential to sustained collaborative work, professional learning, and the development of new habits.

EXAMINE YOUR ASSUMPTIONS

Write your assumptions regarding the significance of emotion generated through vivid stories, images, and experiences, stating them as succinctly and powerfully as possible. For instance, you may believe "The most persuasive way to initiate and sustain change is by providing teachers and administrators with reports that describe the very best scientifically based research." Share your assumptions with colleagues in the spirit of dialogue.

_____

_____

_____

_____

_____

_____

DEEPEN YOUR UNDERSTANDING

Provide examples from your personal and professional lives when you were motivated to action by emotionally compelling stories, images, or experiences. Discuss ways that you could create such images, stories, and experiences to motivate and sustain change in your setting.

_____

_____

_____

_____

_____

_____

ENGAGE IN NEXT ACTION THINKING

Specify what actions will be taken to use images, stories, and experiences to motivate and sustain change, who will take them, and by what date.

_____

_____

_____

_____

_____

_____

REFERENCE

Kotter, J., & Cohen, D. (2002). _The heart of change: Real-life stories of how people change their organizations._ Boston: Harvard Business School Press.

PART IV

Transformation Through Professional Learning and Doing

Leaders are perpetual learners. . . . Learning is the essential fuel for the leader, the source of high-octane energy that keeps up the momentum by continually sparking new understanding, new ideas, and new challenges.

—Warren Bennis & Burt Nanus

The greatest creative challenge is not only to do something different, but to be something different. The most creative act is the modeling of your own life. . . . Those people who experience the greatest joy offer to the world their distinctiveness.

—George Land & Beth Jarman

In far too many classrooms, students miss out on essential knowledge and skills because of poor-quality or mediocre teaching. In addition, far too many students lack meaningful relationships with their peers and with adults. These students leave their K–12 education with a diminished sense of possibilities for their lives.

A related problem is that most teachers experience mind-numbing and demeaning professional development that creates dependency. Even relatively well-executed "pull-out" staff development seldom affects a school's culture, extends to the classroom, or is sustained over enough time to affect instructional practice. In most schools, a large gap exists between what is known about professional learning that affects teaching and improves student achievement and the professional development that teachers and principals regularly experience.

The solution to these problems, I believe, is high-quality, school-based professional learning and collaborative work that affects all teachers virtually every day. Such learning will deepen understanding, transform beliefs and assumptions to support new practices, and provide a continuous stream of powerful goal-focused actions that keeps improvements on track.

Because a great deal has been written about quality professional learning,* the concluding chapters in this book focus on assisting you in developing a clear, compelling point of view about effective professional development to inform the types of conversations described in this book.

As you will see in the chapters that follow, the most powerful forms of professional development:

- Are sustained, focus relentlessly on improving student learning, and provide personalized in-school and in-classroom assistance to teachers;
- Enable schools to focus their efforts on a small number of student-learning goals and use resources more effectively to alter classroom practice;
- Are both practical and intellectually rigorous and produce complex, intelligent behavior that is the hallmark of skillful teaching and leadership;
- Deepen teachers' content knowledge, expand their repertoire of instructional strategies, and connect them to one another in sustained, interdependent ways;
- Engage teachers virtually every day with their colleagues in examining their students' work, considering data, improving their lessons, deepening their understanding of what they teach, and expanding the number of methods available to teach that content successfully to all students;
- Create schools in which teachers feel emotionally connected to a larger, compelling purpose and to each other in a professional community; and
- Energize schools to pull resources toward them that support their continuous improvement to and use the best available knowledge and skills within and around them.

The professional development described in Part III—combined with the professional learning promoted by the type of interpersonal connections advocated in this book—can strengthen the quality of teaching in every classroom and continuously improve student learning. Those are the criteria against which results-focused leadership will ultimately be judged.

---

*Visit www.nsdc.org to study the National Staff Development Council's Standards for Staff Development, NSDC's Code of Ethics, *Designing Powerful Professional Development for Teachers and Principals*, by Dennis Sparks (NSDC, 2002), and many other publications that are available for free downloading.

CHAPTER 36

Design Powerful Professional Learning for All Educators

[T]eachers who know a lot about teaching and learning and who work in environments that allow them to know students well are the critical elements of successful learning.

—Linda Darling-Hammond

Today, people believe that professional development should be targeted and directly related to teachers' practice. It should be site-based and long-term. It should be ongoing—part of a teacher's work week, not something that's tacked on. And it should be curriculum-based, to the extent possible, so that it helps teachers help their students master the curriculum at a higher level.

—James Stigler

My assumptions: Quality professional development focuses on improving the learning of all students, deepens understanding of what is taught and of the most powerful ways of teaching it, affects educators' beliefs about teaching and learning, and produces a coherent stream of actions that continuously improve teaching, learning, and leadership. The most powerful forms of professional learning are embedded in teachers' daily work, address the core tasks of teaching, and support teachers in forming productive relationships with colleagues and students.

The welfare of young people and the future of our nation require that all students have quality teaching each day and are surrounded by supportive relationships with peers and adults. From my perspective, that requires that all teachers participate in team-focused professional learning as part of their daily work.

> Team learning is vital because teams, not individuals, are the fundamental learning unit in modern organization.
>
> —Peter Senge

The most effective professional development has a sustained focus on achieving student-learning goals derived from clear and high expectations for all students. Quality teaching and skillful leadership are manifestations of complex, intelligent behavior, behavior that is refined by continuous, intellectually rigorous professional learning.

Therefore, the most powerful forms of professional development make cognitive demands on teachers and administrators and require the progressive use of increasingly higher-level intellectual skills. That means quality professional learning results from the sustained study of research and other professional literature, the analysis of school and classroom data and other evidence of student performance, and the exchange of professional judgments.

> There is plenty of evidence around that, when teachers know their content and know how to teach it at high levels to all students, "teaching to the test" fades into the background of everyday instruction and learning.
>
> —Anne Lewis

The professional learning advocated here skillfully blends the abstract and intellectual with the concrete and immediately useful. Such learning asks teachers to stand back to look at things from a broader perspective, to dig deeply into the consequences of their actions, and to act in ways that will make a significant difference in the learning of their students.

Powerful professional development hones in on the content knowledge and instructional processes that most affect student learning. When teachers study the subjects they teach and expand their repertoire of strategies to teach that content, they will improve their teaching and student learning. That claim is particularly true, I believe, given the complex instructional challenges of classrooms with increasingly diverse students. Teachers' study of content knowledge and teaching methods is aided when teachers consider how students learn a particular subject and the best ways of teaching that subject (an understanding that some experts call pedagogical content knowledge).

> In all subjects, especially math and science, research indicates that many teachers do not understand the substance well enough to teach concepts, problem formulation and solving, and other higher-order thinking skills now expected as learning outcomes.
>
> —National Institute on Educational Governance, Finance, Policy Making, and Management

Because learning has a strong social component and because the synergy that comes from group problem solving often leads to innovative solutions, the most powerful forms of professional development are centered on teams within schools. Team meetings occur for the most part during the school day because they are an important part of teachers' work responsibilities and benefit from the participation of all teachers, a goal that is difficult to achieve after school and during the summer.

The quality of relationships among adults in schools is a predictor of student learning, particularly in schools that are most challenged by the social ills of poverty and racism. High levels of trust, respectful and honest exchanges of views, and a shared commitment to worthwhile

> To last and to have lasting impact, professional development programs would do well to encourage informed debate and healthy unrest among their participants.
>
> —Mary Ann Smith

goals are some of the most important characteristics of these relationships. Without such relationships, few schools will take full advantage of available resources.

When professional development is well planned and well executed:

- Teachers hold challenging goals for all students and continuously reflect on various forms of evidence regarding student learning.
- Teachers share planning and learning time that promotes meaningful collaboration. Teachers participate in one or more learning teams within which they are mutually accountable for student learning within the broad context of a professional learning community.
- The organization's culture fosters mutual respect, high levels of trust, and innovative solutions to problems. Teachers experience the emotional and social support such communities provide.

- Teachers are intellectually stimulated by their work. Their productive interactions with peers and with various external providers (for instance, district offices, universities, intermediate service agencies, consultants) deepen their understanding of the content they teach, broaden the range of instructional strategies they bring to their classrooms, and improve relationships with students.
- Methods such as classroom coaching, demonstration lessons, lesson study, the examination of student work, and action research ground professional learning in daily practice and its influence on student learning.
- Teachers pursue professional learning through courses, institutes, and conferences when it is important for the achievement of school goals. They may also participate in cross-school networks that strengthen content knowledge and pedagogy.

The *National Staff Development Council's Standards for Staff Development,* the Council's Code of Ethics, and other professional literature are available at www.nsdc.org and can provide materials that can deepen your understanding of these approaches.

Virtually every school can make significant progress in creating such forms of professional learning in a single school year. It is critically important, I believe, that school and district leaders declare high-quality professional learning of the type described here a priority goal within their circles of influence and set about achieving it with the sense of urgency it deserves. Students pass through our schools only once, and they will be the ultimate beneficiaries of the quality teaching such professional learning can produce in every classroom.

EXAMINE YOUR ASSUMPTIONS

Write your assumptions regarding the attributes of quality professional learning. For instance, you may believe "Achieving the kind of professional development described in this chapter will take many years, and the only viable option is to make certain that teacher workshops are relevant to school goals and enjoyed by teachers." Share your assumptions with colleagues in the spirit of dialogue.

_____

_____

_____

_____

_____

_____

DEEPEN YOUR UNDERSTANDING

Describe in detail your long-term goals for the type of professional development you want for all teachers in your school or school system. Discuss which aspects of your vision can be realized in the next school year if the school or district leadership team acts with urgency.

_____

_____

_____

_____

_____

ENGAGE IN NEXT ACTION THINKING

Specify actions that will be taken to make your vision a reality, who will take them, and by what date those actions will be taken.

_____

_____

_____

_____

_____

CHAPTER 37

Match Professional Development Goals and Methods With Student Outcomes

The notes of the lecturer are passed to the notes of the listener—without going through the mind of either.

—Mortimer Adler

To create and sustain for children the conditions for productive growth without those conditions existing for educators is virtually impossible.

—Seymour Sarason

> **My assumptions: Professional development is most effective when to a large extent its goals and methods match the goals and methods teachers are expected to use with their students. The qualities of mind and relationships we wish to create for students depend on creating those same qualities of mind and relationships for their teachers and principals.**

F ar too often, educators experience professional development whose intention and form are disconnected from the recommendations it makes for student learning. For example, teachers sit passively while experts lecture them on the importance of active learning in their classrooms. Or they receive a cursory presentation that skims across the surface of ways to promote students' deep understanding of subject matter. Or they are told to create caring communities within their classrooms while working in schools whose cultures and daily schedules are barriers from them knowing and trusting one another.

I see a critical link between the goals and methods advocated for students and the kinds of professional learning and relationships essential in creating schools in which youngsters and adults experience success.

To prepare for this chapter, I thumbed through several journals from the past few years to find articles that advocated particular student outcomes and instructional approaches for achieving them. The September 2003 issue of *Educational Leadership* provided a rich resource to illustrate my point with a collection of articles on building classroom relationships.

In that issue, Robert Marzano and Jane Marzano tell their readers that relationships within schools cannot be left to chance; Steven Wolk recommends engaged learning and caring teacher-student relationships and classrooms that are interesting, intellectual, creative, communal, and purposeful; Jonathan Erwin describes the power of warm, trusting human relationships; Richard Strong, Harvey Silver, Matthew Perini, and Greg Tuculescu discuss the value of

> In order to offer students the kinds of experiences that reformers want them to have, teachers need to immerse themselves in similar experiences.
>
> —Mary Ann Smith

mastery, understanding, self-expression, and relationships; and Dan Hoffman and Barbara Levak emphasize the importance of knowing, trusting, empowering, connecting with, and honoring all students.

Also in this issue, Ernest Mendes recalls from his teaching experience that "every student with whom I consciously made an effort to establish a rapport or a caring relationship demonstrated dramatic changes in behavior, effort, and performance." Jane Katch writes that she wants her students to "develop empathy, look at a situation from another person's point of view, and form a classroom in which each child is a valued member."

> I don't believe in teacher-proof materials. If a teacher is not a critical thinker, how can we expect our kids to be critical thinkers?
>
> —Diana Lam

If we change words such as *student* or *child* to *teacher* and the location from *classroom* to *school*, we are describing the attributes of professional development and a collaborative work environment that I believe would immensely improve the quality of teaching and student learning. In such schools, caring, respectful, and energizing professional and personal relationships among adults would be cultivated, every person would feel valued, teachers' intellectual and creative capacities would be nurtured, sustained learning would lead to mastery of complex professional skills that would be applied in adult contexts as well as the classroom, and teachers would feel empowered rather than resigned or dependent.

> If teachers decide that their goals for students' learning include understanding, then professional development programs should give them time to think about what they mean by "understanding" and how they engage student in the process of understanding.
>
> —Vicki Jacobs

Schools with these qualities would not only be outstanding places for students, but would attract, retain, and continuously renew talented teachers. Our goal, then, as educational leaders is to create a system of schools each of which would be such an outstanding place for students and adults alike that we would eagerly participate in them even if we did not know in advance whether we would be a student, a teacher, or an administrator nor how long we would remain in those roles. What a wonderful school that would be for everyone who had the good fortune to spend time within it!

EXAMINE YOUR ASSUMPTIONS

Write your assumptions regarding the value of aligning goals and methods advocated for students with those for educators, stating them as succinctly and powerfully as possible. For instance, you may believe "Because teachers are professionals, intellectual stimulation and participation in a strong caring community are unnecessary for them to develop those qualities in their students." Share your assumptions with colleagues in the spirit of dialogue.

_____

_____

_____

_____

_____

_____

_____

DEEPEN YOUR UNDERSTANDING

Describe in detail the broad cognitive, behavioral, and affective outcomes your school or school system seeks to develop in students and the characteristics of the environment in which they would learn each day. Do the same for teachers and administrators. Discuss the alignment between these two sets of qualities.

_____

_____

_____

_____

_____

_____

ENGAGE IN NEXT ACTION THINKING

Determine what actions will be taken to align the goals and methods of adult learning and interaction with those intended for students. Specify who will take those actions and by what date.

_____

_____

_____

_____

REFERENCE

Scherer, M. (Ed.). (2003). Building classroom relationships. *Educational Leadership, 61*(1).

CHAPTER 38

Bridge the Knowing-Doing Gap

What matters to us does not suffer from lack of knowledge or skills. To say we need more skills before we can do anything is usually an excuse.

—Peter Block

The development of real knowledge requires intentional activity. If you wait to know something before you do something, likely neither will happen.

—David Allen

> **My assumptions: Most educators know more about effective practice than they regularly employ in their work. The consistent use of what is already known would lead to significant improvements in leadership, teaching, and learning. Learning by doing is an important and underused method of reducing the knowing-doing gap.**

Most of us know more about teaching, leadership, and ways to improve schools than our actions demonstrate. While that does not mean that there are not important things for us to learn, I believe leadership, teaching, and learning will get quite a bit better when educators more consistently apply what they already know.

I've joked over the years that I've wanted to declare an official year of "no professional learning." During that year, anyone caught learning in the traditional ways would be publicly chastised so that everyone's efforts would be focused on doing what he or she already knows, reflecting on the effectiveness of those actions, and on applying the new learning that would emerge from that action. Sometimes it even seems as if staff development–oriented educators have a default mechanism that moves them toward "head learning" whenever they are faced with a new problem. And because that learning often reveals other gaps in academic knowledge, they engage in even more such learning in the quest for "complete understanding," which further postpones action and the important learning such action can generate.

> Our problem is not a lack of tools. We have more tools than we need, many of them we will never use, so why keep enlarging the workshop instead of producing something we are proud of?
>
> —Peter Block

Jeffrey Pfeffer and Robert Sutton (2000) address this issue in *The Knowing-Doing Gap: How Smart Companies Turn Knowledge into Action.* "[O]ne of the great mysteries in organizational management," they write, is "why knowledge of what needs to be done frequently fails to result in action or behavior consistent with that knowledge. We came to call this the *knowing-doing problem*" (p. 4). They note that " . . . research demonstrates that the success of most interventions designed to improve organizational performance depends largely on implementing what is already known rather than from adopting new or previously unknown ways of doing things" (p. 14).

> We will pay an expert hundreds of dollars an hour for legal, financial, or psychotherapeutic advice, but we're unwilling to pay ourselves the courtesy of trusting that our own instincts and knowledge can guide us to the successful completion of our creative projects. Too often we doubt that we have the right information, ideas, and skills. . . .
>
> —Eric Maisel

Pfeffer and Sutton list numerous organizational processes that substitute for implementing new practices: making a decision to do something as if the decision itself were sufficient to bring about the change, writing a mission statement, engaging in planning, preparing written documents, making presentations and talking "smart" about the change, and so on. While each of these activities may have value, when they are viewed as sufficient in and of themselves, they become sources of the knowing-doing gap, the authors claim.

Here are some additional ideas from the book that have important implications for school leaders:

- "[O]ne of the most important insights from our research is that knowledge that is actually implemented is much more likely to be acquired from learning by doing than from learning by reading, listening, or even thinking" (pp. 5–6).
- "Great companies get remarkable performance from ordinary people" (p. 6).
- "Attempting to copy [from other organizations] just *what* is done—the explicit practices and policies—without holding the underlying philosophy is at once a more difficult task and an approach that is less likely to be successful" (p. 24).
- "[A]t one level, the answer to the knowing-doing problem is deceptively simple: Embed more of the process of acquiring new knowledge in the actual doing of the task and less in formal training programs that are frequently ineffective" (p. 27).
- The "mystique of complexity" employs jargon as a form of status seeking. "The use of complex language hampers implementation even more, however, when leaders or managers don't really understand the meaning of the language they are using and its implications for action. It is hard enough to explain what a complex idea means for action when you understand it and others don't. It is impossible when you use terms that sound impressive but you don't really understand what they mean" (p. 52).

> That individuals, organizations, and countries are not doing very well at converting knowledge to practice is well known in the United States.
>
> —Gerald Nadler & Shozo Hibino

- "You're likely to find talk substituting for action when no follow-up is done to ensure that what was said is actually done; people forget that merely making a decision doesn't change anything; planning, meetings, and report writing become defined as 'action' that is valuable in its own right, even if it has no effect on what people actually do . . . ; complex language, ideas, processes, and structures are thought to be better than simple ones; there is a belief that managers are people who talk and others do; and

> If we are waiting for more knowledge, more skills, more support from the world around us, we are waiting too long. . . . We think there is a right way, that someone else knows what it is, and that it is our job to figure it out. And the world conspires with this illusion, for it wants to sell us an answer.
>
> —Peter Block

internal status comes from talking a lot, interrupting, and being critical of others' ideas" (p. 54).

- "[O]rganizations that were better at learning and translating knowledge into action understood the virtue of simple language, simple structures, simple concepts, and the power of common sense, which is remarkably uncommon in its application" (p. 59).

- "People and the organizations in which they work are often trapped by implicit theories of behavior that guide their decisions and actions. Because the theories are not surfaced or conscious, they can't be refuted with data or logic. In fact, people may not even be conscious of how the theories are directing their behavior. . . . [O]ne of the most powerful interventions we have uncovered to free people from the unconscious power of implicit theory: making people think carefully about the assumptions implicit in the practices and interventions they are advocating. . . . By bringing to the surface assumptions that are otherwise unconscious, interventions and decisions become much more mindful and incorporate what people know" (pp. 91–92).

> People learn best through active involvement and through thinking about becoming articulate about what they have learned.
>
> —Ann Lieberman

Clarity of thought and speech, embedding learning in doing, taking action with accountability, examining our own implicit assumptions and encouraging others to do the same—those are familiar themes of this book.

EXAMINE YOUR ASSUMPTIONS

Write your assumptions regarding the knowing-doing gap, stating them as succinctly and powerfully as possible. For instance, you may believe "A lack of knowledge and skill is the real problem in improving teaching and learning, not the implementation of what is already known." Share your assumptions with colleagues in the spirit of dialogue.

_____

_____

_____

_____

_____

_____

_____

DEEPEN YOUR UNDERSTANDING

Describe ways that you have learned by engaging in action and reflecting on the effects of that action. In addition, discuss ways you have assisted others in considering "the assumptions implicit in the practices and interventions" they regularly employ.

_____

_____

_____

_____

_____

_____

ENGAGE IN NEXT ACTION THINKING

Specify ways in which you will reduce the knowing-doing gap for yourself and for your organization, the actions that will be taken as a result of this discussion, who will take them, and by what date.

_____

_____

_____

_____

_____

_____

_____

REFERENCE

Pfeffer, J., & Sutton, R. (2000). *The knowing-doing gap: How smart companies turn knowledge into action.* Boston: Harvard Business School Press.

CHAPTER 39

Amplify Positive Deviance in Schools

The traditional model for social and organization change doesn't work. It never has. You can't bring permanent solutions in from outside.

—Jerry Sternin

Knowingly or not, commercial publishers, staff development consultants and trainers, and district and state officials have formed an alliance that has repeatedly diminished the ability of local educators to think critically and responsibly. The marketing of answers for schools has kept schools habitually dependent on external authorities.... Members of the local school community are made to believe, or have internalized the belief, that educational change is the province of others . . . External programs, materials, consultants, and research can and should be considered and possibly used when a school makes it own decisions, but a school should look first for resources within.

—Carl Glickman

My assumptions: The quality of teaching and student learning can be significantly improved with the professional expertise that already resides within virtually all schools. Leadership practices and school cultures that "amplify positive deviance" are a primary means by which schools can continuously improve teaching and learning, demonstrate deep appreciation for the talents of staff members, and retain competent teachers.

In a common approach to school reform, researchers identify "best practices," which they disseminate through publications and conferences. In turn, school systems prescribe them to teachers who are monitored carefully for compliance. Little regard is shown for the intelligence and capacities that already reside within schools. Another far less frequently applied approach taps the "positive deviance" that exists in schools and amplifies it across classrooms.

> Even though expert guidance is occasionally helpful, the people involved in a specific situation generally know more about it than outside experts.
>
> —Gerald Nadler & Shozo Hibino

"Positive deviants," Jerry Sternin told me in a Winter 2004 *JSD* interview, "are people whose behavior and practices produce solutions to problems that others in the group who have access to exactly the same resources have not been able to solve. We want to identify these people because they provide demonstrable evidence that solutions to the problem already exist within the community" (p. 46).

Sternin's view is that within virtually every school there are individuals whose behavior enables them to get better-than-average results and that these individuals have discovered pathways to success for the rest of the group. That's contrary to a particularly potent and usually unquestioned assumption in education—and perhaps in other fields as well—that solutions to problems must come from the outside because those on the inside either don't know enough to improve things or don't have the will to do the hard work of change. That view is particularly strong regarding schools that have a history of low performance.

> Most current reforms, rather than seeking to make teachers into co-developers, simply call for them to carry out experts' prescriptions.
>
> —Robert Evans

In the *JSD* interview, I asked Sternin to elaborate on his views regarding outside assistance. "People learn best," he said, "when they discover things for themselves. Knowledge is usually insufficient to change behavior. It is our own discoveries that change behavior. A basic belief of the Positive Deviance Approach is that when someone from the outside provides the solution, those to whom it is directed may not believe it and do not have an investment in it" (p. 48).

Sternin added: "It's natural for people to resist when someone tells them what to do. That's part of human nature. It's like the human immune system's rejection of anything it senses as foreign. It's the same thing as the psychological and emotional levels when an external solution is imposed on us. When the solution comes from within the system, the immune response isn't activated" (p. 48).

The Positive Deviance Approach has six steps: define, determine, discover, design, discern, and disseminate "The group begins its work by defining the problem and describing what success would look like—which is the inverse of the problem statement" Sternin said. "Next, the group determines if there are individuals who have already achieved success. If there are such people, they are the positive deviants. Next, the group discovers the uncommon but demonstrably successful behaviors and practices used by the positive deviants to solve the problem. And finally, the group designs an intervention which enables its members to practice those demonstrably successful but uncommonly applied practices. The process is beautifully simple because its strength lies in the solutions

> We should attach the most importance to improving our teaching methods. Most students are taught by an average teacher, implementing the average method. If we can find a way to make the average method a little bit better, that's going to have a big effect.
>
> —James Stigler

that are discovered and owned by people in the community" (p. 49). The final two steps are discerning the effectiveness of the intervention and sharing the successful intervention with a wider audience.

The physical presence of the positive deviant in the affected community is a significant aspect of the inquiry process. But that presence alone is usually insufficient. For instance, a principal who has heard about positive deviance may invite a teacher who has consistently produced higher reading-test scores to tell her peers how she does it. What often occurs, however, is that the faculty resists and the teacher identified by the principal may even feel shunned by her colleagues.

Sternin explains it this way: "The Positive Deviance Approach requires that community members find the positive deviants within their own community. The community is self-defined and its members always share the same resource base. . . . That's important, and it's a critical distinction between a best-practices approach and positive deviance" (p. 50).

> The very best thing you can do for a superintendent . . . is not to give him more money, more buildings, or a better contract. Instead, give him a tool to make his average teachers just a little bit better, and you'll see a vastly greater impact across the district than any model school or blue-ribbon program will ever bring.
>
> —Superintendent, as quoted by Peter Temes

While the Positive Deviance Approach honors and appreciates the people who engage in it, it may be challenging for traditional "experts" to apply. "Positive deviance," Sternin told me, "is a very empowering approach, but it's one that individuals with lots of degrees on their walls may find it difficult to implement. Positive deviance inquires into what's working and how it can be built upon to solve very difficult problems. It requires that experts relinquish their power and believe that solutions already reside within the system. Our role is to help people discover their answers" (p. 51).

Schools that systematically identify, deeply appreciate, and spread the outstanding practices that already exist within them will also be more effective in using external sources of knowledge, I believe. And schools whose cultures are contrary to such methods will derive few lasting benefits from most externally imposed "solutions." Amplifying positive deviance is a promising, nonprescriptive approach for schools

> Ultimately, no amount of outside intervention can produce the motivation and specificity of best solutions for every setting.
>
> —Michael Fullan

that see value in its premises and are ready to empower teachers through its inquiry process.

Examine Your Assumptions

Write your assumptions about amplifying positive deviance, stating them as succinctly and powerfully as possible. For instance, you may believe "The Positive Deviance Approach cannot work in my setting because teachers have no desire to learn from one another and positive deviant teachers are often ostracized by their peers." Invite others to share their assumptions with you in a spirit of openness to having your views change.

_____

_____

_____

_____

_____

Deepen Your Understanding

Describe in writing or discuss with others the ways in which amplifying positive deviance is the same and different from other types of professional development with which you are familiar. For example, a common approach is for administrators to identify teachers who produce high test scores and ask them to describe their teaching methods at school or district staff development events, a method that does not engage the school community in the process recommended by Jerry Sternin.

_____

_____

_____

_____

_____

_____

ENGAGE IN NEXT ACTION THINKING

Specify what actions you will take to engage the school community in identifying and designing processes to learn from positive deviant teachers and positive deviant schools.

_____

_____

_____

_____

_____

_____

REFERENCE

Sparks, D. (2004). From hunger aid to school reform. An interview with Jerry Sternin. *JSD, 25*(1), 46–51.

CHAPTER 40

Create Professional Learning That Alters Educators' Brains

Learning produces physical change in the brain.

—James Zull

There is now a massive amount of evidence from all realms of science that unless individuals take a very active role in what it is that they're studying, unless they learn to ask questions, to do things hands-on, to essentially recreate things in their own mind and transform them as is needed, the ideas just disappear.

—Howard Gardner

> **My assumptions: Learning physically alters brains. Professional learning, therefore, requires the sustained, active engagement of educators' brains.**

Schools and schools systems do a great many things in the name of professional development that may be important and even essential but do not directly affect the quality of teaching and professional relationships in schools. Among these activities are establishing policies, forming planning committees, writing job descriptions for new teacher leadership roles, hiring instructional coaches, and providing released days. At best, these activities may create conditions favorable to learning but in themselves have little demonstrable affect on teaching and student achievement.

The *final 2%* is the term I have given to the cluster of learning experiences that are sufficiently robust to permanently alter professional practice and relationships in ways that improve teaching and learning in schools. Without these experiences, the initial 98% are to a large degree wasted effort. At the heart of the final 2% is an understanding of how learning occurs within the human brain and the nature of the activities that affect it.

> Teachers . . . must cultivate strategies of problem solving that seem to be quite unusual among adult Americans. They must learn to treat knowledge as something they construct, test, and explore, rather than as something they absorb and accumulate.
>
> —David Cohen

Learning occurs, experts say, when the brain creates new neural networks or reinforces those that already exist. The primary goals of professional development—teachers' deeper understanding of the subjects they teach and of the students with whom they interact, the acquisition of beliefs that support stretching goals for student learning, and new habits of behavior that are demonstrated through instructional practices and relationship skills and routines—are changes in the neural structure of the brain.

> [C]hanges challenge deeply embedded behavioral regularities of classrooms and schools and require teachers to abandon the beliefs, assumptions, habits, and roles of a lifetime.
>
> —Robert Evans

To better understand how the brain changes as humans learn, I asked Pat Wolfe, a highly regarded expert on the application of brain research in schools, to explain this process to me:

> The brain is made of billions of cells called neurons. They connect with one another through synapses. When you learn something, you are making a physiological change in the brain by creating or strengthening an already existing connection. The brain also prunes these connections when they are no longer stimulated.
>
> I am concerned that we too often teach things abstractly before learners have any concrete base to which they can refer. Because there are a lot of things you don't want to concretely experience as a way of learning about them, simulations such as role plays and case studies are a wonderful way to make the abstract more concrete.
>
> Anything with emotion in it makes a stronger connection. Emotion is a double-edged sword, though. Any learning that

has positive or negative emotion is remembered longer. We tend to remember the negative emotions longer, though, because they are often connected with fear. But if the emotion is too high and the person is in the fight-or-flight response, the cortex of the brain, the part that does the problem solving and higher order thinking, becomes less effective. It's important that the environment is both physically and psychologically safe.

Meaning also creates stronger connections among neurons. When we are exposed to a new situation or learning something new, the brain searches through its existing networks to find a place to put the new information within the existing connections. A new concept or idea or exposure to new information causes the brain to determine which existing network it fits into. I call that meaning. If I have no network, no base, in my brain into which I can fit these ideas or concepts, then it becomes necessary to create a new network. That's harder work than using an existing network.

Because the more you make the same connections among neurons, the stronger the connection gets, elaborative rehearsal through processes such as writing, drawing, giving an example, solving a problem with it, and so on increases the strength of the connection. Some of the most powerful teaching tools we have are analogies, similes, and metaphors because they connect new information to existing networks.

Daniel Goleman, Richard Boyatzis, and Annie McKee (2002) emphasized the role of practice in brain reconfiguration in *Primal Leadership: Learning to Lead With Emotional Intelligence.* "The more often a behavioral sequence repeats," they wrote, "the stronger the underlying brain circuits become. People thereby literally rewire their brains: Learning new habits strengthens pathways between neurons, and may even foster neurogenesis—growth of new neurons" (p. 156). The same results, they point out, are obtained from mental rehearsal of new behaviors. "Brain studies have shown that imagining something in vivid detail can fire the same brain cells that are actually involved in that activity" (p. 161).

In *Powerful Designs for Professional Learning,* Lois Easton (2004) and chapter authors described a number of professional learning activities that are especially powerful in engaging educators' brains: action research, design and evaluation of student assessments, case discussions, classroom walk-throughs, critical friends groups, curriculum design, data analysis, lesson study, journal writing, mentoring, peer coaching, portfolios, shadowing of students, tuning protocols, and study groups, to name a few. "The type of staff development featured in this book is powerful because it arises from and returns to the world of teaching and learning," Easton wrote. "It begins with what will really help young people learn, engages those involved in helping them learn, and has an effect on the classrooms (and schools, districts, even states) where those students and their teachers learn" (p. 2).

Meaningful professional learning has the same attributes as other meaningful human learning. It activates the brain in ways that create new neural networks or strengthens those that already exist. Like the brains of their students, teachers' brains are changed when they engage with the concrete tasks of their work in ways that promote meaning, emotion, and reflection through cognitively demanding processes such as reading, writing, observing, listening carefully, speaking thoughtfully, and practicing new habits of mind and behavior until they become habitual.

EXAMINE YOUR ASSUMPTIONS

Write your assumptions regarding the nature of human learning. For instance, you may believe that learning simply means that students are able to demonstrate that they have mastered the content offered by the teacher. Share your assumptions with colleagues in the spirit of dialogue.

_____

_____

_____

_____

_____

_____

DEEPEN YOUR UNDERSTANDING

Engage teachers and other colleagues in sustained discussions of the types of activities that produce lasting and meaningful changes in learners' brains—whether those are the brains of adults or their students—in ways that affect performance.

_____

_____

_____

_____

_____

_____

ENGAGE IN NEXT ACTION THINKING

Discuss with key leaders in your organization ways in which you can ensure that professional learning is sufficiently robust and sustained to alter the brains of teachers and school leaders in ways that change habits of mind and practice.

_____

_____

_____

_____

_____

_____

REFERENCES

Easton, L. (Ed.). (2004). *Powerful designs for professional learning.* Oxford, OH: National Staff Development Council.

Goleman, D., Boyatzis, R., & McKee, A. (2002). *Primal leadership: Learning to lead with emotional intelligence.* Boston: Harvard Business School Press.

CHAPTER 41

Install Next Action Thinking

Our responsibility is not discharged by the announcement of virtuous ends.

—John F. Kennedy

No matter how big and tough a problem may be, get rid of confusion by taking one little step toward solution. Do something.

—George Nordenholt

One of the biggest fears for a creative person is that some brilliant idea will get lost because you didn't write it down and put it in a safe place.

—Twyla Tharp

My assumptions: "Next action thinking" promotes the use of new practices acquired through professional learning, aids in the implementation of plans, and sustains the momentum required to produce valued results. Leaders are more successful when their psychic energy is invested in complex intellectual processes rather than squandered as they worry about whether important tasks have been overlooked by those who have agreed to do them.

"It's not how many ideas you have. It's how many you make happen," a business proclaims in advertisements about its ability to turn "innovation into results." The knowing-doing gap described in Chapter 38 is a manifestation of learning that has simply not been acted upon. Similarly, studies conducted on the effects of strategic planning reveal that less than 10% of well-formulated strategies are successfully implemented. While learning for its own sake and planning for the value of the clarity it produces may be worthy ends in themselves, results are ultimately obtained from actions that we initiate, learn from, and successfully complete.

In this book's Introduction, I noted David Allen's view expressed in *Getting Things Done: The Art of Stress-Free Productivity* (2001) on the power of habitually considering the next action. It bears repeating here: "Over the years, I have noticed an extraordinary shift in energy and productivity whenever individuals and groups installed 'What's the next action?' as a fundamental and consistently asked question" (p. 236). The result, he says, would be that "no meeting or discussion will end, and no interaction cease, without a clear determination of whether or not some action is needed—and, if it is, what it will be, or at least who has responsibility for it" (p. 236). Allen argues that "shifting your focus to something that your mind perceives as a doable, completable task will create a real increase in positive energy, direction, and motivation" (p. 242).

An important aspect of next action thinking and maintaining momentum is making and keeping promises regarding our intentions. Developing agreements about making and keeping promises is important (as discussed more fully in Chapter 19). The options include honoring the agreement, renegotiating it, rescinding it, or breaking the agreement. If an agreement is broken, the protocol may include reporting the breakdown, "cleaning up" the situation in a way that is agreeable to the other person, and recommitting yourself to the agreement, if it is still important to all parties.

Next action thinking is a habit of automatically moving learning and planning into action (more will be said about establishing new habits in Chapter 42). The kinds of professional learning recommended in Part IV of this book will be of little consequence if such habits are not established. Once we have habits and procedures for noting, tracking, and completing agreements and norms of interpersonal accountability, we can be fully invested in results-oriented activities rather than tracking whether others have forgotten or overlooked important tasks.

You could employ sophisticated processes and electronic management systems for project planning. Or you could do something as simple as back-of-the-envelope planning that includes writing the goal, the steps to achieve it, and the dates by which those steps will be taken. For particularly complex long-term goals, however, you may want a clear, detailed vision of the preferred end state, a description of the next several actions, and what you expect will be the last step or two required to achieve the goal. Well-laid plans falter sometimes because no one was paying attention to the last few essential steps for achieving the goal, what some planners call the "final 2%."

EXAMINE YOUR ASSUMPTIONS

Write your assumptions regarding the significance of next action thinking, stating them as succinctly and powerfully as possible. For instance, you may believe "Next action thinking and the interpersonal accountability it promotes are impractical for busy educators who are juggling too many balls to exercise the type of discipline it requires." Share your assumptions with colleagues in the spirit of dialogue.

_____

_____

_____

_____

_____

_____

DEEPEN YOUR UNDERSTANDING

Discuss professional learning or other forms of professional work that were more effective because actions and lines of accountability were clearly specified. Specify the agreements or procedures that contributed to that effort.

_____

_____

_____

_____

_____

_____

_____

Engage in Next Action Thinking

Specify the actions you will take to install the habit of next action thinking and by what dates you will take those actions.

_____

_____

_____

_____

_____

_____

_____

Reference

Allen, D. (2001). *Getting things done: The art of stress-free productivity.* New York: Viking.

CHAPTER 42

Change Habits

[E]ven the most successful leaders can increase their effectiveness by changing certain elements of their behavior.

—Marshall Goldsmith

We are what we repeatedly do; excellence, then, is not an act, but a habit.

—Aristotle

> **My assumptions: Leaders' habits affect the results they achieve. Developing new habits usually requires attention, discipline, and feedback on our progress.**

A foundation of human resourcefulness is our ability at any stage of life to develop new habits of thought and behavior that serve our purposes and values. Clarity regarding our values and purpose has limited significance unless that clarity is followed by commitments to specific actions, a sense of accountability for completing those actions, and the development of habits that sustain those changes over time.

A simple system to use when learning a new habit is to establish a measurable goal regarding the new behavior, determine a method to prompt you to use that behavior, promise someone that you will behave in that way to increase your motivation to acquire the new habit, set up a monitoring system to assess progress, and begin practicing the new behavior. This approach can be applied to any of the beliefs or practices recommended in this book. For instance, if you want to decrease or eliminate your use of obligatory language, state that as a goal, tell coworkers of your intention, ask selected individuals to draw attention to such language whenever it is used, and give yourself a daily letter grade or numerical score that reflects your performance.

> Consultants come in and introduce big bold strategies. Everyone learns what is expected, but over time little seems to change. Everyone slowly reverts to how things have always been done, because the small everyday behaviors that really run the show are never addressed. Everyday behaviors are the glue that keeps organizations stuck in the original form no matter how many big bold initiatives are introduced. Yet, hardly anyone focuses on the small stuff.
>
> —Mikela Tarlow

Executive coach Marshall Goldsmith underscores the importance of creating measurable indicators to motivate and assess progress, even for so-called soft goals. He tells a story about his response to his daughter's complaint that he was inattentive to her when he was home during respites from his busy work-related travel schedule. He set a goal to increase the number of days in which he spent at least four hours interacting with his family without the common distractions of TV, movies, or the telephone. The first year he recorded 92 days of "unencumbered interaction," which grew to 135 days over the next four years. (He says that he later recalibrated his goal when his teenage children said they were seeing too much of him.)

Goldsmith also describes a process he calls "feed forward" in which individuals select behaviors they believe will make a positive difference in their lives, ask coworkers for suggestions, listen to their ideas, thank them for their contributions. "No on is allowed to critique suggestions or to bring up the past," he notes (p. 103).

Kerry Patterson, Joseph Grenny, Ron McMillan, and Al Switzer (2002) offer another approach in *Crucial Conversations: Tools for Talking When Stakes Are High.* They suggest four general principles for "turning ideas into action": (1) mastering the content, (2) mastering the related skills, (3) enhancing motivation, and (4) watching for cues to apply the new knowledge and skills. To *master knowledge and skills*, they suggest digging more deeply into an area of particular interest, teaching the skill to someone else, rehearsing with a friend, and selecting a low- or medium-risk situation in which to apply the learning. To *enhance motivation*, they suggest using incentives, celebrating improvements, and making intentions known so others may assist you and provide a disincentive to not following through on the commitment. *Cues to assist in changing habits* include carrying note cards as reminders of the goal, posting small notes around your office or home, and placing large posters or signs to signal your intention to you and to others.

EXAMINE YOUR ASSUMPTIONS

Write your assumptions regarding the significance of developing new habits as a means of creating the results you desire, stating them as succinctly and powerfully as possible. For instance, you may believe "Because behavior is shaped more by organizational culture and structures that surround people than it is by personal habits, leaders will have the greatest impact by focusing on those factors." Share your assumptions with colleagues in the spirit of dialogue.

_____

_____

_____

_____

_____

_____

DEEPEN YOUR UNDERSTANDING

Describe habits that have enabled you to achieve your goals. Discuss the methods you have found most useful in developing new habits of thought and behavior. Consider methods you may have used such as daily reminders posted on a mirror or your desk or a daily diary or log related to changes in diet or exercise habits.

_____

_____

_____

_____

_____

_____

Engage in Next Action Thinking

Specify one or more habits you would like to develop, the methods you will use to prompt the new behavior and to monitor your progress, and the date by which you will begin.

_____

_____

_____

_____

_____

_____

_____

References

Goldsmith, M. (2004, May). Leave it at the stream. *Fast Company, 82,* 103.

Patterson, K., Grenny, J., McMillan, R., & Switzer, A. (2002). *Crucial conversations: Tools for talking when stakes are high.* New York: McGraw-Hill.

CHAPTER 43

Sustain the Conversation

All learning is social. It is with our peers that we will ultimately find our voice and change our world. It is in community that our lives are transformed. Small groups change the world.

—Peter Block

[A]ll individuals, in conditions of stress, benefit from interpersonal support. Research has shown that the more isolated people are, the more vulnerable they are to stress; support not only makes people feel better, it helps them think better, improving their problem-solving ability.

—Robert Evans

My assumptions: Clear and deeply felt values, a passionate sense of purpose, and meaningful connections with others generate energy to sustain the momentum of continuous improvement. Ongoing recognition of "small wins" maintains motivation and enthusiasm as teachers and administrators learn, create, innovate, and develop new habits.

A story is told in which the composer George Gershwin approaches Maurice Ravel to ask permission to study with him. Ravel responds, "Why would you wish to be a second-rate Ravel when you can be a first-rate Gershwin?" Becoming deeply ourselves—our first-rate selves—is a prerequisite to fulfilling our unique role in creating first-rate organizations. Doing so means finding and using our "voice"—gaining clarity about our most deeply felt values and purposes and consistently and courageously representing our point of view in many venues through well-considered words and actions.

Becoming our first-rate selves, however, requires a lifetime of attention and persistence. Our original sense of purpose may wane and our initial enthusiasm diminish. More urgent priorities may claim our attention and take precedence for our time. Even if we are able to stay focused on our goals amidst the press of competing demands, we may become discouraged by setbacks and interpersonal challenges that typically accompany important individual and organizational changes.

> Look around you for people whose conversations are memorable, people who wake you up and provoke your learning—people who are real.
>
> —Susan Scott

This chapter describes numerous ways to sustain the new habits acquired in previous chapters. It describes ways we can deepen our learning, remain in meaningful dialogue, maintain our enthusiasm, and act consistently with our purposes and values to achieve the results most important to us. In addition, I encourage you to invent other ways that draw on your strengths to sustain new habits and extend your learning on these subjects. Here are a few suggestions:

• Stay in tune with your fundamental choices, values, purposes, and intentions and consistently align your actions with them. Clarity regarding values and goals provides energy that fuels our effort in the face of the adversity that almost always accompanies the development of new habits and significant change in individual and organizational practices. Have a laserlike focus on actions that are closely linked to the values and purposes most important to you.

• Apply daily what you have learned in previous chapters about next action thinking and changing habits. For the most part, our professional and personal lives may be viewed as a bundle of habits. What we think about educational matters, the intellectual processes we most commonly use, our manner of speaking, and how we relate to others can be shaped to match our values and purposes. Next action thinking reminds us that the most important action we can take is the next one and that the impetus gained from that action will help shape the one that follows. Taken together, this chain of actions forms our habits and professional practice. No part of our lives is too large or small to benefit from this step-by-step approach to creating the results we desire.

• Have conversations with others in the ways described in this book to focus and sustain your work. High-quality connections with others are a fundamental source of direction and energy for your work and your life. Conversations rich in candor, clarity, purposefulness, committed listening, and dialogue can have a profound effect on individuals and schools.

One way to create interpersonal connections related to your most important goals is to identify individuals or designate a personal "board of directors" to provide emotional and social support and bring diverse perspectives to the creative and improvisational venture that is our lives. Another way some leaders maintain their focus is to seek the services of executive coaches (also called life coaches or results coaches). While these specialists may charge a fee for their services, the benefit of such one-on-one support can be worth the costs. A less-expensive substitute is to ask mentors or friends to serve you in

> There was no single defining action, no grand program, no one killer innovation, no solitary lucky break, no wrenching revolution. Good to great comes about by a cumulative process—step by step, action by action, decision by decision, turn by turn of the flywheel—that adds up to sustained and spectacular results.
>
> —Jim Collins

this capacity by practicing the committed listening skills described in Chapter 16 and trusting your ability to find ways to achieve pathways to your goals.

Celebrate progress as well as the accomplishment of your goals. While I emphasized the value of stretch goals and the deep changes they often require in our beliefs and behavior in Chapter 3, motivation for achieving such demanding goals is sustained as we define, achieve, and recognize the accomplishment of each of the subordinate goals that comprise the larger goal. One way to do so is to begin with easy-to-achieve goals—"low-hanging fruit"—to gain a feeling of success and momentum. (However, resist the temptation to stop here thinking that the completion of these low-level activities is the same as accomplishing your larger purpose.) Another process of defining and achieving these smaller goals is the "Swiss cheese method"— poking holes in the larger goal as opportunities present themselves until very little remains to be done. Whatever your approach, recognize and, when appropriate, reward completion of milestones on the journey.

Consciously apply these skills in many settings to expand your influence. Each interaction with others is an opportunity for transformation when approached with a clear sense of what you want to accomplish and the skills you wish to apply in the conversation.

Everything you have learned in this book can be practiced in one-on-one conversations with parents, colleagues, supervisors, and those you supervise; in telephone conversations with parents; as a participant in grade-level, department, school, and district instructional meetings; and in school improvement or professional development committee meetings. These ideas and skills can also be applied when you facilitate meetings or make presentations at faculty meetings, staff development sessions, or parent events.

My hope is that you will use what you have learned in this book to help create schools in which quality teaching occurs in every classroom and teachers and students alike experience success, joy, and satisfaction each day. Such schools are grounded in relationships and intellectual tasks that honor and challenge every member of the community to more fully develop his or her talents to serve both individual and collective purposes. Those are the schools to which I believe we would all happily send our own children.

EXAMINE YOUR ASSUMPTIONS

Write your assumptions regarding the most powerful methods of sustaining energy and enthusiasm for change over time, stating them as succinctly and powerfully as possible. For instance, you may believe "The professional lives of educators are too busy and fragmented these days to expect them to pay attention to their values and purposes, let alone find time to stay connected with others who share their deepest commitments." Share your assumptions with colleagues in the spirit of dialogue.

_____

_____

_____

_____

_____

_____

DEEPEN YOUR UNDERSTANDING

List individuals you have known or learned about who have lived in alignment with their deepest values and aspirations. Consider individuals whom you have known personally or those you have come to know through biography or works of fiction. Reflect on the methods they used to achieve that alignment. Discuss barriers that you anticipate arising in your life and ways that they may be addressed.

_____

_____

_____

_____

_____

_____

ENGAGE IN NEXT ACTION THINKING

Specify actions you will take to continue your professional learning and sustain your efforts over many months and years and by what dates you will initiate them.

_____

_____

_____

_____

_____

_____

Index

CORWIN
PRESS

The Corwin Press logo—a raven striding across an open book—represents the union of courage and learning. Corwin Press is committed to improving education for all learners by publishing books and other professional development resources for those serving the field of PreK–12 education. By providing practical, hands-on materials, Corwin Press continues to carry out the promise of its motto: **"Helping Educators Do Their Work Better."**

NSDC's mission is to ensure success for all students by serving as the international network for those who improve schools and by advancing individual and organization development.

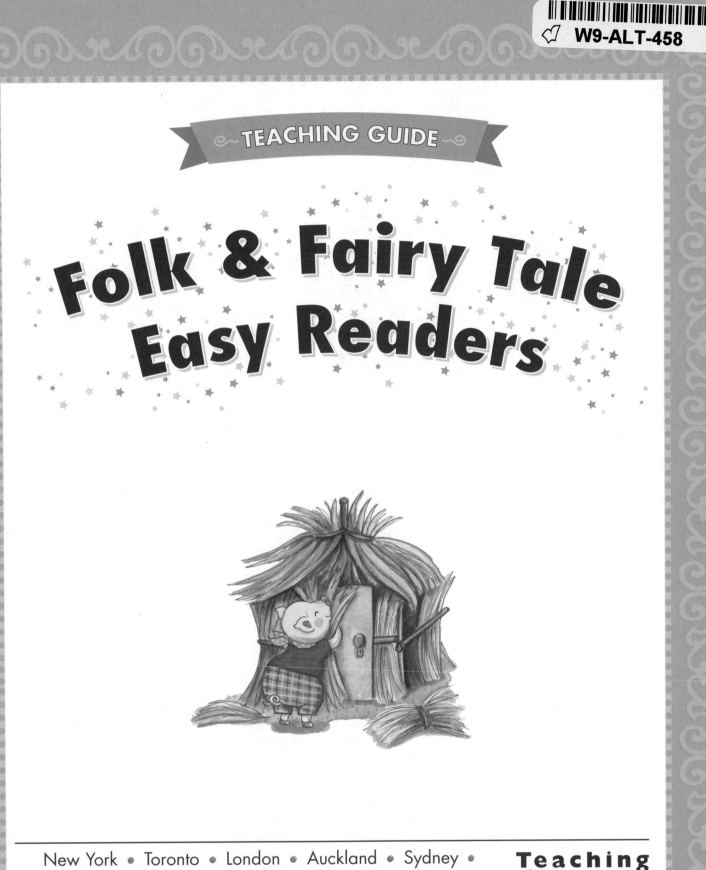

TEACHING GUIDE

Folk & Fairy Tale Easy Readers

New York • Toronto • London • Auckland • Sydney •
New Delhi • Mexico City • Hong Kong • Buenos Aires

Teaching *Resources*

SCHOLASTIC

Cover design by Maria Lilja
Interior design by Grafica
Preface, Sample Lesson Routine, and Guided Reading Grid by Wiley Blevins
All other text by Liza Charlesworth

ISBN: 0-439-77394-6

Contents

Preface

One of my favorite childhood memories involves a collection of books that was tucked away in the corner of our school's library. This collection, by Virginia Haviland, was entitled *Favorite Folktales From Around the World*. Since I lived in a small rural community and our school library consisted of only a few shelves in the corner of our gymnasium's stage, these books were my passport to the world beyond. I was fascinated. Intrigued. I wanted more.

The stories we have collected in *Folk & Fairy Tale Easy Readers* are those classic stories all children should know; those tales that I enjoyed so many years ago. According to E.D. Hirsch, Jr., these are the stories that help to create our children's cultural literacy—the stories they need to know and will want to pass on to their children. However, many of our students come to school with limited exposures to print, including little or no exposure to these tales.

This collection, therefore, offers a readable and engaging introduction to these timeless tales. The repetitive, patterned nature of the text adds rhythm and ensures accessibility. The generous dialogue will engage young readers and help bring these stories to life for them.

Whether you use these books in small-group reading lessons or simply place them in a special bin in your classroom library, they will make a wonderful addition to your curriculum. And who knows? Perhaps one day those youngsters sitting in your classroom will be in their homes telling these classic tales to their children. The tradition continues.

Enjoy!

Wiley Blevins
Reading Specialist

Introduction

$\mathscr{O}$nce upon a time...

That familiar opening line had the power to
enchant children hundreds of years ago.
And it has the same effect on kids today.
Folk and fairy tales are still a joyful rite of
passage for every young learner. And it's no
surprise. These timeless tales invite children to
take a break from the hectic pace of the modern
world and spend a few minutes savoring a super-
engaging story with a meaningful message. After all,
who can resist the foolish big bad wolf, the endearing ugly
duckling, or the tenacious little red hen? Nothing compares to the magical
experience of enjoying a classic tale—especially when kids can read that tale all by themselves!

That's the big idea behind *Folk & Fairy Tale Easy Readers*. This unique collection was developed to
put easy-to-read classics into the hands of every child you teach, by providing a critical mass of time-
honored tales housed in a handy storage box. In the box, you'll find five copies of each of these titles:

* *The Little Red Hen*

* *The Three Little Pigs*

* *Martina the Cockroach*

* *The Tortoise and the Hare*

* *The Three Billy Goats Gruff*

* *The Gingerbread Man*

* *Stone Soup*

* *The Ugly Ducking*

* *Goldilocks and the Three Bears*

* *The Spider and the Beehive*

* *The City Mouse and
   the Country Mouse*

* *The Elves and the Shoemaker*

* *The Princess and the Pea*

* *The Nightingale*

* *Cinderella*

The multiple copies will enable your students to enjoy these classics during guided-reading time, independent-reading time—or anytime. But that's not all! We've also provided this complete teaching guide to help tailor your teaching to fit your specific needs. In this resource, you'll find:

❀ A rationale for making *Folk & Fairy Tale Easy Readers* a part of your reading program, including a handy **Standards Box** showcasing the important skills your students will meet with these 15 titles (see page 9)

❀ A step-by-step **Guided Reading Lesson Routine** for *The Little Red Hen,* which shows how to seamlessly incorporate this title (and the others) into your guided-reading program in order to boost a network of literacy skills including decoding, phonics, comprehension, vocabulary, writing, and fluency (see pages 12–13)

❀ A helpful **Book-by-Book Guided Reading Grid** stocked with guided reading levels, word counts, focus lessons, supportive and challenging features, and teaching strategies for each title (see pages 14–19)

❀ Four reproducible, comprehension-boosting **graphic organizers** and two sheets of special fairy-tale **stationery** to use with every title (pages 22–27)

❀ **Instant activities** for extending whole-class learning, including tips for using the collection as the centerpiece for an in-depth study of folk and fairy tales (see page 30)

❀ A special **Teaching Page** for each title, filled with background information, book links, activities, discussion questions, and a ready-to-use companion reproducible (see pages 31–116)

❀ And last but not least, **reproducible mini-book versions of all 15 titles**, enabling you to send the stories home for kids to enjoy with their families (see pages 33–120)

In short, we've provided everything you'll need to put *Folk & Fairy Tale Easy Readers* to work in your classroom right away and ensure a literacy-rich—and rewarding—learning experience.

Now, it's time to read

. . . happily ever after!

—The Editors

Tips and Strategies for Great Teaching

Why Teach With *Folk & Fairy Tale Easy Readers*?

Welcome to *Folk & Fairy Tale Easy Readers*! There are so many great reasons to use this collection of classic stories to teach reading. Take a look!

Reason 1: They Present Important Cultural Touchstones

One of the most compelling reasons to add *Folk & Fairy Tale Easy Readers* to your classroom routine is to expose children to 15 essential cultural touchstones. Fads come and go, but folk and fairy tales such as "The Three Billy Goats Gruff" and "The Princess and the Pea" have endured for hundreds of years. In fact, most of the 15 classics included in this collection were passed down orally from generation to generation long before they were ever committed to paper. That's no fluke. The stories were too important to fall by the wayside. These stories were—and are—so wonderful that they retain the power to render children of any era wide-eyed with engagement. That's because they feature absorbing, clearly delineated characters, settings, and plotlines. They also feature a clearly stated message to ponder and, in some instances, debate.

Folk and fairy tales are everywhere! Classic stories are quoted, referenced, revisited, and revised each and every day. There would be no *The True Story of the 3 Little Pigs!* by John Scieszka, for example, without "The Three Little Pigs" by Anonymous. And children would not have the proper context to delight in Scieska's witty yarn without exposure to its antecedent. Likewise, children would not have the context for understanding a term like "a real Cinderella story," if they never had the opportunity to enjoy "Cinderella." Folk- and fairy-tale allusions are so ubiquitous, they're practically woven into the fabric of our culture. Simply stated: To navigate our world, it's important to have a firm knowledge of these oft-told tales. *Folk & Fairy Tale Easy Readers* not only grants students access to 15 of the most beloved folk and fairy tales, it also empowers kids to read them independently.

Reason 2: They Help You Meet Key Standards

In today's ambitious classrooms, teachers are expected to justify each and every learning experience. Your *Folk & Fairy Tale Easy Readers* set is a practical way to meet essential language-arts standards with a minimum of stress. Take a look at the important standards they'll help you meet:

Connections to the K–2 Language-Arts Standards

Child uses general skills and strategies of the reading process including:

❋ Understands that print conveys meaning

❋ Understands how print is organized and read (e.g., identifies front and back covers, title pages, author; follows words from left-to-right and from top-to-bottom; knows the significance of spaces between letters, words, and sentences; understands the use of capitalization and punctuation as text boundaries)

❋ Creates mental images from pictures and print

❋ Uses basic elements of phonetic analysis to decode unknown words

❋ Understands level-appropriate sight words and vocabulary

❋ Uses self-correction strategies

❋ Reads aloud familiar stories with fluency and expression

Child uses reading skills and strategies to understand and interpret a variety of literary text including:

❋ Uses reading skills and strategies to understand a variety of folktales, fairy tales, and fables

❋ Knows the basic characteristics of folktales, fairy tales, and fables

❋ Understands setting, main characters, main events, and sequence in stories

❋ Understands the main idea and theme of a story

❋ Relates stories to personal experiences

Source—*Content Knowledge: A Compendium of Standards and Benchmarks from K-12 Education* (3rd ed.) (Mid-Continent Research for Education and Learning, 2000).

Reason 3: They Help You Teach Reading Your Way

Your *Folk & Fairy Tale Easy Readers* set was created specifically to support, motivate, and teach reading to young learners. Toward that end, the titles in this set were carefully designed to match the specific needs of burgeoning readers by presenting these developmentally appropriate characteristics:

* ✳ Two to five lines of text per page
* ✳ Clear, high-support illustrations
* ✳ Patterned text
* ✳ Natural syntax
* ✳ Repeated and recognizable high-frequency words
* ✳ Consistent print placement
* ✳ A full range of punctuation
* ✳ Familiar, engaging story lines

And here's more good news: The collection allows for flexible use and is very easy to incorporate into your independent or guided-reading routines.

• For Independent Reading

Folk & Fairy Tale Easy Readers are the perfect addition to your independent-reading library. Simply place the storage box on a countertop or, if you prefer, remove the books and place them in a basket labeled "Folk and Fairy Tales." Then invite children to peruse and select their favorite titles to enjoy during sustained silent reading time. Or, boost fluency by slipping the storybooks into a self-sealing bag filled with an array of on-level titles selected for each student.

• For Guided Reading

Folk & Fairy Tale Easy Readers are also excellent for guided reading. All of the titles in this collection have been correlated with guided-reading levels E through I (see grid on page 14–19). This enables you to select just-right titles for each student—and guided reading group—you teach. What constitutes "just right"? Experts agree that a book is on level when children are able to read and understand most of the text. And when they encounter unknown words, they are able to decode the majority of the words independently, using familiar strategies. Reading a healthy number of just-right books provides children with a wealth of opportunities to be both challenged *and* successful—a winning combination that helps fine-tune a network of critical reading strategies including:

* ☀ controlling word-by-word matching of print and voice

* ☀ predicting what will happen next in the story

* ☀ understanding characters and their motivations

* ☀ noticing the language patterns and style of the text

* ☀ using known words as anchors to navigate the text

* ☀ noticing unfamiliar words and using context clues and/or decoding skills to arrive at their meaning

* ☀ returning to the text to confirm understanding

* ☀ connecting the text to other stories and their own lives

* ☀ forming opinions about the books they read

How should you use *Folk & Fairy Tale Easy Readers* in the context of your guided reading groups? While there is no definitive way to teach early reading, following is a Guided Reading Lesson Routine for *The Little Red Hen* (see pages 12–13), which you can adapt to meet your individual classroom needs. It offers a step-by-step lesson plan for using this title— and by example, the 14 other titles in the *Folk & Fairy Tale Easy Readers* set—to develop key literacy skills in the areas of decoding, phonics, comprehension, fluency, and more.

In addition, we've, provided a Book-by-Book Guided Reading Grid (see pages 14–19). This handy chart provides at-a-glance information on each title in the collection, including guided reading levels, word counts, and supportive and challenging features, plus plenty of quick activities to help you get the most out of your reading lessons.

Guided Reading Lesson Routine: **The Little Red Hen**

First Reading

First Reading

Routine	Sample
Teacher Preview • Read book for content and vocabulary demands. • Scan book for supportive and challenging text features.	**Summary:** "The Little Red Hen" is the classic story of the hardworking hen and her lazy pals. **Supportive Features:** The repetitive, patterned nature of the text will make the book easy to read for most children. **Challenging Features:** Some children will need help reading the dialogue throughout the book. Teach children the use of quotation marks in dialogue and model how to read sample dialogues from the story. In addition, some children may be unfamiliar with the concept of growing and grinding wheat, and the process of making bread.
Introduce Book • Display and discuss cover. Read author's and illustrator's names. • Browse the first few pages of the story and have children predict what the story will be about.	• Display the cover of the book. Read aloud the title and author and illustrator's names. • Tell children that this is a retelling of the popular story "The Little Red Hen." • Ask children if they are familiar with the story. If so, allow them to retell what they remember. • Distribute copies of the book and allow children to browse. Elicit any comments children have, such as how the story compares to the version they know or what difficult words they might see.
Pre-Teach Vocabulary • Introduce key vocabulary words using the book's glossary and illustrations.	• Have children turn to the glossary at the end of the book. • Point to each word, read it aloud, and have children repeat it. • Then discuss the meaning of each word. Use each word in context in a sentence. If a picture is shown, discuss it with the children. For nouns, look for additional pictures in the story to illustrate the word. For verbs and adjectives, act out the word when appropriate. • Conclude by asking questions to help children think about and use the new words. Use these and other prompts: ✓ Which word names a chicken? ✓ Finish this sentence, "When I feel lazy, I____." ✓ Show me how you grind something.
Read Book • Guide children through the reading of the book. • Assist children with decoding issues. • Check comprehension.	• Have children read softly to themselves one to two pages at a time. • Circulate and listen in. Assist children with decoding any difficult words. • While children read, you may wish to stop periodically and ask the following questions to monitor comprehension: **Page 3:** Who are the characters in the story? **Page 4:** What did the little red hen do first? Who helped her? **Page 5:** What word has the /u/ sound? What letter is used to write the sound? **Page 8:** What does it mean to grind wheat? How does the picture help you understand this? **Page 12:** Where have we seen these sentences before? **Page 16:** Why didn't the little red hen share her bread with her friends? Do you agree with her decision?

12

Revisit and Reinforce

Routine	Sample
Teach Comprehension Strategy • Select a key comprehension strategy to model. • Use a graphic organizer to practice and reinforce the skill.	**Sequencing** • Explain to children that thinking about the order in which things happen helps readers understand and remember a story. Draw children's attention to the order of events from beginning to end. Ask: ✓ What did the little red hen do first? Who helped her? ✓ What did the little red hen do after she planted the wheat? Who helped her? ✓ What did the little red hen do next? ✓ What did the little red hen do last? ✓ Tell children that words and phrases such as *first, next, last,* and *before long* are signal words. They help the writer tell the story in order. • Distribute the Sequencing Chart on page 22. Have the children complete the chart using the story events.
Teach Phonics • Select decodable words from the book and focus on phonics patterns children need for instruction on and/or to practice with. • Do blending and word-building activities with the decodable words.	**Short Vowels** Guide children to blend words with short vowels. • Write on the board the following sentences from the story: "Who will help me cut this?" asked the little red hen. "Not me!" said the dog. "Not me!" said the cat. "Not me!" said the duck. • Point to the letter *a* in *cat.* Tell children that the letter *a* stands for the /a/ sound. Then slowly model how to blend the word *cat.* Ask: "What other words have the /a/ sound?" • Repeat the procedure with /e/ and *hen,* /i/ and *will,* /o/ and *not,* and /u/ in *duck.* • Begin a short-vowel word chart on the board. Under each letter, write the following word families: at, an, en, ell, ill, ip, op, ot, ug, uck. Have children generate words for each word family. When finished, ask children to chorally read the word list.
Writing Option • Select one or two writing options to check children's understanding of the story and extend the learning.	**Check Understanding** • Write a letter to the cat, dog, and duck explaining why they did not deserve to eat the bread. **Extend Learning** • Write the steps in making a favorite food, such as a peanut butter and jelly sandwich.
Building Fluency • Model at least one key aspect of fluency: speed, accuracy, or expression. • Do repeated reading activities to develop fluency.	**Model Reading Dialogue** Read aloud pages 2 and 3 from the story. Tell children that you will read the dialogue (the words in between the quotation marks) as if the characters are saying the words. Ask the children to echo your reading, sentence by sentence. They should use the same expression and pace as you do. **Repeated Reading: Readers Theater** Provide or make masks for each character. Have children chorally read the narrator's portion of the story. Each character reads and acts out his or her part.

Book-by-Book Guided Reading Grid

Title	Level	Word Count	Vocabulary	Supportive Features	Challenging Features
The Little Red Hen	E	**259**	grind, hen, lazy, quite, wheat	repetitive, patterned text	concept of planting and grinding wheat, and the process of making bread; dialogue
The Three Little Pigs	F	**243**	chimney, cozy, dashed, stew, straw	repetitive, patterned text; familiar story	long sentences, use of commas, phrases such as "Quick as a wink"
Martina the Cockroach	F	**264**	cockroach, couple, perfume, whistle	repetitive, patterned text	onomatopoeia, setting, dialogue
The Tortoise and the Hare	G	**252**	by and by, grinned, hare, steady, tortoise	few sentences on a page; mostly short sentences	use of interior commas, moral of tale, dialogue
The Three Billy Goats Gruff	G	**239**	clomp, cranky, rammed, troll	repetitive, patterned text	long sentences, use of commas, difficult adjectives and verbs (*cranky, clomp, sneaky, rammed*), dialogue

Comprehension Strategy	Phonics	Writing	Fluency
Use this book with the Sequencing Chart on page 22.	short vowels (*a: cat, plant, asked, jam; e: red, hen, help; i: will, it, this, with, o: dog, not, on, top; u: duck, cut, just*)	Have children write a letter to the cat, dog, and duck explaining why they did not deserve to eat the bread.	Provide or make masks for the little red hen, dog, cat, and duck, and assign four children these roles. Have each character read his/her part; have the children chorally read the narrator's portion of the story.
Use this book with the Problem/Solution Chart on page 24.	short vowels (*a: bad, and, as, ran, at, back, that; e: yelled, then, them, when; i: pig, big, quick, sticks, bricks, in; o: upon, not, pot, hot, bottom, u: huffed, puffed, lunch, jumped, up*)	Invite children to pretend they are the big bad wolf and write a letter to the pigs explaining his point of view.	Have partners reread the story taking turns reading one page at a time. Circulate and listen in. Model how to read dialogue that is in all caps, such as "OUCH!"
Use this book with the Comprehension Quilt on page 23.	consonant blends and digraphs (*pretty, sweeping, floor, dress, smelled, frog; cockroach, while, should, she, shoes, share, thank, then, whistle*)	Ask children to create a wedding invitation for Martina and the mouse. They can even include a picture of the happy couple.	Using text on page 7, model reading sentences with different punctuation. Then have children chorally read the story, paying special attention to punctuation.
Use this book with the Sequencing Chart on page 22.	long *a (ay, ai, a_e): named, always, snail, race, day, way, take, wake, may;* words with *–ed: teased, decided, hopped, napped, passed, yelled, jumped, crossed, cheered, grinned*	Have children draw a picture of the tortoise and the hare. Above each, have kids make a speech bubble. Ask them to write inside the bubble a conversation that the two characters might have.	Using page 12, model reading sentences with different punctuation. Then have children chorally read the story, paying special attention to punctuation.
Use this book with the Problem/Solution Chart on page 24.	long *e (e, ea, ee, y): three, billy, decided, eat, sweet, mean, cranky, sneaky, green*	Have children write "Little," "Middle," and "Big" on a large sheet of paper. Beside each word, ask them to draw a picture of that billy goat and describe it in a sentence.	Provide or make masks for each character. Have children chorally read the narrator's portion of the story. Then, have the students portraying each character read and act out their parts.

Book-by-Book Guided Reading Grid

Title	Level	Word Count	Vocabulary	Supportive Features	Challenging Features
The Gingerbread Man	G	276	clever, dashed, fibbed, munched, naughty	repetitive, patterned text; few lines of text per page	some difficult adjectives and verbs: *clever, naughty, dashed, fibbed, munched*; dialogue
Stone Soup	G	261	broth, cabbage, sniff, village	repetitive, patterned text; few lines of text per page	concept of tricking the villagers, dialogue
The Ugly Duckling	G	287	curious, geese, heron, pecked	repetitive, patterned text; short sentences	use of interior commas, dialogue, moral of tale
Goldilocks and the Three Bears	G	311	porridge, rude, slurp, tidy	repetitive, patterned text; familiar story	long sentences; up to four sentences on a page; use of commas and dialogue
The Spider and the Beehive	G	297	entire, golden, hive, talent, village	repetitive, patterned text; familiar story	unfamiliar setting

Comprehension Strategy	Phonics	Writing	Fluency
Use this book with the Sequencing Chart on page 22.	long i (y, igh, i_e): time, right, might, try, while, like	Have children write directions for decorating a gingerbread man.	Model how to read dialogue. Then read aloud the story. Stop when you get to dialogue, and have children chorally read it back to you. Provide feedback and additional modeling as needed.
Use this book with the Comprehension Quilt on page 23.	soft c and g: nice, place, except, once, danced; village, giant, cabbage	Invite children to write a summary of the story. It should be no longer than four sentences and should tell about the main events.	Have children chorally read the story as volunteers act it out. As an alternative, have children use the story's dialogue to write and perform a play version of the story.
Use this book with the Compare/Contrast Venn on page 25.	final e: time, five, cute, while, came, face, spoke, made, lake	Have children draw a picture of the ugly duckling after it has grown into a beautiful swan. Around the picture, ask children to write words to describe the swan, such as white and feathery.	Have partners reread the story, taking turns to read one page at a time. Circulate and listen in. Model how to read the longer sentences, which contain phrases or clauses separated by commas.
Use this book with the Sequencing Chart on page 22.	dipthong /ou/, ou, ow: house, found, down, our, growled; words with -ed: decided, named, opened, tried, growled, screamed	Have children write a letter to the three bears as if they were Goldilocks. The letter should be an apology for what she did to their home.	Invite children to chorally read the narrator's portion of the story. Assign volunteers to read the dialogue of each character.
Use this book with the Problem/Solution Chart on page 24.	long e (e, ee, ee, y, ey): tricky, sweetest, hungry, me, agreed, deep, tree, greedy, every, honey, squeezed, sweet, treat, he, week, finally; variant vowel /ô/ phonograms (au, aw, all, alk): small, all, walked, always	Tell children to draw a picture of the story's setting. Ask them to describe the setting for someone who has never been to Africa or seen it in books.	Have children softly reread the book. Circulate and listen in. Model how to read difficult words or longer sentences.

Book-by-Book Guided Reading Grid

Title	Level	Word Count	Vocabulary	Supportive Features	Challenging Features
The City Mouse and the Country Mouse	H	366	finest, hikes, nibbled, roam, wrinkled	many short sentences	use of ellipses, dialogue, moral of story
The Elves and the Shoemaker	H	382	curious, deeds, jig, shoemaker, tattered	amount of text on page increases gradually, mostly common one-syllable words	up to five lines of text per page, dialogue
The Princess and the Pea	H	279	boulder, rude, shivering, snoozed, stormy	some short sentences, simple story structure, consistent structure	combination of short and long sentences, dialogue
The Nightingale	I	412	healed, nightingale, palace, servant, trusted	strong text-to-picture match	unfamiliar setting, long sentences, four to five lines of text per page, multisyllabic words
Cinderella	I	446	alas, chores, coach, spell, vowed	familiar story, predictable structure	long sentences, four to five lines of text per page, multisyllabic words

Comprehension Strategy	Phonics	Writing	Fluency
Use this book with the Compare/Contrast Venn on page 25.	Variant vowel *oo*: *food, took, room, stood, good-bye*; words with *-le*: *little, nibble, wrinkle, table*	Have children write a letter from the city mouse to the country mouse telling about his experience during his visit.	Have partners reread the story, alternating pages. Circulate and listen in. Evaluate children's speed, accuracy, and expression.
Use this book with the Sequencing Chart on page 22.	Short *e* (*ea*): *leather, already, instead*; variant vowel /$\overline{oo}$/ phonograms (*ew, oe*): *shoemaker, grew, shoes, new*	Have the children write thank-you notes from the shoemaker to the elves.	Have the partners reread the story, taking turns to read one page at a time. Circulate and listen in. Evaluate children's reading—speed, accuracy, and expression.
Use this book with the Comprehension Quilt on page 23.	*r*-controlled vowels: *girl, shivering, first, third, turned, after, stormy, morning*; silent letters: *knock, knee*	Have children write a "Princess Wanted" ad for the newspaper.	Using the sentences on pages 12 and 13, model how to read dialogue. Then have children chorally read the narrator's portion of the story. Select two volunteers to read the parts of the prince and the princess aloud. Repeat with other students.
Use this book with the Sequencing Chart on page 22.	Two- to three-syllable words: *upon, palace, China, behind, forest, sweetly, servant, singing, Japan, inside, forget, sadly, music, window, nightingale, beautiful, unwanted, forever*	Have children write a letter from the king to the nightingale asking the bird to come back and sing for him.	Have children read the story into a tape recorder. Ask them to listen to their recording with a partner and evaluate the speed, accuracy, and expression of their reading.
Use this book with the Comprehension Quilt on page 23.	Long *o* (*oo, oa, ow, o_e*): *hoped, coach, old, broken, no, home, low, owner*; words with *-ed*: *named, lived, helped, curled, appeared, turned, agreed, danced, vowed, knocked, lied, nodded, asked, invited*	Have children write their own version of the story. Encourage them to include as many details as possible.	Have partners time each other reading the story, writing down their times. Ask children to read the story a few more times, then record themselves again to see if their pace has increased.

Instant Teaching Tools

On the pages that follow, you'll find a wealth of teaching materials to enrich your *Folk & Fairy Tale Easy Readers*, including age-perfect graphic organizers, standards-based activities, engaging discussion questions, and skill-building reproducibles. In addition, you'll find mini-book versions of each and every storybook. Here are some quick tips for getting the most out of these valuable resources.

Using the Graphic Organizers

Research shows that using language-arts graphic organizers is an excellent way to develop key comprehension, critical-thinking, fluency, and writing skills because graphic organizers challenge children to reflect meaningfully—and analytically—on what they've read. On the next five pages, we've provided four customized charts that can be used with all 15 storybooks. They were specially designed for young learners who have very little writing experience. Invite emergent writers to draw or dictate their responses to you, a teacher's aide, or parent volunteer. Invite competent writers to fill in the graphic organizers on their own or with a reading buddy.

• Sequencing Chart

Make reproducible copies of the Sequencing Chart on page 22 and distribute to children. Develop kids' sequencing skills by asking them to retell the story in their own words. They can do this by condensing the main events into a "bite-size" beginning, middle, and end. Kids can respond in words, pictures, or a combination of the two.

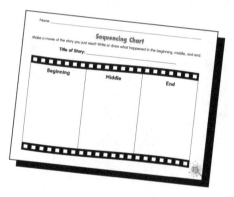

• Comprehension Quilt

Make reproducible copies of the Comprehension Quilt on page 23 and distribute to children. Develop an early awareness of literary elements by asking students to fill in each square of the quilt by responding to these four questions:

❋ Who were the main characters?

❋ Where did the story take place?

❋ What did you think of the story?

❋ How much did you like the story?

❋ Kids can then rate the tale by shading in one to five magic wands.

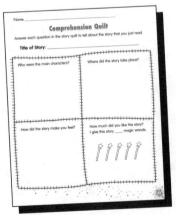

• Problem/Solution Chart

Make reproducible copies of the Problem/Solution Chart on page 24 and distribute to children. Develop an understanding of story structure by challenging students to record the story's main problem in the Problem Box and the subsequent solution in the Solution Box.

• Compare/Contrast Venn

Make reproducible copies of the Compare/Contrast Venn on page 25 and distribute to children. This opened-ended Venn Diagram can be used to compare and contrast characters within a story. It can also be used to compare and contrast the basic elements of two different stories. First, ask students to label their graphs to indicate the intent. Then challenge them to fill in each circle with exclusive attributes and the overlapping circles with shared attributes.

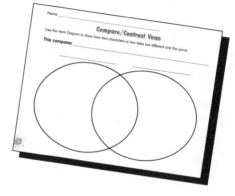

• Folk & Fairy Tale Stationery

Make copies of the reproducible Folk and Fairy Tale Stationery on pages 26–27, storing a plentiful supply in a basket or folder. (We've included both lined and unlined sheets.) Then, turn to the stationery to motivate your young writers. Kids can use it to craft responses to the discussion questions (included on each Teaching Page), compose original tales, or do anything they choose!

Name _____

Sequencing Chart

Make a movie of the story you just read! Write or draw what happened in the beginning, middle, and end.

Title of Story: _____

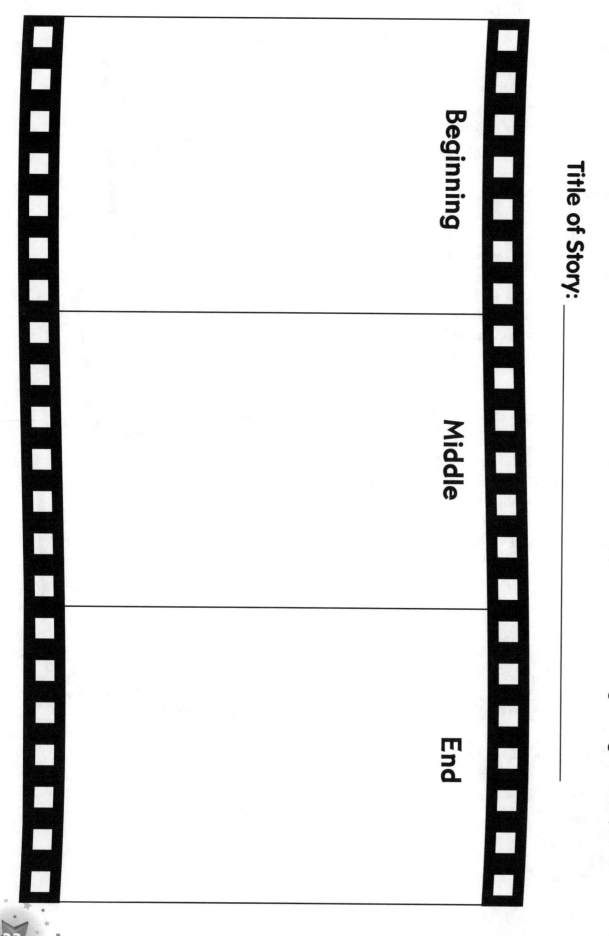

| Beginning | Middle | End |

22

Name _____

Comprehension Quilt

Answer each question in the story quilt to tell about the story that you just read.

Title of Story: _____

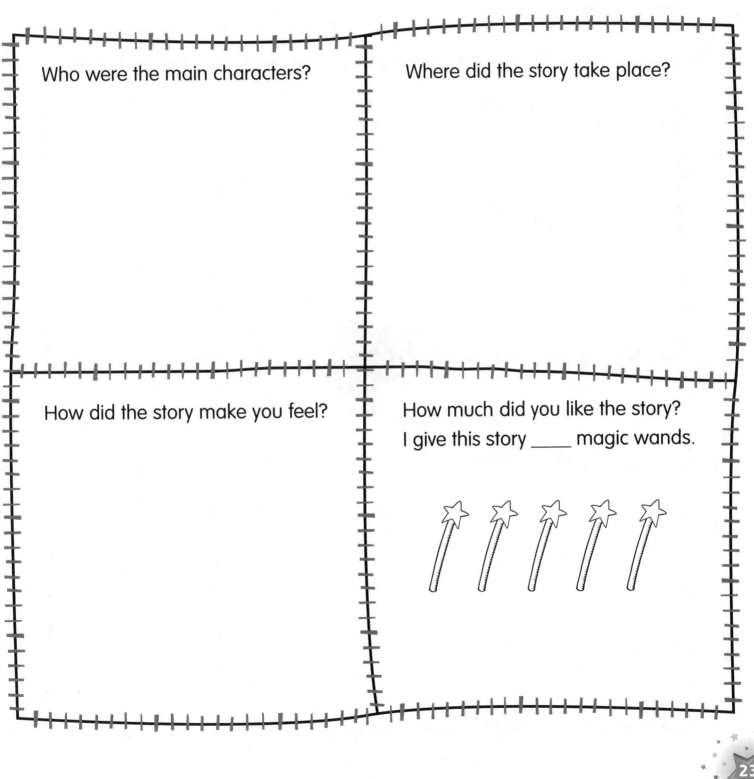

Who were the main characters?

Where did the story take place?

How did the story make you feel?

How much did you like the story?
I give this story ____ magic wands.

Scholastic • Folk & Fairy Tale Easy Readers Teaching Guide • page 23

Name _____

Problem/Solution Chart

Write or draw the main problem of the story in the Problem Box. Then, write or draw how it was solved in the Solution Box.

Title of Story: _____

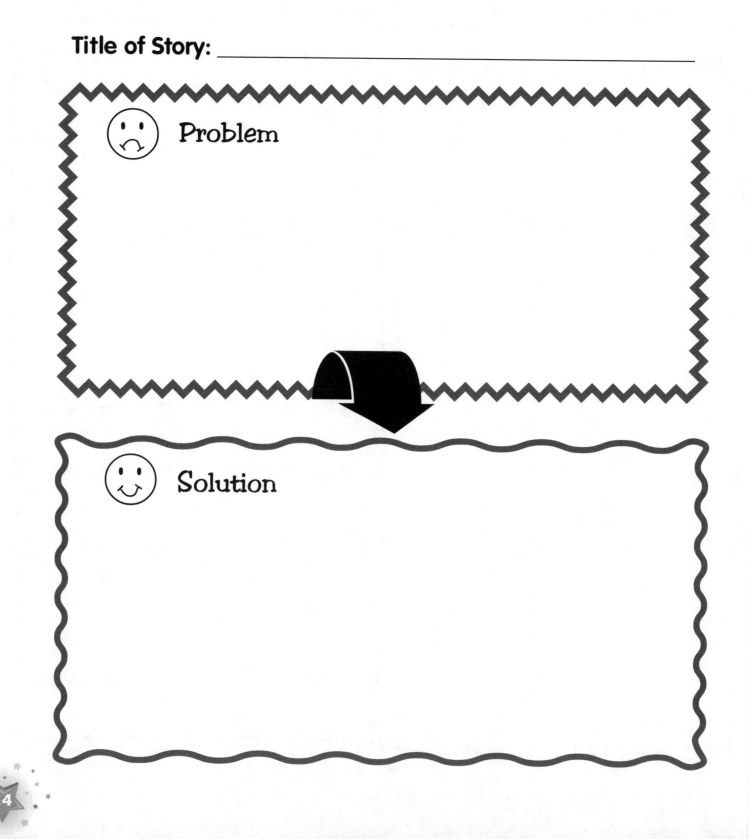

Name _____

Compare/Contrast Venn

Use the Venn Diagram to show how two characters or two tales are different and the same.

This compares: _____

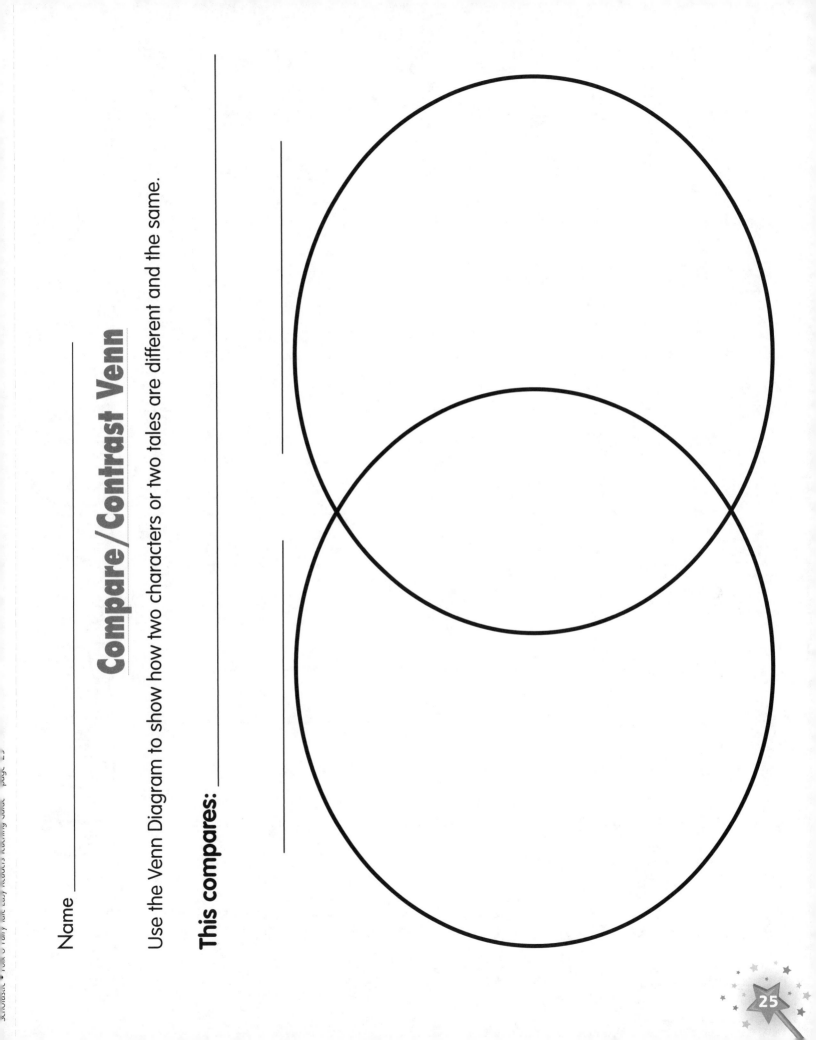

25

Using the Teaching Pages, Reproducibles, & Mini-Books

We know you're eager to create compelling and purposeful lesson plans to use with your *Folk & Fairy Tales Readers*. Toward that end, we've included ready-to-use Teaching Pages for each of the 15 storybooks in the collection. On them, you'll find information about the history of each tale plus three recommended trade-book versions to share with students during read-aloud time. Research shows that multiple exposures to the same story help kids internalize its structure and gain a deeper understanding of each author's unique voice and writing intent.

In addition, we've provided age-perfect discussion questions and a handy grid, which will enable you to put each title to work in your reading groups right away. The grid includes the title's guided reading level, word count, supportive features, challenging features, *plus* effective comprehension, phonics, and fluency-related activities developed by a reading specialist.

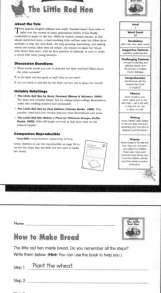

Finally, we've offered a literacy-boosting—and engaging—reproducible to accompany each of the 15 *Folk & Fairy Tale Easy Readers*. These were designed to help your students develop key reading and writing skills independently or with a buddy.

Mini-Book Tips

Using the reproducible mini-books is an excellent way for kids to hone their reading skills and enjoy each story again and again. For how-tos on making the mini-books, see the box on page 29. In the meantime, here are some quick tips for using the mini-books in and out of the classroom:

• In the Classroom

Ask each child to bring in a shoe box from home. Set out a variety of art materials and invite children to decorate the boxes. Kids can then use the boxes to house their very own collection of *Folk & Fairy Tale Easy Readers*. Encourage kids to turn to these tales during independent-reading time, recess, or when they finish their work early.

• At Home

Let children take the mini-books home to read with family members. Encouraging kids to share these classic stories will give them the golden opportunity to show off their reading know-how. If the students are confident readers, reproduce and use the "Let me read _____ to you!" badge on page 29. If students are less-confident readers and the story is still a bit challenging, use the "Let's read _____ together!" badge. Either way, you're sure to spur at-home reading enthusiasm and promote fluency.

Making the Mini-Books

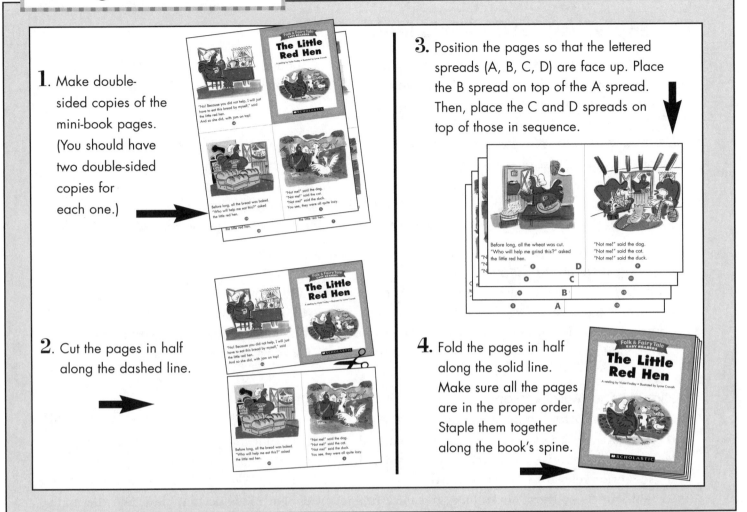

1. Make double-sided copies of the mini-book pages. (You should have two double-sided copies for each one.)

2. Cut the pages in half along the dashed line.

3. Position the pages so that the lettered spreads (A, B, C, D) are face up. Place the B spread on top of the A spread. Then, place the C and D spreads on top of those in sequence.

4. Fold the pages in half along the solid line. Make sure all the pages are in the proper order. Staple them together along the book's spine.

Book Badge Reproducibles

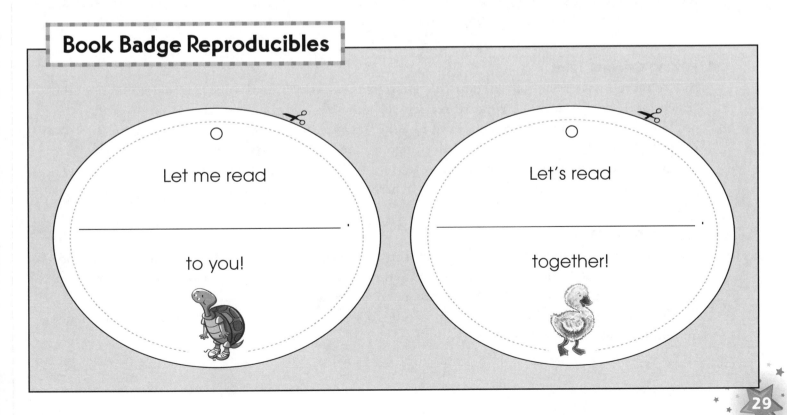

Let me read

_____

to you!

Let's read

_____

together!

Five More Ways to Enrich Learning

Make *Folk & Fairy Tales Easy Readers* a part of your classroom routine, and you'll have the double benefit of building reading skills and exposing kids to important cultural touchstones. In addition, here are five more ways to maximize learning mileage:

1. Crafting a Special Word Wall

Nurture reading, writing, spelling, and vocabulary skills by creating a special word wall just for folk and fairy tales! Designate a bulletin board or, better yet, cut a giant gingerbread-man shape out of craft paper. Then hang it on the wall and use it to display special words and terms associated with classic stories—*once upon a time, happily ever after, by and by, cozy,* and so on.

2. Creating a Listening Center

To help your young learners gain fluency, create a special listening center where children can listen to the stories on tape as they scan the text in the books. To make the tales extra-compelling, add some simple sound effects or distinctive voices for the dialogue segments. TIP: If you like, invite confident readers to tape their own renditions to share with their classmates.

3. Highlighting Moral Lessons

The Brothers Grimm published stories in the early 1800s while the fables of Aesop date back more than 2,500 years. One reason these tales have flourished is that many present timeless moral lessons. What can we learn from "The Tortoise and the Hare" or "The Little Red Hen"? How are these stories relevant to kids' own lives and to your classroom? Invite children to discuss and/or write about these thoughts in folk- and fairy-tale journals. Or, make a chart that lists the main message of each tale. Are there any messages that children disagree with? What do these stories tell us about the gender roles of boys and girls in the era in which these tales were created?

4. Writing Original Tales

After children have read *Folk & Fairy Tale Easy Readers*, they'll have a basic understanding of the "rules" of these classic tales. What better way for kids to show what they know than to craft original stories? Before children sit down to write, go over the common elements of the tales you've read—for example, most begin with "Once upon a time," many feature talking animals, a lot include the number three, and all of them teach a lesson. Then invite children to use the writing process—plan, write, revise, edit, publish—to arrive at a thoughtful, polished final product.

5. Tossing a Tea Party

After children have enjoyed the 15 books in this collection, the time is right to throw a celebratory bash. Work with students to plan and execute the perfect party, complete with festive decorations, punch, and gingerbread cookies. Invite kids to come dressed as their favorite characters. Then, host a reading in which kids share their favorite folk and fairy tales—or original works—for friends and family members!

The Little Red Hen

About the Tale

This popular English folktale was orally "handed down" from teller to teller over the course of many generations before it was finally committed to paper in the late 1800s by author Joseph Jacobs. In this simple patterned story, a hard-working little red hen asks her fellow farm animals—a dog, cat, and duck—for help growing, harvesting, and baking wheat into bread. After they all refuse, *she refuses* to share her bread with them! This story, with its firm position on laziness, is sure to strike a chord with most young learners.

Discussion Questions

1. What words would you use to describe the little red hen? What about the other animals?

2. Is the little red hen good or bad? Nice or not nice?

3. Do you think it was fair for the little red hen *not* to share her bread?

Notable Retellings

※ *The Little Red Hen* by Barry Downard (Simon & Schuster, 2004). The story line remains intact, but its unique photo-collage illustrations make this retelling modern and memorable.

※ *The Little Red Hen* by Paul Galdone (Clarion Books, 1985). This popular, tried-and-true version features clear illustrations and prose.

※ *The Little Red Hen Makes a Pizza* by Philemon Sturges (Puffin Books, 2002). Kids will laugh out loud at this zany twist on the beloved classic!

Companion Reproducible

Focus Skills: Comprehension, Sequencing, Writing

Invite children to use the reproducible on page 32 to record the steps that the little red hen uses to make her bread.

Level
E

Word Count
259

Vocabulary
grind, hen, lazy, quite, wheat

Supportive Features
repetitive, patterned text

Challenging Features
concept of planting and grinding wheat, and the process of making bread; dialogue

Comprehension
Use this book with the Sequencing Chart on page 22.

Phonics
short vowels (*a: cat, plant, asked, jam; e: red, hen, help; i: will, it, this, with; o: dog, not, on, top; u: duck, cut, just*)

Writing
Have children write a letter to the cat, dog, and duck, explaining why they did not deserve to eat the bread.

Fluency
Make masks for the little red hen, dog, cat, and duck and assign four children these roles. Have each character read his/her part; have the children chorally read the narrator's portion of the story.

Name _____

How to Make Bread

The little red hen made bread. Do you remember all the steps?
Write them below. (**Hint:** You can use the book to help you.)

Step 1: _____Plant the wheat._____

Step 2: _____

Step 3: _____

Step 4: _____

Now you are ready to eat! What do you like to put on top of your bread?

_____

Draw a picture of it.

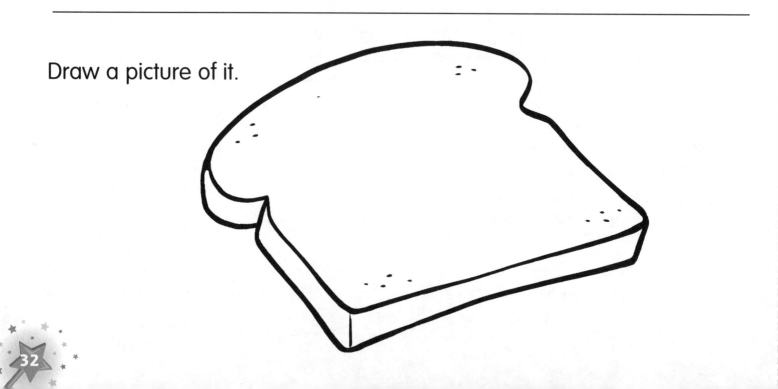

"No! Because you did not help, I will just
have to eat this bread by myself," said
the little red hen.
And so she did, with jam on top!

16

The Little Red Hen

A retelling by Violet Findley • Illustrated by Lynne Cravath

SCHOLASTIC

Before long, all the bread was baked.
"Who will help me eat this?" asked
the little red hen.

14

"Not me!" said the dog.
"Not me!" said the cat.
"Not me!" said the duck.
You see, they were all quite lazy.

3

Once upon a time, a little red hen decided to plant some wheat.
"Who will help me plant this?" she asked.

2

A

"Me!" said the dog.
"Me!" said the cat.
"Me!" said the duck.

15

"I will just have to plant it by myself," said the little red hen.

4

B

"I will just have to bake it by myself," said the little red hen.

13

"Not me!" said the dog.
"Not me!" said the cat.
"Not me!" said the duck.

12

Before long, all the wheat was tall.
"Who will help me cut this?" asked
the little red hen.

5

"I will just have to grind it by myself," said
the little red hen.

10

"I will just have to cut it by myself," said
the little red hen.

7

"Not me!" said the dog.
"Not me!" said the cat.
"Not me!" said the duck.

6

C

Before long, all the wheat was ground.
"Who will help me bake this into bread?"
asked the little red hen.

11

Before long, all the wheat was cut.
"Who will help me grind this?" asked
the little red hen.

8

D

"Not me!" said the dog.
"Not me!" said the cat.
"Not me!" said the duck.

9

The Three Little Pigs

About the Tale

Although we'll never know who invented the story of "The Three Little Pigs," historians credit James Orchard Halliwell with being the first person to publish it. In 1849, he included the tale in his tome *Popular Rhymes and Nursery Tales*. Since then, the classic has been retold—and interpreted—by everyone from the Brothers Grimm to fractured-fairy-tale specialist John Scieszka. Today, this engaging story of three house-building pigs and the huffing, puffing big bad wolf is probably the most widely told children's story in the English-speaking world.

Discussion Questions

1. Why did the big bad wolf want to blow down the pigs' homes?

2. The pigs put a pot of hot stew at the bottom of the chimney. Do you think that was fair? Why or why not?

3. The are three pigs in this story. Can you think of some other stories that have three characters?

Notable Retellings

✳ **The Three Little Pigs by James Marshall (Puffin Books, 1996)**. Via funny dialogue and exuberant cartoons, Marshall breathes new life into this favorite.

✳ **The Three Pigs by David Wiesner (Clarion Books, 2001)**. Don't miss this Caldecott Award–winning retelling stocked with incredible pictures and a super-zany plotline.

✳ **The True Story of the 3 Little Pigs! by John Scieszka (Puffin Books, 1996)**. Get kids giggling and teach point of view with this fractured classic told from the wolf's perspective.

Companion Reproducible

Focus Skills: Critical and Creative Thinking, Making Personal Connections, Writing

Distribute copies of the reproducible on page 38. Then invite each child to complete the poem and add an illustration.

Level
F

Word Count
243

Vocabulary
chimney, cozy, dashed, stew, straw

Supportive Features
repetitive, patterned text; familiar story

Challenging Features
long sentences, use of commas, phrases such as "Quick as a wink"

Comprehension
Use this book with the Problem/Solution Chart on page 24.

Phonics
short vowels (*a: bad, and, as, ran, at, back, that; e: yelled, then, them, when; i: pig, big, quick, sticks, bricks, in; o: upon, not, pot, hot, bottom; u: huffed, puffed, lunch, jumped, up*)

Writing
Invite children to pretend they are the big bad wolf and write a letter to the pigs explaining his point of view.

Fluency
Have partners reread the story, alternating each page. Circulate and listen in. Model how to read dialogue that is in all caps, such as "OUCH!"

Name _____

Build a House

The three little pigs used straw, sticks, and bricks to build their homes. What would you use? Fill in the poem. Then draw a picture of yourself inside your house!

To keep the Big Bad Wolf away,

I would not build a house of hay.

Instead, I'd build a house of _____ .
(object)

Then in my happy home I'd stay!

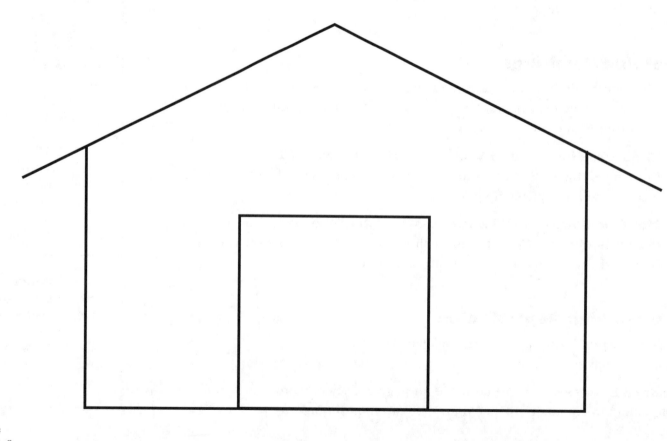

After that, the three little pigs lived safe and sound in their cozy house of bricks. And the big bad wolf never bothered them again.

16

Folk & Fairy Tale
EASY READERS

The Three Little Pigs

A retelling by Violet Findley • Illustrated by Keiko Motoyama

■ SCHOLASTIC

When the wolf came down the chimney, he landed right in the pot.
"OUCH! OUCH! OUCH!" he yelled.

14

One day, each pig decided to build a house to keep safe from the big bad wolf. You see, the wolf loved to eat little pigs.

3

Once upon a time, there lived three little pigs.

2

Then, quick as a wink, he dashed out the door and ran far, far away.

15

A

The first pig built a cozy house of straw.

4

B

"Please do!" said the pigs sweetly.
You see, they had put a pot of very hot stew at the bottom of the chimney.

13

"I'm coming down the chimney to eat you for dinner!" said the wolf.

12

But the big bad wolf huffed and puffed and blew the house down.

5

The third little pig built a cozy house of bricks. He invited the two other pigs to live with him.

10

The second little pig built a cozy house of sticks.

7

Quick as a wink, the first little pig ran away before he became breakfast.

6

The big bad wolf huffed and puffed and huffed and puffed. But he just could not blow the brick house down.

11

C

But the big bad wolf huffed and puffed and blew the house down.

8

D

Quick as a wink, the second little pig ran away before he became lunch.

9

Martina the Cockroach

About the Tale

This enchanting Latin-American tale is as familiar to Puerto Rican and Cuban youngsters as the "Three Little Pigs" is to American kids. And it's no surprise. After all, what child can resist the antics of a pesky insect? In this humorous tale, a glamorous cockroach named Martina dabs on some perfume, puts on a pretty dress, and waits patiently as an assortment of noisy animals parade by to propose marriage. Who will win her hand? Why, the dapper mouse, of course, because only he makes the perfect sound— "Kiiiii, Kiiiii."

Discussion Questions

1. Why does Martina decide to marry the mouse?

2. Do you think a mouse would make a good husband for a cockroach? Why or why not?

3. Do you think this story could happen in real life? Why or why not?

Notable Retellings

✳ *La Cucaracha Martina* by Daniel Moreton (Turtle Books, 1999). These humorous and colorful illustrations are super eye-peeling!

✳ *Perez and Martina* by Pura Belpré (Penguin Books, 2004). Students will delight in this detailed version translated from the work of Belpré, a renowned South-American storyteller.

✳ *Señor Cat's Romance and Other Folk Stories From Latin America* by Lucia M. Gonzalez (Scholastic, 2001). This terrific collection includes a charming version of Martina, illustrated by the great Lulu Delacre.

Companion Reproducible

Focus Skills: Critical and Creative Thinking, Making Personal Connections, Writing

Distribute to each student a copy of the reproducible on page 44. Then invite kids to complete the poem to tell what animal sound they like best, and draw a companion picture.

Level
F

Word Count
264

Vocabulary
cockroach, couple, perfume, whistle

Supportive Features
repetitive, patterned text

Challenging Features
onomatopoeia, setting, dialogue

Comprehension
Use this book with the Comprehension Quilt on page 23.

Phonics
consonant blends and digraphs (*pretty, sweeping, floor, dress, smelled, frog; cockroach, while, should, she, shoes, share, thank, then, whistle*)

Writing
Ask children to create a wedding invitation for Martina and the mouse. They can even include a picture of the happy couple.

Fluency
Using the text on page 7, model reading sentences with different punctuation. Then have children chorally read the story, paying special attention to punctuation.

Name _____

My Favorite Animal Sound

Martina loves the sound that a mouse makes. What animal sound do you like? Fill in the poem below. Then draw a picture to go with it.

The sound of a _____

(animal)

Makes me want to cheer!

Because it goes " _____ "

(sound it makes)

Which is music to my ears!

Kiiii, kiiii.

Martina and the mouse lived happily ever after. And his soft sound was always music to her ears.

16

Folk & Fairy Tale EASY READERS

Martina the Cockroach

A retelling by Kama Einhorn • Illustrated by Patrick Girouard

SCHOLASTIC

Martina and the mouse got married the next day.

14

One day she found a gold coin while sweeping her floor.

3

Once upon a time there was a pretty cockroach named Martina. She lived in a nice little house.

2

All of their friends came to the wedding. The mouse's friends sang to the couple.

15

What should she buy? Should she buy shoes? Should she buy candy? "No, I will buy perfume," she said.

4

"Oh, I love that sound! It is like a whistle! It is like music!" said Martina.

13

"What sound do you make?" asked Martina.
"Kiiii, kiiii," he said.

12

She bought perfume and put it on. Then she fixed her hair and put on a pretty dress.

5

A dog came by and said, "Marry me!"
"What sound do you make?" asked Martina.
"Woof, woof!" he said.
"No, thank you," she said.

10

A cat came by and said, "Marry me!"
"What sound do you make?" asked Martina.
"Meow, meow!" he said.
"No, thank you," she said.

7

Martina looked and smelled beautiful!
Now, she was ready to get married.
But she did not want to share her home
with a noisy husband.

6

C

Then a mouse came by and said,
"Marry me!"

11

A rooster came by and said, "Marry me!"
"What sound do you make?" asked Martina.
"Cock-a-doodle-doo!" he said.
"No, thank you," she said.

8

D

A frog came by and said, "Marry me!"
"What sound do you make?" asked Martina.
"Ribbit, ribbit!" he said.
"No, thank you," she said.

9

The Tortoise and the Hare

Level
G

Word Count
252

Vocabulary
by and by, grinned, hare, steady, tortoise

Supportive Features
few sentences on a page; mostly short sentences

Challenging Features
use of interior commas, moral of tale, dialogue

Comprehension
Use this book with the Sequencing Chart on page 22.

Phonics
long a (ay, ai, a_e): named, always, snail, race, day, way, take, wake, may; words with –ed: teased, decided, hopped, napped, passed, yelled, jumped, crossed, cheered, grinned

Writing
Have children draw a picture of the tortoise and the hare. Above each, have kids make a speech bubble. Ask them to write inside the bubble a conversation that the two characters might have.

Fluency
Using page 12, model reading sentences with different punctuation. Then have children chorally read the story, paying special attention to punctuation.

About the Tale

For more than 2,500 years, the sly wit of Aesop's fables have entertained children the world over. And the important lessons of these tales have seeped into the very fabric of our cultures, turning up in many expressions including "sour grapes," and "slow and steady wins the race." In *The Tortoise and the Hare*, a quick rabbit challenges a slow turtle to a race, convinced that he cannot lose. But the hare's confidence leads him to take a long nap—a mistake that allows the plodding turtle to cross the finish line first! Besides being funny, this well-loved story serves as a great reminder to never give up.

Discussion Questions

1. Why does the tortoise win the race?

2. What do you think the author is trying to tell us in this story?

3. Would you rather be the hare or the tortoise?

Notable Retellings

❋ *Hare and Tortoise Race to the Moon* by Oliver J. Corwin (Harry Abrams, 2002). Children will adore this updated tale in which the two rivals race to the moon.

❋ *The Tortoise and the Hare* by Janet Stevens (Holiday House, 1985). This tried-and-true retelling features easy-to-read text and simple yet amusing illustrations.

❋ *The Tortoise and the Hare* by Helen Ward (Millbrook Press, 1999). Don't miss the stunning, detailed pictures in this contemporary classic.

Companion Reproducible

Focus Skills: Comprehension, Critical and Creative Thinking, Writing

Invite children to use the reproducible on page 50 to write a letter to the hare offering advice on what he should do—or not do—to win his new race with a snail.

49

Racing Tips

Hare is going to have a race with Snail! Write Hare a letter telling him what he should do to win.

Dear Hare,

_____

_____

_____

_____

_____

_____

Your friend,

_____

"How did you ever beat the hare?"
asked the horse.
The tortoise grinned, "The hare may be
fast, but slow and steady wins the race."

16

Folk & Fairy Tale
EASY READERS

The Tortoise and the Hare

A retelling by Violet Findley • Illustrated by Jackie Snider

SCHOLASTIC

But it was no use. The tortoise crossed
the finish line first.

14

The hare, who was very fast, always teased
the slow tortoise.
"Ha, ha, ha! Even a snail is faster than
you!" he said.

3

Once upon a time, there lived a tortoise and a hare.

②

"The tortoise won! The tortoise won!" all the animals cheered.

⑮

A

The tortoise did not like the teasing one bit. Finally, he decided to do something about it. "Let's have a race," he said.

④

B

After a while, the hare woke up.
"Oh, no! The tortoise is winning!" he yelled.
He jumped up and hopped along the path.

⑬

But as the hare napped, the tortoise walked.
Slow, slow, slow. And guess what? By and
by, the tortoise passed the hare!

The hare fell down laughing.
"OK, but you know I will win," he said.
"We will see," said the tortoise.

"Ha, ha, ha! I can take a nap and still wake
up in time to beat the tortoise," said the hare.

The hare hopped. Fast, fast, fast.
The tortoise walked. Slow, slow, slow.

On the day of the big race, all of the animals came to watch.
"On your mark, get set, go!" said the fox.

6

So he did. Snore, snore, snore.

11

The hare hopped. Fast, fast, fast.
The tortoise walked. Slow, slow, slow.

8

Soon the hare was way ahead of the tortoise.

9

The Three Billy Goats Gruff

About the Tale

This kid-pleasing tale, which originated in Norway many hundreds of years ago, gained worldwide acclaim after it was written down by the authors Asbjornsen and Moe. These two Norwegians published the oral stories swirling around them just as they Brothers Grimm did. "The Three Billy Goats Gruff" tops a long list of "beast fables" in which animals talk, reason, and have human traits. When each of the three goats attempts to cross the bridge, the mean troll threatens to eat them up. But—surprise, surprise—the canny brothers manage to outwit him in the end.

Discussion Questions

1. How does each goat trick the troll into allowing him to cross the bridge?

2. What does *cranky* mean? Why do you think the troll is so cranky?

3. What makes you feel cranky?

Notable Retellings

✸ *The Three Billy Goats Gruff* by Ellen Appleby (Scholastic, 1992). This whimsically illustrated, straightforward retelling is perfect for the K–2 crowd.

✸ *The Three Billy Goats Gruff* by Stephen Carpenter (Harper Festival, 1998). Build phonemic awareness with the fun, repetitive rhymes in this lively picture book.

✸ *The Three Billy Goats Gruff/Just a Friendly Troll* (Steck-Vaughn, 1995). Kids will love this unique version that tells the story from the point of view of the goats *and* the troll.

Companion Reproducible

Focus Skills: Vocabulary Development, Critical and Creative Thinking, Writing)

Invite children to use the reproducible on page 56 to draw a picture of their very own troll. They should then write five words to describe the creature.

Level
G

Word Count
239

Vocabulary
clomp, cranky, rammed, troll

Supportive Features
repetitive, patterned text

Challenging Features
long sentences, use of commas, difficult adjectives and verbs (*cranky, clomp, sneaky, rammed*), dialogue

Comprehension
Use this book with the Problem/Solution Chart on page 24.

Phonics
long e (*e, ea, ee, y*): *three, billy, decided, eat, sweet, mean, cranky, sneaky, green*

Writing
Have children write "Little," "Middle," and "Big" on a large sheet of paper. Beside each word, ask them to draw a picture of that billy goat and describe it in a sentence.

Fluency
Provide or make masks for each character. Have children chorally read the narrator's portion of the story. Then, have the students portraying each character read and act out their parts.

Name _____

My Troll

Use your imagination to draw a troll. Give your troll a name.
Then write five words to describe him or her.

Troll Name _____

Words to describe my troll:

1. _____

2. _____

3. _____

4. _____

5. _____

After that, the three brothers crossed the bridge whenever they liked. And, my, the sweet green grass was delicious!

16

"Stop there! I am going to eat you up!" yelled Troll.
"OK," said Big Billy, for he had a sneaky plan.

14

One day, they decided to cross the bridge to eat the sweet grass on the other side.

3

Once upon a time, there lived three billy goat brothers. Their names were Little Billy, Middle Billy, and Big Billy.

2

A

When Troll climbed up on the bridge, Big Billy rammed him so hard that he fell into the water with a giant splash!

15

There was only one problem. A mean troll lived under it.

4

B

Clomp, clomp, clomp! Big Billy started across the bridge. Then he heard a cranky voice.

13

"What a fine idea," said Troll, licking his lips. And with that, Middle Billy crossed the bridge.

12

Clomp, clomp, clomp! Little Billy started across the bridge. Then he heard a cranky voice.

5

"Stop there! I am going to eat you up!" yelled Troll.

10

"Wait for my brother. He is bigger and much more delicious than I!" cried Little Billy.

7

"Stop there! I am going to eat you up!" yelled Troll.

6

C

"Wait for my brother. He is bigger and much more delicious than I!" cried Middle Billy.

11

"What a fine idea," said Troll, licking his lips. And with that, Little Billy crossed the bridge.

8

D

Clomp, clomp, clomp! Middle Billy started across the bridge. Then he heard a cranky voice.

9

The Gingerbread Man

About the Tale

There are literally hundreds of published adaptations of this timeless European tale. In the earliest ones—produced in Norway in the mid-1800s—the fleeing confection is a pancake. But somehow, as the story was shared between countries and continents, the lead character morphed into a gingerbread man. And we Americans wholeheartedly embrace this cookie version! In the story, a clever gingerbread man hops off a tray and outruns several hungry pursuers before finally getting gobbled up by a crafty fox. What child—or adult for that matter—could resist such a deliciously silly treat?

Discussion Questions

1. Is the gingerbread man good or bad? Tell why you think so.

2. How did the fox trick the gingerbread man into becoming his snack?

3. If you could write a story about a runaway food, what would it be?

Notable Retellings

※ *The Gingerbread Man* by Jim Aylesworth (Scholastic, 1998). Clever wordplay and charming "old-fashioned" pictures combine in this kid-pleasing version.

※ *The Gingerbread Man* by Karen Schmidt (Scholastic, 1980). This simply illustrated, straightforward retelling makes for an excellent read-aloud.

※ *The Musubi Man: Hawaii's Gingerbread Man* by Sandi Takagama (Bess Press, 1997). Kids will laugh out loud at this Hawaiian-flavored yarn, in which a runaway Musubi Man encounters a famished surfer.

Companion Reproducible

Focus Skills: Comprehension, Understanding Dialogue, Writing

Invite children to use the reproducible on page 62 to create their very own gingerbread man. They can then imagine something he would say and write it in the speech balloon.

Level
G

Word Count
276

Vocabulary
clever, dashed, fibbed, munched, naughty

Supportive Features
repetitive, patterned text; few lines of text per page

Challenging Features
some difficult adjectives and verbs: *clever, naughty dashed, fibbed, munched*; dialogue

Comprehension
Use this book with the Sequencing Chart on page 22.

Phonics
long i (y, igh, i_e): *time, right, might, try, while, like.*

Writing
Have children write directions for decorating a gingerbread man.

Fluency
Model how to read dialogue. Then read aloud the story. Stop when you get to dialogue, and have children chorally read it back to you. Provide feedback and additional modeling as needed.

My Gingerbread Man

Use your imagination to draw your very own gingerbread man.
Then write something your cookie might say.

Scholastic • Folk & Fairy Tale Easy Readers Teaching Guide • page 62

CRUNCH! The fox munched the cookie
in one bite.
"My, what a tasty treat!" he said.
And that was the end of the poor
Gingerbread Man.

16

Folk & Fairy Tale
EASY READERS

The Gingerbread Man

A retelling by Violet Findley • Illustrated by Hector Borlasca

SCHOLASTIC

"I don't like cookies," fibbed the clever fox.
"I just want to help you get across this river.
Hop on my shoulder! I promise you will not
get wet."

14

But the naughty cookie jumped off the plate
and dashed out the door.

3

Once upon a time, an old woman baked a gingerbread man. She put it on a plate to cool.

2

"OK," said the cookie.
So he did.

15

A

"Run, run, as fast as you can. You can't catch me. I'm the Gingerbread Man!" he sang.

4

B

"Don't even think about eating me up. I ran away from an old woman and a dog and a cow. And I will run away from you, too!" said the cookie.

13

After a while, the cookie came to a fox standing by a river. The fox was licking his lips.

12

The cookie was right. Try as she might, the old woman was just too slow.

5

"Run, run, as fast as you can. You can't catch me. I'm the Gingerbread Man!" sang the cookie.

10

"Run, run, as fast as you can. You can't catch me. I'm the Gingerbread Man!" sang the cookie.

7

After a while, the cookie came to a dog.
"I'm going to eat you up!" said the dog.

6

The cookie was right. Try as he might, the cow was just too slow.

11

The cookie was right. Try as he might, the dog was just too slow.

8

After a while, the cookie came to a cow.
"I'm going to eat you up!" said the cow.

9

Stone Soup

About the Tale

This charming cumulative tale originated in Europe where it spread from country to country. Many versions exist in French, Swedish, Russian, English, and a host of other languages. In it, a stranger (or a group of strangers) comes to town and "tricks" the towns-folk into adding a variety of vegetables to a pot, which contained hot water and a single stone. As you may have imagined, the resulting soup is rich, delicious, and plentiful enough to be eaten by one and all. "Stone Soup" is not only an engaging story, but also a gentle reminder of the great benefit of sharing.

Discussion Questions

1. What would stone soup taste like *without* any vegetables?

2. Was it fair or unfair of the soup-maker to trick the people of the village into adding their vegetables?

3. What lesson does this story teach us?

Notable Retellings

✳ *Stone Soup* by Marcia Brown (Aladdin, 1997). Originally published in 1947, this wonderful Caldecott-Honoree still stands the test of time.

✳ *Stone Soup* by Jon Muth (Scholastic, 2003). In this richly illustrated version, the story in transplanted from Europe to wartorn China.

✳ *Stone Soup* by Tony Ross (Puffin, 1990). Get silly with this rib-tickling take starring a crafty hen and gullible wolf.

Companion Reproducible

Focus Skills: Comprehension, Critical and Creative Thinking, Writing

Distribute copies of the reproducible on page 68. Then invite each child to write the directions for making stone soup.

Level
G

Word Count
261

Vocabulary
broth, cabbage, sniff, village

Supportive Features
repetitive, patterned text; few lines of text per page

Challenging Features
concept of tricking the villagers, dialogue

Comprehension
Use this book with the Comprehension Quilt on page 23.

Phonics
soft *c* and *g*: *nice, place, except, once, danced; village, giant, cabbage*

Writing
Invite children to write a summary of the story. It should be no longer than four sentences and should tell about the main events.

Fluency
Have children chorally read the story as volunteers act it out. As an alternative, have children use the story's dialogue to write and perform a play version of the story.

Name _____

My Recipe for Stone Soup

What would you put in stone soup? Add it on the line.
Then, write the directions for making the soup.

Stone Soup

Feeds: A village

Ingredients:

- Stone
- Carrots
- Beans
- Cabbage
- Corn
- _____

Directions for making: _____

_____

_____

_____

_____

Scholastic • Folk & Fairy Tale Easy Readers Teaching Guide • page 68

From then on, the people in the village shared. And their very favorite thing to share was stone soup!

16

Stone Soup

A retelling by Kama Einhorn • Illustrated by Necdet Yilmaz

■SCHOLASTIC

The soup cooked and cooked. Finally, it was ready. Everyone ate a big bowl. "This is delicious!" they all said.

14

One day a visitor came to town.
"Hello! Does anybody have food to share?" he asked.
"NO!" said everyone.

3

Once upon a time, there was a village.
It was a nice place to live except for one
thing. People did not like to share.

2

The soup made them so happy that they
danced and sang all night long.

15

"That's OK," said the visitor. "I will make
stone soup for everyone."
Then he took a stone and dropped it into
a giant pot.

4

A girl brought beans and put them in the pot.

13

Then the visitor said, "I once had stone soup with cabbage and carrots and corn and beans. It was delicious!"

12

The visitor sniffed his broth. Some people came outside to see what he was doing. Some watched from their windows.

5

Then the visitor said, "I once had stone soup with cabbage and carrots and corn. It was delicious!"

10

That gave one man in the village an idea. He brought a cabbage and put it in the pot.

7

"Mmmm, I love stone soup. The only thing better is stone soup with cabbage!" said the visitor.

6

A boy brought corn and put it in the pot.

11

C

Then the visitor said, "I once had stone soup with cabbage and carrots. It was delicious!"

8

D

A woman brought carrots and put them in the pot.

9

The Ugly Duckling

About the Tale

Hans Christian Andersen was born in the small Danish town of Odense, in 1805. Like the ugly duckling, he was awkward and special. With nothing to sustain him but sheer determination, Hans headed for Copenhagen. There, he went to college and later wrote an assortment of plays, novels, articles, and his beloved children's tales. He penned "The Ugly Duckling" in 1844. This lovely story of a homely bird that "blooms" into a gorgeous swan has been translated into dozens of languages—English among them. It remains one of Anderson's most celebrated works.

Discussion Questions

1. Why do the other birds make fun of the ugly duckling?

2. Why is the ugly duckling afraid to show his face to the swans?

3. At the end of the story, the ugly duckling decides "to be kind to all living things, from peacocks to potato bugs." Why?

Notable Retellings

※ *The Ugly Duckling* by Hans Christian Anderson (Mineditions, 1995). This faithful translation of Anderson's fluid tale is a bit melancholy, but oh-so beautiful.

※ *The Ugly Duckling* by Lorinda Bryan Cawley (Voyager Books, 1979). Charming pictures and text combine for a lively read-aloud.

※ *The Ugly Duckling* by Jerry Pinkney (HarperCollins, 1999). Kids are sure to respond to the wonderful art of this Caldecott-Honor book.

Companion Reproducible

Focus Skills: Following Directions, Vocabulary Development, Writing

Distribute copies of the reproducible of page 74. Then invite each child to fill in the blanks to write their own customized Animal Tale inspired by "The Ugly Duckling."

Level
G

Word Count
287

Vocabulary
curious, geese, heron, pecked

Supportive Features
repetitive, patterned text; short sentences

Challenging Features
use of interior commas dialogue, moral of tale

Comprehension
Use this book with the Compare/Contrast Venn on page 25.

Phonics
final *e*: *time, five, cute, while, came, face, spoke, made, lake*

Writing
Have children draw a picture of the ugly duckling after it has grown into a beautiful swan. Around the picture, ask children to write words to describe the swan, such as *white* and *feathery*.

Fluency
Have partners reread the story, taking turns to read one page at a time. Circulate and listen in. Model how to read the longer sentences, which contain phrases or clauses separated by commas.

Name _____

My Animal Tale

Fill in the blanks to write your own tale.

Once upon a time, a little _____ went

animal

for a walk. He met some mean _____s.

different animal

"You are ugly! Go away." They said.

Next, he met some mean _____s.

different animal

"You are ugly. Go away," they said.

Finally, he met some nice _____s.

different animal

"Don't look at me. I am ugly," he said.

"You are not ugly. You are just different. Let's be

friends!" they said.

Then, they all went out for _____

flavor of ice cream

ice cream and lived happily ever after!

🙲 THE END 🙰

From that day on, the once ugly duckling
lived happily ever after. And he was always
kind to all living things, from peacocks to
potato bugs.

16

Scholastic • Folk & Fairy Tale Easy Readers Teaching Guide • page 73

The Ugly Duckling

A retelling by Violet Findley • Illustrated by Susan Chapman

SCHOLASTIC

That made the ugly duckling curious.
He looked into the shiny water.

14

Out popped five little ducklings. Four were
fluffy and cute. One was gray and ugly.

3

Once upon a time, five eggs began to hatch. Crack! Crack! Crack! Crack! Crack!

2

Wow! He had grown into a beautiful swan, just like them!

15

The cute ducks were mean to their ugly brother. They pecked at him.
They said, "You are ugly. Go away!"

4

B

A

The swan laughed, "Have you looked in a mirror lately?"

13

One day, a swan swam over and spoke to him.
"Why are you so shy?" he asked.
"Because I am ugly," said the ugly duckling.

12

One day, the ugly duckling did go away.
He swam and swam. After a while, he met
some geese.

5

When the swans swam near, the ugly
duckling hid his face and cried. He did not
want them to see how ugly he was.

10

Once again, the ugly duckling did go away.
He swam and swam. After a while, he met
some herons.

7

But the geese were just as mean as the ducks. They pecked at him.
They said, "You are ugly. Go away!"

6

Life went on like this for many months. The ugly duckling stayed by himself. He also grew and grew.

11

C

But the herons were just as mean as the geese. They pecked at him.
They said, "You are ugly. Go away!"

8

D

Once again, the ugly duckling did go away. He swam and swam. After a while, he came upon some swans. They were the most beautiful birds he had ever seen.

9

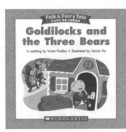

Goldilocks and the Three Bears

About the Tale

Like many European folktales, this widely told yarn revolves around the number three. There are three bears, three bowls of porridge, three chairs, and three beds. While scholars are not sure why three plays such a prevalent role in folklore, many believe it has something to do with the fact that three animals or objects lend themselves to easy comparison such as big, small, and medium, or hot, cold, and "just right." While we await a definitive explanation, one thing is for certain: The tale of naughty Goldilocks is sure to be three times the fun!

Discussion Questions

1. Which bear's things did Goldilocks like best?

2. Do you like or not like Goldilocks? Tell why.

3. This story contains many sets of three. Can you find them all? Make a list.

Notable Retellings

✳ *Goldilocks and the Three Bears* by Jim Aylesworth (Scholastic, 2003). Combine a playful retelling with quaint illustrations, and you've got one crowd-pleasing read-aloud.

✳ *Goldilocks and the Three Bears* by Jan Brett (Putnam, 1996). This talented author-illustrator breathes new life into the classic with her trademark illustrations featuring detailed borders.

✳ *Goldilocks Returns* by Lisa Campbell Ernst (Aladdin, 2003). This campy, kid-pleasing sequel has an older and wiser "Goldi" returning to the scene of her crime.

Companion Reproducible

Focus Skills: Comprehension, Critical and Creative Thinking, Writing

Invite children to use the writing prompt on page 80 to tell whether or not they think Goldilocks should go inside a house owned by three little pigs.

Level
G

Word Count
311

Vocabulary
porridge, rude, slurp, tidy

Supportive Features
repetitive, patterned text; familiar story

Challenging Features
long sentences; up to four sentences on a page; use of commas and dialogue

Comprehension
Use this book with the Sequencing Chart on page 22.

Phonics
dipthong /ou/, *ou, ow*: *house, found, down, our, growled*; words ending with *-ed*: *decided, named, opened, tried, growled, screamed*

Writing
Have children write a letter to the three bears as if they were Goldilocks. The letter should be an apology for what she did to their home.

Fluency
Invite children to chorally read the narrator's portion of the story. Assign volunteers to read the dialogue of each character.

Name _____

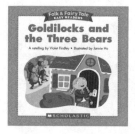

Should Goldilocks Go Inside?

After Goldilocks runs away from the bears, she sees a house that belongs to three little pigs. Do you think she should go inside? Tell why or why not. Then draw a picture to go with your writing.

_____

_____

_____

_____

_____

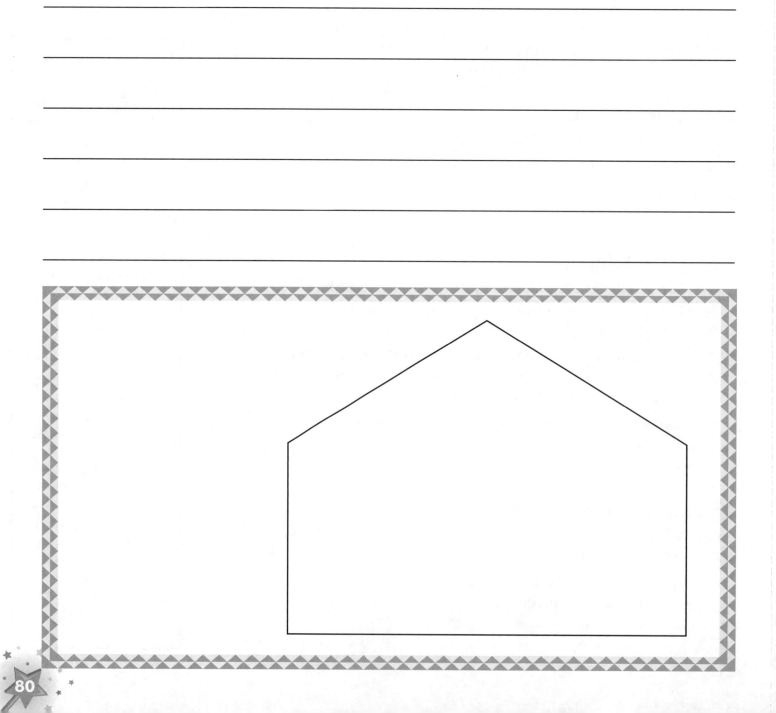

Then, quick as a wink, she ran out the door.
And the three bears never saw that rude
girl again.

16

Folk & Fairy Tale
EASY READERS

Goldilocks and
the Three Bears

A retelling by Violet Findley • Illustrated by Jannie Ho

SCHOLASTIC

The bears went into the bedroom to lie
down. "Someone has been sleeping in our
beds!" said Papa Bear and Mama Bear.

14

By and by, a girl named Goldilocks saw
their house.
"What a nice home!" she cried.
Then she opened the door and went inside.

3

Once upon a time, a family of three bears decided to go for a walk. They shut the door of their tidy house and off they went.

2

"And someone is still in mine!" cried Baby Bear.
With that, Goldilocks opened up her eyes and screamed.

15

In the kitchen, Goldilocks found three bowls of porridge. She tried the big bowl. It was too hot. She tried the middle bowl. It was too cold.

4

"And someone broke mine into bits!" cried Baby Bear.

13

The bears went into the living room to
sit down.
"Someone has been sitting in our chairs!"
said Papa Bear and Mama Bear.

12

Slurp!

Finally, she tried the little bowl. It was just
right, so she ate it up. Slurp!

5

By and by, the bears came back to their
house to have breakfast.
"Someone has been eating our porridge!"
said Papa Bear and Mama Bear.

10

Crack!

Finally, she tried the little chair. It was just
right, so she sat down. But the chair broke
into bits. Crack!

7

In the living room, Goldilocks found three chairs. She tried the big one. It was too hard. She tried the middle one. It was too soft.

6

c

"And someone ate mine all up!" cried Baby Bear.

11

In the bedroom, Goldilocks found three beds. She tried the big one. It was too hard. She tried the middle one. It was too soft.

8

D

Finally, she tried the little bed. It was just right, so she lay down and went to sleep. Zzzzz!

9

The Spider and the Beehive

About the Tale

This story comes to us from West Africa, where a spider named Anansi was invented and spun into a series of lively, often side-splittingly funny tales. In this one, the spider tricks a boy into sharing his cache of delicious plums, bananas, and honey. The only problem is that the greedy spider eats too much and finds himself stuck inside a beehive. "The Spider and the Beehive" is known as a "trickster tale" because the main character—in this case, the spider—is a cunning yet compelling trickster we love despite his misdeeds.

Discussion Questions

1. Why did the spider get stuck in the beehive?

2. Do you think this spider is good or bad? Explain.

3. "The Spider and the Beehive" is called a "trickster tale." Can you figure out why?

Notable Retellings

✳ *Anansi the Spider: A Tale from Ashanti* by Gerald McDermott (Henry Holt, 1987). Kids will be captivated by this lively read-aloud— especially the evocative illustrations.

✳ *Anansi and the Talking Melon* by Eric Kimmel (Holiday House, 1995). In this laugh-out-loud tale, Anansi finds himself stuck in a melon after a big day of bingeing.

✳ *A Story, a Story* by Gail E. Haley (Aladdin, reprinted 1988). This beautiful story of Anansi won the Caldecott back in 1971, but it's still a star!

Companion Reproducible

Focus Skills: Following Directions, Vocabulary Development, Writing

Distribute copies of the reproducible on page 86. Then invite each child to fill in the blanks to write their own customized trickster tale!

Level
G

Word Count
297

Vocabulary
entire, golden, hive, talent, village

Supportive Features
repetitive, patterned text; familiar story

Challenging Features
unfamiliar setting

Comprehension
Use this book with the Problem/Solution Chart on page 24.

Phonics
long e (e, ee, ee, y, ey): *tricky, sweetest, hungry, me, agreed, deep, tree, greedy, every, honey, squeezed, sweet, treat, he, week, finally*; variant vowel /ô/ phonograms (au, aw, all, alk): *small, all, walked, always*

Writing
Tell children to draw a picture of the story's setting. Ask them to describe the setting for someone who has never been to Africa or seen it in books.

Fluency
Have children softly reread the book. Circulate and listen in. Model how to read difficult words or longer sentences.

85

Name _____

My Trickster Tale

The Spider and the Beehive

Fill in the blanks to write your own tricky spider tale.

Once upon a time, there was a spider. He loved to trick

everyone. One day, he put on his _____ mask
                                        animal

and went to visit his friend, the monkey. He knocked on the

monkey's door _____ times. When the
                      number

door opened, the monkey turned bright _____
                                              color

and screamed for _____ minutes.
                         number

"Don't worry. It's just me," said the spider, taking off his mask.

"Don't scare me like that again!" said the monkey.

The spider said he was sorry and promised not to trick

the monkey again.

Then the spider said, "I have an idea. Let's play a trick

on _____!"
        your name

CB THE END CB

And from that day on, the spider always shared his fruit with his friends.

16

Folk & Fairy Tale
EASY READERS

The Spider and the Beehive

A retelling by Kama Einhorn • Illustrated by Stephen Lewis

SCHOLASTIC

The spider yelled and yelled. But nobody could hear his cries. He was too far from the village. For an entire week, the spider sat in that hive.

14

The boy had a special talent. He was able to find the biggest, sweetest fruit in all the jungle.

3

Once upon a time, there was a small African village. In it, lived a little boy and a tricky spider. The spider thought he was smarter than everyone else.

2

A

Then, finally, he squeezed out.

15

One day the spider was hungry, so he asked the boy, "Will you take me to the best plums?"
The boy agreed.

4

B

The boy said, "You have not been very nice to me. Good-bye, greedy spider!"
Then off he went.

13

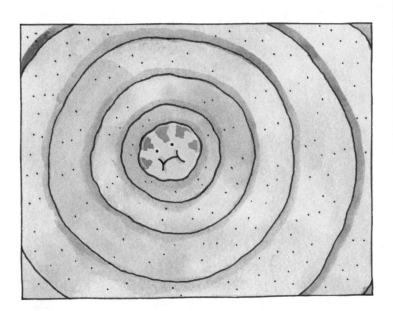

The spider was ready for the next treat.
But when he tried to climb out of the hive,
he was stuck. His belly had become too big!
"Help! Get me out!" he cried.

12

They walked deep into the jungle to the
boy's favorite plum tree. The spider felt
greedy. He ate up every single plum and
did not share any!

5

Then the boy said, "Inside this hive is the
most delicious honey in the world."

10

They walked to the boy's favorite banana
tree. The spider ate up every single banana
and did not share any!

7

The spider rubbed his belly.
He said, "Now, can you take me to the
best bananas?"

6

C

The spider squeezed into a hole in the
hive. He ate up all the sweet golden
honey and did not share any!

11

His belly was full, but the spider said,
"Now, can you take me to the best honey?"

8

D

The spider and the boy walked farther
and farther into the jungle.

9

The City Mouse and the Country Mouse

About the Tale

Aesop is widely credited with originating this story and dozens more. Although little is known about this wise and witty storyteller, scholars believe he was born into slavery in 620 B.C., somewhere in Greece. Upon being freed by his master, he became part of the court of King Croesus. It was there that he wove his timeless tales, including "The Tortoise and the Hare," "The Lion and the Mouse," and, of course, "The City Mouse and the Country Mouse." Aesop's stories qualify as fables because they are short, humorous, and teach important lessons by way of example. Despite being created thousands of years ago, they remain as relevant today as they were then.

Discussion Questions

1. Why does the country mouse decide to go to the city?

2. Why does the country mouse decide to go back to the country?

3. What lesson is the author trying to teach us in this tale?

Notable Retellings

※ *Bernelly and Harriet* by Elizabeth Dahlie (Little Brown 2002). In this perky twist on the favorite tale, two mouse cousins come to discover that there is no place like home.

※ *The Town Mouse* by Nigel Brooks (Walker and Co., 2000). Kids will delight in this sweet, old-fashioned version, filled with lovingly rendered pictures.

※ *Town Mouse City Mouse* by Jan Brett (Putnam, 2003). Brett applies her unique style of illustration to the classic tale, with winning results.

Companion Reproducible

Focus Skills: Comparing and Contrasting, Making Personal Connections, Writing

Distribute copies of the reproducible of page 92. Then invite children to fill in the T chart to compare the benefits of country and city living.

Level
H

Word Count
366

Vocabulary
finest, hikes, nibbled, roam, wrinkled

Supportive Features
many short sentences

Challenging Features
use of ellipses, dialogue, moral or story

Comprehension
Use this book with the Compare/Contrast Venn on page 25.

Phonics
variant vowel *oo*: *food, took, room, stood, good-bye*; words ending with *-le*: *little, nibble, wrinkle, table*

Writing
Have children write a letter from the city mouse to the country mouse telling about his experience during his visit.

Fluency
Have partners reread the story, taking turns to read one page at a time. Circulate and listen in. Evaluate children's speed, accuracy, and expression.

Name _____

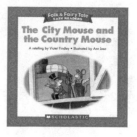

City and Country T Chart

What are some good things about living in the country? What are some good things about living in the city? Fill in the T chart. Then tell which place you would rather live and why.

Good Things About the Country	Good Things About the City

I would choose to live in the _____
country/city

because_____

_____

_____.

Then the country mouse jumped on a train and went back to the country.
"No matter where I roam, there is no place like home," he said.

16

Folk & Fairy Tale EASY READERS

The City Mouse and the Country Mouse

A retelling by Violet Findley • Illustrated by Ann Iosa

■ SCHOLASTIC

Quick as a wink, the mice jumped off the table and ran into a little hole. The country mouse had never been so scared.
"I'm going back home," he said.

14

One day, his city friend came to visit.
"Welcome," said the country mouse.
"Glad to be here," said the city mouse.

3

Once upon a time, there was a little mouse.
He lived in the country.

2

A

"Do you really want to leave all this fine
food?" asked the city mouse.
"The city is nice, but corn and safety are
better than cherry pie and danger," said
the country mouse.
The two mice hugged good-bye.

15

The two mice had a great time. They played
tag. They climbed trees. They took long
hikes. All of this made them very hungry.

4

B

. . . in came a cat! In came a dog! In came
a person!
"Run for your life!" said the city mouse.

13

"Mmmm!" said the city mouse.
"Mmmm!" said the country mouse.
But just as they started to nibble the food...

12

So they went into the fields and began to
nibble some corn and beans. But after a
while, the city mouse wrinkled up his nose.

5

The two mice had a great time. They
listened to music. They played games.
They ran from room to room. All of this
made them very hungry.

10

The next day, the two mice jumped on
a train and went to the city.

7

"This food is so boring. In the city, I eat the finest meat, cheese, and pie. Do you want to go there with me?" asked the city mouse. The country mouse licked his lips. "Oh, yes!" he said.

6

C

So they went into the dining room. There stood a table filled with meat and cheese and a whole cherry pie!

11

They walked to a tall building and took an elevator to the tippy top. This was where the city mouse lived.

8

D

The home was fit for a king! It was big and very fancy. "Welcome," said the city mouse. "Glad to be here," said the country mouse.

9

The Elves and the Shoemaker

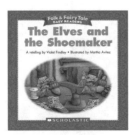

About the Tale

We have Jacob and Wilhelm Grimm to thank for immortalizing this heartwarming tale. These German-born brothers studied law and collaborated on a dictionary, but are best known for their 1814 publication of *Nursery and Household Tales*. In these two thick volumes, the Grimms retold more than 200 oral folktales—"The Elves and the Shoemaker" among them. Although the brothers' initial intention was to create a scholarly work for adults, their collection soon fell into the hands of story-hungry children and the rest, as they say, is history.

Discussion Questions

1. Why do you think the elves might have decided to help the shoemaker?

2. How did the shoemaker and his wife grow very, very rich?

3. After the elves get their new clothes, they never return again. Where do you think they went? What do you think they did?

Notable Retellings

※ *The Bootmaker and the Elves* by Susan Lowell (Orchard Books, 1997). Kids will adore this rib-tickling version, in which the action takes place in the rootin' tootin' Wild West.

※ *The Elves and the Shoemaker* by Paul Galdone (Clarion, 1986). Light-hearted text and humorous illustrations combine for a lively and accessible read-aloud.

※ *The Elves and the Shoemaker* by the Brothers Grimm (Chronicle Books, 2003). Rich, evocative illustations bring this charming, old-world retelling to life.

Companion Reproducible

Focus Skills: Vocabulary Development, Critical and Creative Thinking, Writing

Distribute copies of the reproducible on page 98. Invite children to imagine they're elves, then decorate and write about the shoes they'd create.

Level
H

Word Count
382

Vocabulary
curious, deeds, jig, shoemaker, tattered

Supportive Features
amount of text on page gradually increases, mostly common one-syllable words

Challenging Features
up to five lines of text per page, dialogue

Comprehension
Use this book with the Sequencing Chart on page 22.

Phonics
Short *e* (*ea*): *leather, already, instead;* variant vowel /o͞o/ phonograms (*ew, oe*): *shoemaker, grew, shoes, new*

Writing
Have the children write thank-you notes from the shoemaker to the elves.

Fluency
Have the partners reread the story, taking turns to read one page at a time. Circulate and listen in. Evaluate children's reading—speed, accuracy, and expression.

Name _____

My Amazing Shoes

Pretend you are an elf. First, design an amazing pair of shoes.
Then, describe them in writing.

_____

_____

_____

_____

_____

The shoemaker and his wife never saw the two elves again. But thanks to their good deeds, all four of them lived happily ever after.

16

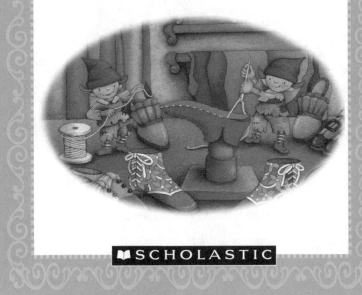

Folk & Fairy Tale EASY READERS

The Elves and the Shoemaker

A retelling by Violet Findley • Illustrated by Martha Aviles

SCHOLASTIC

They put the new clothes on the table and hid. When the clock struck midnight, in came the two elves.

14

One day, they had only enough leather to make a single pair of shoes.

3

Once upon a time, there lived a kind
shoemaker and his wife. Times were hard
and they became very, very poor.

2

The elves were surprised to see the fine
clothes instead of the leather. Zippity, zip!
They put on the shirts, pants, and shoes.
Then they danced a joyful jig and left.

15

The shoemaker put the leather on his table.
"Tomorrow, I will make one last pair of
shoes to sell at the market," he said sadly.

4

All day, the shoemaker and his wife worked
and worked. She made two tiny outfits. He
made two tiny pairs of shoes.

13

"Two elves have been making the shoes!"
said the shoemaker.
"Did you see their tattered clothes? Let's
make them some new ones to say thank
you," said his wife.

But a magical thing happened. When the
shoemaker woke up, the leather had already
been turned into a fancy pair of shoes!
"Wow! I will sell these at the market," he said.

The shoemaker and his wife were happy,
but also very curious. Who was making all
the fancy shoes? One night, they decided
to find out. Instead of going to bed, they
hid behind a curtain.

The shoemaker put the leather on his table.
The next morning, he found two fancy
pairs of shoes!
"Wow! I will sell these at the market," he said.
And so he did.

The shoemaker sold the shoes for a bag of gold. With the gold, he bought more leather.

6

C

When the clock struck midnight, in came two little elves. Zippity, zip! They made 100 pairs of the fanciest shoes ever seen. Then they danced a joyful jig and left.

11

Again, the shoemaker used the gold to buy more leather. He put the leather on the table. The next morning, he found three fancy pairs of shoes!

8

D

Life went on like this for many months. In time, the shoemaker and his wife sold many shoes and became very, very rich.

9

The Princess and the Pea

About the Tale

Danish writer Hans Christian Anderson is credited with popularizing "The Princess and the Pea" when he included an adapted version in his *Tales for Children*, published in 1835. Since then, the story of the super-sensitive princess and the pesky pea that has her tossing and turning all night has been interpreted in many books and even a long-running Broadway musical called *Once Upon a Mattress*. Today, it remains a favorite among children who like their fairy tales with a large dose of humor!

Discussion Questions

1. Where does the prince place the pea?

2. How does the prince know his visitor is a real princess?

3. Do you think it was fair for the prince to "trick" the princess? Why or why not?

Notable Retellings

✳ *The Princess and the Pea* by Harriet Ziefert (Puffin, 1996). Cartoony art and uncluttered text come together for a kid-pleasing read-aloud.

✳ *The Princess and the Pea-ano* by Mike Thaler (Scholastic, 1997). Replace the pea with a pea-ano and you've got one funny fractured fairy tale!

✳ *The Very Smart Pea and the Princess-to-Be* by Mini Grey (Knopf, 2003). Kids will adore this clever tale told from the pea's point of view.

Companion Reproducible

Focus Skills: Following Directions, Vocabulary Development, Writing

Distribute copies of the reproducible of page 104. Then invite each child to fill in the blanks to write his or her own customized version of "The Princess and the Pea."

Level
H
Word Count
279
Vocabulary
rude, shivering, snoozed, stormy, yawn
Supportive Features
some short sentences; simple story structure, consistent structure
Challenging Features
combination of short and long sentences, dialogue
Comprehension
Use this book with the Comprehension Quilt on page 23.
Phonics
r-controlled vowels: *girl, shivering, first, third, turned, after, stormy, morning;* silent letters: *knock, knee*
Writing
Have children write a "Princess Wanted" ad for the newspaper.
Fluency
Using the sentences on pages 12 to 13, model how to read dialogue. Then have children chorally read the narrator's portion of the story. Select two volunteers to read the parts of the prince and the princess aloud. Repeat with other students.

Name _____

My Funny Fairy Tale

Fill in the blanks to write your own funny fairy tale.

Once upon a time, a girl named _____
                                                    girl's name

knocked on a prince's door. "I'm a princess.

Can I stay here tonight?" she asked.

"OK," said the prince. Could she really be a princess?

The prince had a plan to find out. He put some

_____s on a bed. Then he covered them
          food

with _____ mattresses and _____ quilts.
        large number   large number

"Here is your bed. Good night!" said the prince.

The next day the prince asked the girl how she slept.

"Terrible! I tossed and turned all night." she said.

"Great! Now I know you are a real princess!" he said.

 THE END

The girl said yes, of course. Then they both lived, and snoozed, happily ever after.

16

Folk & Fairy Tale
EASY READERS

The Princess and the Pea

A retelling by Violet Findley • Illustrated by Rebecca Thornburg

SCHOLASTIC

The prince smiled. Then, he got down on one knee and asked the girl to marry him.

14

The prince looked high and low for the perfect wife, but had no luck. He could not find a real princess anywhere!

3

Once upon a time, there lived a prince. He was very lonely and wanted to get married.

2

A

Why? He knew that only a real princess could feel a tiny pea under 20 mattresses and 20 quilts!

15

One stormy night, there was a knock on his door. When the prince opened it, he saw a girl. Her hair was wet. Her clothes were muddy. And she was shivering.

4

B

"I don't mean to be rude, but I slept very badly. It felt like there was a boulder under my back!" she said with a yawn.

13

The next morning, the prince invited the girl to have some pancakes.
"How did you sleep?" he asked.

12

"Hello. I am a princess. May I stay here tonight?" she asked.
"Of course," he said kindly.

5

"Here is your bed. Sweet dreams," he said.

10

The girl seemed very nice. Could she really be a princess? The prince had a plan to find out.

7

The prince invited the girl in.
"Come warm yourself by the fire.
Have a cup of hot chocolate," he said.
"Thank you," she said sweetly.

6

C

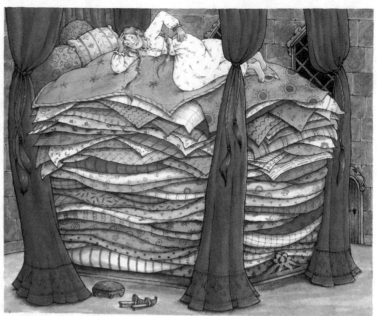

But the girl's dreams were not sweet. She
tossed and turned. She barely slept at all.

11

First, he put a tiny pea on a bed.

8

D

Second, he piled 20 mattresses on top of
the pea. Third, he piled 20 quilts on top
of the mattresses.

9

The Nightingale

About the Tale

"The Nightingale" originated in Asia hundreds of years ago, where it was passed down verbally from generation to generation. Although centuries old, the fairy tale was not widely known in the West until Hans Christian Andersen published his lyrical retelling in 1835. We are thankful he did. This beautiful story of an emperor who selfishly cages a nightingale in order to capture its sweet singing is among Andersen's very finest tales. And the people of China agree. Today, Hans Christian Andersen is nearly as popular there as he is in his native Denmark.

Discussion Questions

1. Why does the king put the nightingale in a cage?

2. Why does the nightingale decide to fly away?

3. Do you think the king is good or bad? What lesson does he learn at the end of the story?

Notable Retellings

✳ *Fairy Tales of Oscar Wilde* **by Oscar Wilde (Nautier Beall Miniustchine Publishing, 2004)**. The master applies his storytelling gifts to "The Nightingale" with stunning results.

✳ *The Nightingale* **by Stephen Mitchell (Candlewick Press, 2002)**. Kids will love this melodic retelling and the Asian-inspired brush paintings.

✳ *The Nightingale* **by Jerry Pinkney (Dial Books, 2002)**. In this lavishly illustrated picture book, the story is relocated to exotic Morocco.

Companion Reproducible

Focus Skills: *Vocabulary Development, Making Personal Connections, Writing*

Distribute copies of the reproducible on page 110. Then invite children to decorate and describe their own windup birds.

Level
I
Word Count
412
Vocabulary
healed, nightingale, palace, servant, trusted
Supportive Features
strong text-to-picture match
Challenging Features
unfamiliar setting, long sentences, four to five lines of text per page, multisyllabic words
Comprehension
Use this book with the Sequencing Chart on page 23.
Phonics
two- to three-syllable words: *upon, palace, China, behind, forest, sweetly, servant, singing, Japan, inside, forget, sadly, music, window, nightingale, beautiful, unwanted, forever*
Writing
Have children write a letter from the king to the nightingale, asking the bird to come back and sing for him.
Fluency
Have children read the story into a tape recorder. Ask them to listen to their recording with a partner and evaluate the speed, accuracy, and expression of their reading.

Name _____

My Windup Bird

Use your imagination to decorate your own fancy windup bird. Then choose five words to describe it.

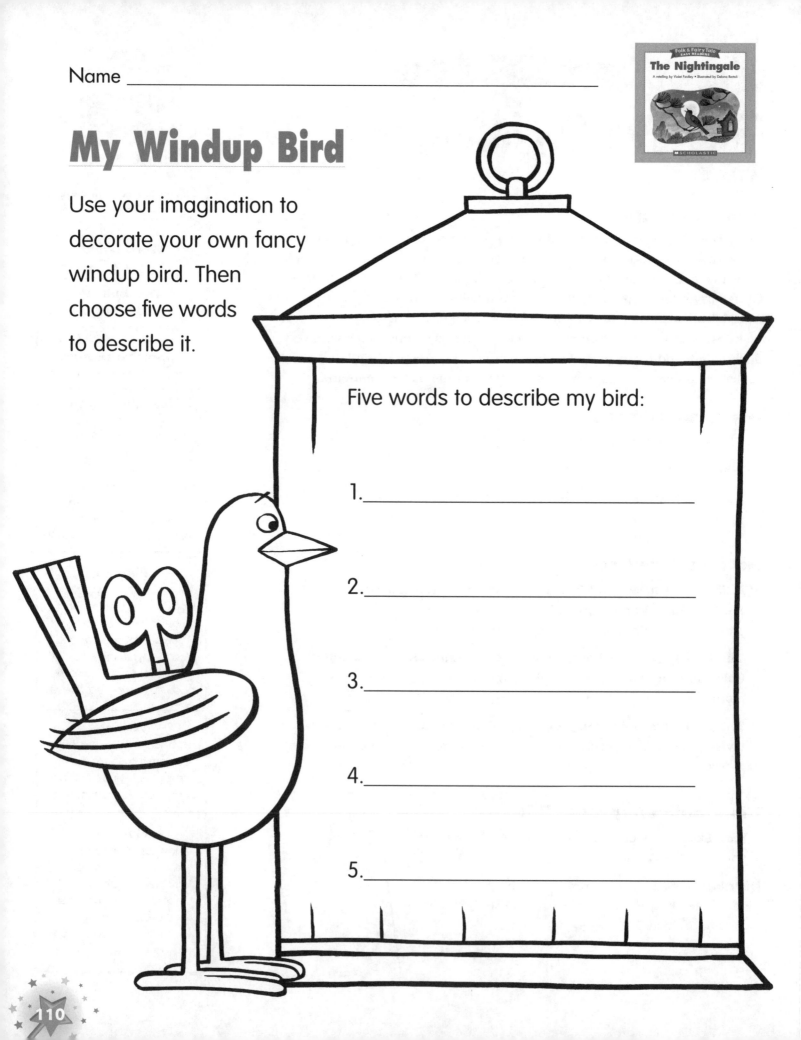

The Nightingale
A retelling by Violet Findley • Illustrated by Dakota Bertoli
SCHOLASTIC

Five words to describe my bird:

1._____

2._____

3._____

4._____

5._____

"No, keep the toy bird," said the nightingale.
"I like the forest, but I will come to your
window every night to sing."
So he did. And his sweet music brought joy
to everyone in the palace forever more.

16

Folk & Fairy Tale
EASY READERS

The Nightingale

A retelling by Violet Findley • Illustrated by Delana Bettoli

■ SCHOLASTIC

By and by, the real nightingale heard that
the king was sick and flew to his window.
There, he sang a song so sweet that the
king was quickly healed.

14

Behind the palace was a forest. In the forest
lived a nightingale.

3

Once upon a time, there was a king.
He lived in a beautiful palace in the land
of China.

2

"Dear nightingale, you made me well.
Come back! I will throw away the toy bird.
Then you can live in the cage all by yourself,"
said the king.

15

The nightingale sang so sweetly that he was
known far and wide. People even wrote
books about him. One day, the king read
one of the books.

4

Years passed and the king grew very sick.
"My only wish is to hear the music of a
nightingale," he said.
He begged the toy bird to sing. But, of
course, it did not.

13

Every night the king listened to the toy bird sing. But one day, it broke.
"It will never sing again," the servant said sadly.

12

"This bird lives in the forest behind my palace, but I have never heard him sing. I must!" said the king.
So he sent his most trusted servant to bring back the nightingale.

5

The king wound up the toy bird and it sang. "This is so pretty! I will place it in the cage with the real nightingale," he said.
So he did.

10

"Will you come to the palace and sing for the king?" asked the servant.
"Of course," said the nightingale.

7

The servant went into the forest. By and by, he came upon a plain brown bird singing a sweet song. It was the nightingale!

6

C

At the palace, the nightingale sang and sang. The king loved the music so much that he cried. "I will buy you a fancy cage so you can sing for me always," he said.
So he did.

8

D

By and by, the king seemed to forget all about the real nightingale. Feeling unwanted, he flew back to the forest.
"No matter. The toy bird is better," said the servant.

11

By and by, a present came from the king of Japan. Inside was a toy nightingale. It was made of gold and covered with jewels.

9

Cinderella

About the Tale

The story of Cinderella is perhaps the most widely told tale in the world, with adaptations cropping up in numerous countries including China, Korea, South Africa, Egypt, France, Germany, Ireland, England, and of course, North America. Just how many Cinderellas are there on the planet? Scholars estimate the number to be somewhere between 300 and 3,000. While it would be impossible for you to read every one, there are literally dozens of wonderful versions readily available for your class to share, compare, and relish.

Discussion Questions

1. Do you think Cinderella was treated fairly by her stepsisters?

2. What happened when the clock struck midnight?

3. Cinderella stories are told all over the world. Why do you think this is so?

Notable Retellings

※ *Cinderella* by Charles Perrault (Nord-Sd Velag, 2002). This exquisitely illustrated translation of Perrault's classic "Cinderella" makes for a magical read-aloud indeed.

※ *The Rough-Face Girl* by Rafe Martin (Putnam, 1998). Kids are sure to be engaged by this moving tale of a Native American girl with a rough face but a very tender heart.

※ *Yeh-Shin: A Cinderella Story From China* by Ai-Ling Louie (Putnam, 1996). Ed Young's misty, marvelous illustrations bring this Asian Cinderella tale to life.

Companion Reproducible

Focus Skills: Making Personal Connections, Critical and Creative Thinking, Writing

Distribute copies of the reproducible on page 116. Then invite each child to write—and draw—about what they would wish for if they had a fairy godmother like Cinderella's.

Level
I
Word Count
446
Vocabulary
alas, chores, coach, spell, vowed
Supportive Features
familiar story, predictable structure
Challenging Features
long sentences, four to five lines of text per page; multisyllabic words
Comprehension
Use this book with the Comprehension Quilt on page 23.
Phonics
long o (oo, oa, ow, o_e): hoped, coach, old, broken, no, home, low, owner; words ending with -ed: named, lived, helped, curled, appeared, turned, agreed, danced, vowed, knocked, lied, nodded, asked, invited
Writing
Have children write their own version of the story. Encourage them to include as many details as possible.
Fluency
Have partners time each other reading the story, writing down their times. Ask children to read the story a few more times, then record themselves again to see if their pace has increased.

Name _____

My Wonderful Wish

Poof! You fairy godmother has just appeared! Write about what you will wish for. Then, draw a picture to go with it.

_____

_____

_____

_____

_____

_____

Cinderella had a great big wedding and
even invited her mean stepsisters. Then,
she and the handsome prince lived happily
ever after.

16

Folk & Fairy Tale
EASY READERS

Cinderella

A retelling by Violet Findley • Illustrated by Lynne Cravath

SCHOLASTIC

Just then, Cinderella came into the room.
"Will you please try on this shoe?" asked
the prince.
Cinderella nodded.

14

One morning, an invitation came. The
handsome prince was having a ball! The
mean stepsisters were very excited. You see,
they both hoped to meet and marry him.

3

Once upon a time, there was a beautiful girl named Cinderella. She lived with two stepsisters, who were very mean. They made her dress in rags and do all the chores.

2

A

The shoe fit perfectly! At last, he had found the girl from the ball.
"Will you marry me?" asked the prince.
"Of course," said Cinderella.

15

On the day of the ball, Cinderella helped her stepsisters get ready. She ironed their dresses. She curled their hair. They were so mean they didn't even say thank you.

4

B

Finally, the prince knocked on one last door. Cinderella's mean stepsisters answered. Both lied and said the shoe was theirs. But, try as they might, it was too small to fit their big feet.

13

True to his word, the prince went from house to house. He tried the shoe on every girl he met. But, alas, it didn't fit any of them.

12

"I wish I could go to the ball, too," cried Cinderella.
Poof! A lady with a magic wand appeared.
It was Cinderella's fairy godmother!
"I will help you," she said.

5

Bong! The clock struck midnight and the spell was broken. Cinderella's coach turned back into a pumpkin. Her dress turned back into rags.
"I guess I will just have to walk home," she said sadly.

10

"You look lovely! There is only one rule. You must be home by midnight or the spell will be broken," said the fairy godmother. Cinderella agreed. Then she waved goodbye.

7

Poof! The fairy godmother turned a pumpkin into a coach. She turned mice into horses. She turned Cinderella's rags into a fancy dress and her old shoes into glass slippers.

6

C

A minute later, the prince ran out to find Cinderella. But all that was left of her was a glass slipper.
"I will search high and low to find the owner of this shoe," he vowed.

11

Cinderella was the star of the ball. Everyone thought she was amazing, especially the prince. He quickly fell in love with her and they danced all night.

8

D

Cinderella had such fun she forgot to look at the clock until it was almost midnight. Oh, no! There was no time to say good-bye to the prince. She ran outside so fast that she lost one of her glass slippers.

9